Richmond
First Certificate
Course

first

Student's Book

Diana L Fried-Booth

Richmond PUBLISHING

CONTENTS MAP

WRITING	GRAMMAR	UNIT MONITOR	EXAM ADVICE	FCE PLUS
Informal letter: using narrative	Reported speech 1 Gerunds 1: after certain verbs	(incorporating **Learning record** and **FCE Checklist**) *Key vocabulary* Education and studying	Use of English, Part 4 Reading, Part 2	Reading, Part 2; Gerunds 1; Revision of articles; Vocabulary: matching words and meanings; Use of English, Part 4; Reported speech 1; Revision of present tenses
Article: organising ideas and making notes	Phrasal verbs Zero and first conditional patterns	*Key vocabulary* Family and relationships *Recycling* Gerunds 1: after certain verbs – multiple choice	Writing, Part 2: article Reading, Part 3	Writing: introducing, linking and concluding; Writing, Part 2: article; Reading, Part 3; Revision of adjectival order; Revision of adverbs; Vocabulary: word groups; Phrasal verbs
Formal letter 1	Word building 1: suffix *-ation* Second conditional Modal verbs 1: expressing possibility and certainty	*Key vocabulary* Occupations *Recycling* Phrasal verbs: multiple choice	Writing, Part 2: non-transactional letter Use of English, Part 2	Use of English, Part 4; Second conditional; Writing, Part 2: letter of application; Modal verbs 1; Word building 1; Revision of past tenses 1; Use of English, Part 2
Article: organising information	Gerunds 2: gerund or infinitive Reported speech 2 Expressing wishes and regrets; complaints	*Key vocabulary* Food and drink *Recycling* Zero, first and second conditionals	Writing, Part 2: composition Use of English, Part 5	Reading, Part 2: Gerunds 2; Writing, Part 2: composition; Reported speech 2; Use of English, Part 5; Revision of past tenses 2
Formal letter 2	Linking conditional sentences Word building 2: suffixes *-ment, -ance, -ence* Verbs followed by the infinitive	*Key vocabulary* Environment, space *Recycling* Direct and reported speech	Use of English, Part 1 Writing, Part 1: transactional letter	Use of English, Part 1; Revision of future tenses 1; Verbs followed by the infinitive; Revision of *too/enough* (+ *for*) + infinitive; *so* + *that*; Vocabulary: matching words and meanings; Writing, Part 1: transactional letter
Article: describing plans	Using the passive Verb + infinitive without *to* Gerunds 3: after prepositions Word building 3: suffix *-ness*	*Key vocabulary* Health, sport *Recycling* Word building 1 and 2	Reading, Part 4 Use of English, Part 3	Revision of future tenses 2; Reading, Part 4; Using the passive; Writing, Part 2: composition; Gerunds 3; Use of English, Part 3
Formal letter 3	Word building 4: suffixes *-ability; -ibility* *would rather; it's time* Modal verbs 2: expressing obligation and necessity; permission and prohibition	*Key vocabulary* Science, technology, motoring *Recycling* Verbs followed by prepositions (+ gerunds)	Reading, Part 1 Listening, Part 1	Revision of comparatives and superlatives; Use of English, Part 2; Revision of *used to, be used to, get used to*; Writing, Part 1: transactional letter; Modal verbs 2
Report	Third conditional *have/get something done* Word building 5: negative prefixes Using *it*	*Key vocabulary* The Arts *Recycling* *would rather; it's time*	Writing, Part 2: report Listening, Part 2	Use of English, Part 5; Writing, Part 2: report; Use of English, Part 4; Phrasal verbs and nouns; Third conditional; Reading, Part 1
Narrative composition: writing a story Formal letter 4	Link words *so* and *such* Question tags Using determiners to express quantity	*Key vocabulary* Weather, transport and travel *Recycling* Negative prefixes	Writing, Part 2: article Listening, Part 3	Reading: story sequence and multiple choice; Writing, Part 2: article; Use of English, Part 1; Phrasal verbs; Link words
Article: writing a description	Relative clauses: identifying and non-identifying Phrasal and compound nouns Making comparisons	*Key vocabulary* Crime, law and order *Recycling* Link words	Listening, Part 4 Speaking	Reading, Part 2; Relative clauses; Use of English, Part 5; Phrasal verbs and nouns; compound nouns; Use of English, Part 2; Writing, Part 2: article
Narrative composition: writing a story	Participles and participle clauses Compound adjectives *make/let/allow*	*Key vocabulary* Clothing and parts of the body *Recycling* Relative clauses	Writing, Part 2: set texts Using computerised answer sheets	Use of English, Part 3; *do* or *make*; Writing: story review and recommendation; Use of English, Part 4; Participles and participle clauses; Reading, Part 3

Appendix 1: Irregular verbs page 232   Appendix 2: Phrasal verbs and phrasal nouns page 233

INTRODUCTION

This course is designed to help you prepare for the five papers which make up the Cambridge First Certificate in English examination.

The book is divided into eleven units which cover the kinds of topics you can expect to come across in the examination. Each unit gives you plenty of practice in the four skills – speaking, listening, reading and writing. From the very beginning of the course you are also learning how to use these skills in tackling the questions in the examination. Moreover, each unit gives you practice in learning and revising the grammar and the main vocabulary which you need to know in relation to the topics at this level.

In addition to developing your language skills, the course includes various strategies to help you develop your confidence so that by the time you take the FCE you are completely familiar with what to expect. Towards the end of each unit you will find the following seven sections:

Key vocabulary brings together the topic-related vocabulary which you need to know and which you will not have come across in the remainder of the unit.

Vocabulary in context gives you practice in *using* the vocabulary which you have learnt during the unit.

Recycling gives you further practice in revising some of the grammar which you have already covered in the previous unit.

Learning record helps you check that you have understood the main grammatical focus of the unit and gives further opportunity to check vocabulary.

FCE Checklist helps you familiarise yourself with the various parts of the five papers of the FCE so that by the end of the course you are completely sure of what to expect in each paper.

Exam advice helps you learn how to deal with the different kinds of questions in the papers. You should read these tips before going on to practise the questions.

FCE Plus consists of supplementary exercises and exam-type questions to give you further practice in the grammar which you cover in each unit. The exam-type questions give practice in the kinds of questions which appear on Papers 1, 2 and 3 of the FCE.

At the end of the book you will find the following three sections:

Grammar reference summarises the grammar covered in the course.

Appendix 1 lists the irregular verbs you need to know at this level.

Appendix 2 covers some of the most common phrasal verbs and phrasal nouns and puts them in sentences so that you can see how they are used and what they mean.

When the FCE was revised in December 1996, one of the most important changes involved the Speaking paper (Paper 5). This will always be taken by candidates in pairs, with two examiners present, one of whom carries out the interview while the other examiner carries out the assessment. Throughout this course you will have many opportunities to work together with a partner. It is important that you get used to doing this, as it will help you prepare for the Speaking test from the very beginning of the course.

The course ends with a Practice exam, which your teacher will give you shortly before you take the actual FCE.

I hope you enjoy the course and pass the FCE.

Good luck!

FCE OVERVIEW

Before you begin this course, you may need to know about the Cambridge First Certificate in English examination: how many papers there are in the examination, what the various papers are called and what kinds of task you can expect in each paper.

Look at the table very carefully and be prepared to refer back to it as you work through the course. This will help you to understand how each unit in the book is related to the preparation for the examination.

The FCE has 5 different papers.

Paper 1 **READING**	*Content* 35 questions based on 4 long texts or 3 long texts and 2 or more short texts. The paper is between 1,900 and 2,300 words long *Time* 1 hour 15 minutes

Part	*Task*
1	6 or 7 questions which require selecting items from a list and matching them to sections of a text
2	7 or 8 4-option multiple choice questions on a text
3	6 or 7 questions reordering sentences or paragraphs which have been removed from a text
4	13–15 questions which require selecting items from a list and matching them to sections of a text(s)

Paper 2 **WRITING**	*Content* 2 writing tasks: 1 compulsory and 1 from a choice of 4 different tasks which include a question based on set texts *Time* 1 hour 30 minutes

Part	*Task*
1	Writing a letter based on written information which may occasionally include illustrations or other visual material (120–180 words)
2	A choice of questions based on: a short story, a description, an informal letter, a report, a composition, an article or a set text (120–180 words)

Paper 3 **USE OF ENGLISH**	*Content* 65 questions based on 5 separate parts *Time* 1 hour 15 minutes

Part	*Task*
1	15 questions based on a text containing 15 gaps with 4-option multiple choice questions for each gap
2	15 questions based on a text with 15 missing words to be supplied

3   10 questions based on completing a sentence using a key word (which is supplied) so that the rewritten sentence means the same as the original one

4   15 questions based on picking out errors in a text by recognising which lines in a text are correct, and which lines contain an unnecessary word

5   10 word building questions based on completing missing words in a text, using the root of the word which is printed in the margin beside each gap

Paper 4 LISTENING

Content

30 questions based on 4 recorded texts drawn from a variety of sources: talks, advertisements, interviews, phone messages, lectures, speeches, announcements, news broadcasts, conversations, etc.

Time

approximately 40 minutes

Part	Task
1	8 3-option multiple choice questions based on 8 short recordings with 1 or 2 speakers
2	10 gap-fill questions based on a recording with 1 or 2 speakers
3	5 multiple match questions based on listening to 5 short recordings (with 1 or 2 speakers) and selecting the correct answer from a list of 6 options
4	7 questions based on a recording with 1 or more speakers; the questions may be True/False, Yes/No, or 3-option multiple choice

Paper 5 SPEAKING

Content

4 parts taken in pairs with 2 examiners present, one who conducts the interview and one who assesses

Time

14 minutes

Part	Task
1	Giving personal information and talking about oneself
2	Expressing opinions and attitudes in response to colour photos and taking turns to talk for up to a minute each
3	Talking to each other in response to a visual stimulus, e.g. diagram, drawing, etc.
4	Talking to the interviewer based on the discussion arising out of Part 3

Each paper is worth 40 marks, and the marks for the individual papers are added together to form a total mark out of 200.

There are three pass grades: A, B, C; and three fail grades: D, E and U. A minimum grade C pass corresponds to approximately 60% of the total mark.

When you get your results, you will be notified if you have done particularly well or badly on individual papers.

You can take the examination twice a year: in June and December.

X SPEAKING

Is the world getting smaller?

1 Modern travel means that within a few hours you can be on the other side of the world, experiencing a completely different way of life.

What about the new language? Would you learn a few phrases beforehand? Would you try to use sign language? Would you hope to find someone who could speak your language?

You have a few minutes to identify as many of these languages as you can. There are 18 different languages altogether – you may not recognise more than a few, so try to make sensible guesses!

學期報告

স্কুল রিপোর্ট

Rapporti Sulle Scuole

Tuairisc na Scoileanna

Học bạ

Έλεγχος σχολείων

Schoolverslag

Adroddiadau Ysgol

Доклад о школах

Rapport ya classe

Izveštaj o školama

سکول کی رپوٹ

Koulujen Raportti

Avaliações Escolares

Relatio De Ludis

Schulberichte

学校報告

Rapport sur les écoles

Compare answers with another pair.

2 Work with a new partner and fill in this questionnaire.

QUESTIONNAIRE

❶ How many languages do you speak? .....
What are they? ....

❷ Do you think it's important to learn foreign languages?
YES ☐   NO ☐

❸ If *yes*, why? ....

❹ If *no*, why not? ....

❺ What other foreign languages would you like to learn?
....

3 Find three other people who share similar reasons to those which your partner gave for Questions 3 or 4.
Discuss the reasons which people have given.
Does any one reason seem more important than any other?
Find out how many people gave the same answer to Question 5.

4 Make questions to ask your partner from the prompts below.
Then fill in the information about **yourself**.

PERSONAL FACT FILE

Length/time learning English: ....

Family/from: ....

Length/time/live/town: ....

Hobbies/interests: ....

Plans/future: ....

READING
Studying abroad

1 Even without knowing the language very well, many people are attracted to studying in a foreign country.
Maybe you have already studied abroad or been to a school in a foreign country for a few weeks. If you have, did you enjoy the experience?
If you haven't studied abroad yet, would you like to?

2 🗵 Write down as many advantages and disadvantages as you can think of for studying abroad. Be ready to discuss them with the class.

3 The articles below are about students' experiences of being at a foreign university.

Before you read the first article in detail, try to find the answers to the following questions as quickly as you can.

What nationality is Peter Quinn?
How long has he been in Spain?

Peter Quinn, 19, from Dublin in Ireland is studying translation and interpretation at ICADE, part of Universidad Pontificia Comillas

1 I am a typical Hispanophile. As a child I spent a lot of holidays on the *costas*, and at my school there were lots of Spanish students, so I developed a love for the place.

2 The social life is very easy. My Spanish has really improved in the year and a half I've been living here. I spoke textbook Spanish before I came, but now I speak much better colloquial Spanish. Watching TV is a great help. The people are very open and very warm – from the first day I was 'Peter', I wasn't a foreigner.

3 I was offered a place in Dublin to study arts, but I came to Spain to do a Spanish course at the University of Alcala. At the same time I was studying

for *selectividad* – the Spanish university entrance exam. It was very hard but I passed, and I was accepted at two places. I chose Comillas.

4 I'm living in a rented room in a house out of the centre. I'd rather live centrally – if I want to go shopping at the moment, I have to take the metro. I don't know whether I'll have to pay the rent through the summer yet, though. Accommodation in Madrid is a problem – I'd like to have my own place one day, but it's very expensive. Getting grants isn't easy for foreign students.

VOCABULARY

4 Find words or phrases in the text which mean:

1 someone who loves Spain (para. 1)
2 got better (para. 2)
3 informal, idiomatic (para. 2)
4 unreserved, friendly (para. 2)
5 accommodation belonging to someone else and paid for on a weekly basis, for example (para. 4)
6 sums of money provided by a government or public fund (para. 4)

5 Now look again at the last paragraph from the article about Peter Quinn. This time it contains a number of words which should not be there. One of the skills you need to develop for the FCE is the ability to spot mistakes in a text. In the paragraph below all the wrong words are underlined, with the exception of the last line. Discuss why you think these words should not be there.

Pick out the word in the last line which should not be there.

I'm living in a rented room in a house out of the centre. I'd rather <u>to</u> live centrally – if I want to go shopping at the moment, I <u>do</u> have to take the metro. I don't know <u>for</u> whether I'll have to pay the rent through the summer yet, though. Accommodation in <u>the</u> Madrid is a problem – I'd like to have my own place one day, but it's very <u>much</u> expensive. Getting grants isn't quite easy for foreign students.

6 Now look at the second article. In some lines there is a word which should not be there. As you read, find the words which are incorrectly included. The first one has been done for you.

Mariann Grønnestad, 26, from Stavanger in Norway, is studying medicine in Munich.

1 THERE WERE TWO REASONS WHY I WANTED TO COME TO SOUTHERN GERMANY TO STUDY. I WANTED TO BE AT THE CENTRE OF EUROPE, 5 WITHIN EASY REACH OF OTHER COUNTRIES, AND CITIES SUCH AS PARIS AND PRAGUE.

2 The other <u>one</u> reason was that I was finding it very difficult to 10 find a place to study medicine in Norway, where there are only three medical schools.

3 I have spent my last two years at a boarding school, where I 15 made lots of friends and learned to look after myself and integrate in with other people. I was 19 when I left, and those two years had changed me; I 20 knew I could cope with student life in another country.

4 First I had to learn German. I went to Munich in September, a month before the term started 25 out, and spent three weeks on a language course. I stayed with a German family and was able to practise speaking the language with them. Nobody spoke 30 Norwegian, of course, so it was a great help to find that there were other students from Norway at the university. I made plenty friends with some 35 of them and we were able to help one another during the first few weeks in a new city.

5 After six months I moved into my own self apartment; there is 40 a wonderful mix of cultures and I have made many friends from different places. For three years I did had a Norwegian boyfriend who was also 45 studying to be a doctor, but that ended when he left.

6 I would recommend studying abroad to anyone. You must get a chance to learn another 50 language and to understand the culture and traditions of another country. Munich is a fantastic city for us students, especially as beer is the 55 favourite drink of students everywhere. I didn't like beer before, but if you live in Munich, there really is no alternative, and now I have 60 acquired the taste. In a winter I prefer to visit cafes and talk with friends, but in summer my favourite place is the *Englisher Garten*, with its lake and park 65 and lots of bars. The city's beer halls are generally full of students and tourists.

7 At weekends I often go to skiing in the Austrian Alps with 70 friends. We pile into a couple of cars and rent an apartment.

8 This all costs money, and, like the most students, I am living on a loan from the 75 government. By the time I take my final exams I shall have a big debt which must be repaid with interest. If I don't find no work, I shall have serious 80 problems.

9 I hope to get a job in a hospital near Oslo. I worked there last summer, while earning up the money to go to Nepal, 85 Thailand and Vietnam for three months.

10 We are a high medical family. My mother and my elder sisters are nurses, but my father is the 90 odd one out: he runs a hairdressing salon.

1 line 9	..*one*..	6 line 40	....	11 line 69	....
2 line 14	....	7 line 44	....	12 line 74	....
3 line 18	....	8 line 49	....	13 line 79	....
4 line 26	....	9 line 54	....	14 line 84	....
5 line 35	....	10 line 61	....	15 line 88	....

7 Find words or phrases in the text which mean:

1 close to (para. 1)
2 manage (para. 3)
3 option (para. 6)
4 usually (para. 6)
5 get into (in a disorganised way) (para. 7)
6 money which is owed (para. 8)

Now answer the following questions by choosing the best answer from A, B, C or D.

1 Mariann was attracted to studying abroad because
  A she wanted to eventually work in Germany.
  B it was easier to get onto a medical course.
  C she was influenced by boarding school.
  D Germany had offered her a university grant.

2 What does Mariann like about studying abroad?
  A She meets people of different nationalities.
  B German social life is cheaper than in Norway.
  C Her boyfriend is at the same university.
  D Accommodation is provided by the government.

3 Why is unemployment particularly worrying for Norwegian students?
  A Government benefits are very low for the unemployed.
  B They may find themselves unable to get out of debt.
  C The number of people out of work is increasing.
  D The interest rates on student loans are increasing.

4 Which word best describes Mariann's attitude to life?
  A hardworking
  B pessimistic
  C escapist
  D adventurous

SPEAKING

Imagine you can spend some time studying abroad.
Decide where you would each like to go.
What would you like to study? How long would you want to be there?
What kind of accommodation would you like?
What difficulties (if any) do you think you would experience?
What do you think you would enjoy most about studying abroad?

1  Look back at the questions you asked your partner in the questionnaire on page 10.

1 *How many languages do you speak?*
You asked your partner how many languages she/he spoke.

2 *Do you think it's important to learn foreign languages?*
You also asked if she/he thought it was important to learn foreign languages.

What changes when the questions are reported? Do the changes only affect the verbs? What else do you need to change when you want to report what someone has asked or said?

---

2 Look at the picture. An interviewer is talking to an English student called Paul who is living and studying in Moscow. Report what Paul said to the interviewer.

I: Do you like living in Moscow?

P: Yes, very much.

Example

Paul said that he really liked living in Moscow.

I: Is there anything you miss?

P: Yes, I miss my girlfriend.

I: How long will you stay in Moscow?

P: Probably about three years.

I: Can you speak fluent Russian?

P: Not yet – but I'm learning!

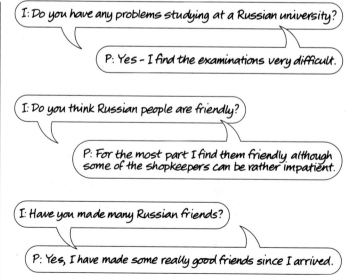

I: Do you have any problems studying at a Russian university?

P: Yes – I find the examinations very difficult.

I: Do you think Russian people are friendly?

P: For the most part I find them friendly although some of the shopkeepers can be rather impatient.

I: Have you made many Russian friends?

P: Yes, I have made some really good friends since I arrived.

3 Now report three of the answers your partner gave you in the questionnaire.

While you were waiting to go through passport control in a foreign country, the person in front of you in the queue was involved in an argument. Read the dialogue and then write and tell your friend what happened by continuing the letter below.

IMMIGRATION OFFICIAL	I'm afraid your visa has expired, sir.
YOUNG MAN	But I've only been away a few days.
OFFICIAL	You should have renewed your visa before you left the country.
MAN	But it expired while I was away.
OFFICIAL	Then you should have applied to renew it before returning.
MAN	I didn't have time and yesterday the office was closed.
OFFICIAL	I'm sorry, but you are not allowed entry without a valid visa.
MAN	But I have to be back at university tomorrow. Can't you stamp it for me?
OFFICIAL	No. You have to apply through the embassy.
MAN	But I can't afford another ticket to go home.
OFFICIAL	Will you step to one side please and I'll call a senior officer. There is a queue behind you of people waiting to come through.
MAN	This is ridiculous – I've been at university here for two years.

Dear ....,

I arrived here safely, and although everyone at the university is very helpful, it all feels rather strange. I had to wait ages at the airport because there was a problem at passport control. The person in front of me had an argument with the immigration officer, who told him

LISTENING

1   You are going to hear some foreign students who are being interviewed on a radio programme. They are talking about why they have chosen to study English in Australia.
Before you listen, try to guess which student is most likely to give which reason.

2   As you listen, write down the country each student comes from and match what they say with their main reason A–E for studying abroad.

Student	Country	Reason
Sirkka	....	....
Tatsuo	....	....
Eugenia	....	....
George	....	....
Irma	....	....

A a relative already in Sydney

B to fulfil an ambition

C good weather

D to gain independence

E a different teaching method

3   If only one of these students could receive a visa to remain in Australia to study, who do you think it should be?
Decide which student has the best reasons for studying in Sydney. Compare decisions with other students in the class.

1 🔲 Look back at the article on page 12 about Mariann Grønnestad.

In lines 48–49 she says:
I would recommend studying abroad to anyone.

Is it possible to say:
I would recommend to study abroad to anyone.

How did you decide? Can you think of any other words which must be followed by the *-ing* form of the verb?

2 Now complete these sentences with an appropriate verb form.

1 I denied .... his pen – I hadn't been near his desk.

2 They delayed .... into their new house until the painters had completely finished.

3 Can you imagine .... an astronaut and walking on the moon?

4 Would you mind .... the teacher that I'll be late for the lesson?

5 I can never resist .... clothes in a sale even if I don't need them.

6 She admitted .... the money in order to help her boyfriend.

7 You must finish .... your letter as the last post leaves in ten minutes.

8 He keeps .... me when I'm talking – I wish he'd be quiet.

9 My work for the Red Cross involves .... many different countries.

10 As this is the first day of the holiday, I suggest .... a party to celebrate.

3 Look at the pictures of various activities and tell your partner how you feel about these things.

Example
I loathe waiting for a bus in the rain.
I adore watching an old movie.

How many other things can you think of that you can't stand doing, that you don't mind doing or that you enjoy doing?

UNIT MONITOR

Key vocabulary

Apart from the vocabulary practised within this unit, you also need to know the following words in connection with education and studying.
Use your dictionary to look up any words you don't know.

Rearrange the words below under the four headings. You can add to the lists if there is anything missing which applies to your own learning situation.

Places	Subjects	Qualifications	People

art   kindergarten   music   nursery (school)
physics   certificate   primary (school)   science
degree   junior (high school)   sociology   diploma
senior (high school)   secondary (school)
boarding school   college   university   director
biology   lecturer   business studies   GCSE 16 (UK)
principal   chemistry   Advanced Level 18 (UK)
professor   computing   pupil   design   student
economics   teacher   geography   history
information technology   languages   mathematics

Vocabulary in context

Fill in the missing words in the sentences below. Each word has been started for you, but you can refer back to the Introduction on pages 5–7 if you need further help.

1 If you f _ _ _ your examination, you can always take it again.
2 Maria was delighted when she pa _ _ _ _ _ her First Certificate examination.
3 When do you get the re _ _ _ _ _ _ of your examination?
4 Matthias got very good m _ _ _ _ _ in his test at the end of term.
5 In the FCE examination there are three pass gr _ _ _ _ _: A, B and C.

Learning record

When you have finished Unit 1, try filling in this record of what you have learnt.

1 Write down ten new words you have learnt.
....
....

2 Write down one of the basic rules for changing direct speech into reported speech.
....

3 Write down five verbs you can remember which take the gerund.
....

4 Can you guess what an *Anglophile* is?
....
A Francophile?
....

FCE Checklist

Look back at the description of what the FCE examination comprises on pages 6–7 and then answer the questions.

▶ How many papers make up the FCE?
....
▶ What are the papers called? ....
....
▶ How many times a year can you sit the FCE? ....
▶ Do all the papers carry equal marks? ....
▶ Which paper is divided into 2 parts?
....
▶ Which paper is divided into 5 parts?
....
▶ How many parts do the remaining papers have? ....

EXAM ADVICE

1 Use of English, Part 4

The Use of English paper is divided into 5 parts with 65 questions. All your answers are written on a separate answer sheet (see page 237 for the sample).

Part 4 consists of a passage in which some lines are correct, and some are incorrect; the exercise requires you to pick out the extra or unnecessary words.

- The kinds of words which will be incorrectly included will focus on your understanding of the grammatical structure of the sentence. This means you need to concentrate on things like articles, prepositions, verbs, link words, pronouns, etc. and pay less attention to vocabulary.

- Read through the passage very carefully so that you understand the general meaning.

- Then re-read the passage very slowly pausing at the end of every sentence.

- Some of the errors may seem obvious, but it is easy to overlook small errors like the wrong preposition or an unnecessary article.

- Although the number of errors is not fixed, no single line will contain more than one error. If you think that you have found more than one error in a line, then check again!

- If you only find two or three errors in the whole passage, the chances are that you have missed quite a few, as on average you can expect to find about ten errors in the fifteen numbered lines.

- If a line is correct, then all you have to do is **put a tick (✓)** against the line number on your separate answer sheet.

- If a line is incorrect, then you must **copy the incorrect word** against the line number on your separate answer sheet.

- This exercise will always begin with two examples showing you how to complete your answer sheet. Look carefully at these two examples to remind yourself what you should focus on when answering this question.

2 Reading, Part 2

The Reading paper consists of 4 parts and 35 questions. Although the number of questions in each part may vary very slightly from one session to another, the total number will always remain the same. It is also possible for one part to have two shorter (but related) reading texts instead of one long text. The number of words which you will have to read overall in the paper will range between 1,900 and 2,300, and each text will range between 350 and 700 words. Part 2 consists of a passage with 7 or 8 multiple choice questions.

- Read the instructions carefully as they will tell you what the passage is going to be about.

- Read the passage through carefully without looking at the questions.

- Don't spend ages worrying about words which you don't know. It may be that you will be able to answer the questions without knowing a few of the words anyway.

- Look at the questions. Each multiple choice question has four possible answers. You have to **choose the one correct alternative** from the optional answers A, B, C or D and mark this letter on your answer sheet.

- When you first look at a question, you may already have an idea of the answer from what you have read. Don't be tempted to guess, but go back to the passage and focus on the part of the text which contains the information to answer the question.

- If the question is testing your understanding of the whole passage, skim through the complete passage and don't just focus on part of the text.

- The 'wrong' options will be written in such a way that they could almost be right and they will also use the information which is contained in the passage.

- If you are unsure of the correct option, then try working out why the other answers could be wrong; there can only be one correct answer.

- If you try and fill in two answers on your answer sheet, you will get no marks even if one of them is the correct answer!

1 Reading PART 2

You are going to read an article about the differences between male and female brains. For questions **1–4**, choose the answer (**A, B, C** or **D**) which you think fits best according to the text.

A couple driving in unfamiliar territory get lost. The man wants to look at the map; the woman wants to stop and ask directions. An argument develops.

Why does this happen so often, regardless of nationality, age or education? Research across Europe suggests that the cause is neither culture nor upbringing, but the result of the different ways in which men's and women's brains are organised.

A neurobiologist working in Holland has found that from the age of five until adolescence, one part of the brain develops differently in boys and girls, resulting in different adult brain structures. The key region is the hypothalmus, the part of the brain which controls appetite, sleep, body temperatures and mood. In other words, it influences the way we operate. It is clear that there are sex differences in the brain and that men and women have a biological reason to think, and therefore act, differently. It seems that scientists are finding that the standard ideas of male and female behaviour may have some scientific basis: men tend to be attracted to football and video games and women to artistic interests and personal conversations because their brains make them think that way.

If the upbringing of boys and girls was built on social behaviour, you would expect differences between cultures. But this is not the case. Some scientists believe that there may be more similarities in the thinking patterns of Italian and Swedish girls than in a boy and girl from the same country. Men's interest in rough and risky activities, from rugby to rock climbing, is universal. In all societies, they are attracted to aggressive, energetic and competitive activities. But most girls reject boys' games from a young age, preferring those involving talking and sharing.

1 The writer suggests that the behaviour between the sexes

    A varies from one country to another.   **C** is dependent on biological causes.
    B changes from one culture to another.   **D** is a result of children's upbringing.

2 According to the article, why are men likely to be attracted to football?

    A They believe it makes them strong.   **C** They think it proves their superiority.
    B They can't help wanting to play it.   **D** They regard it as the best sport there is.

3 What does the writer say about Italian and Swedish girls?

    A The way they think is related to where they grow up.
    B The way they behave depends on cultural influences.
    C They develop different brain structures as they grow up.
    D They seem to have almost identical thought processes.

4 What is the point of the opening paragraph of the article?

    A It explains why women are more thoughtful than men.
    B It gives an example of the sexes' reactions to things.
    C It shows that men are more likely to enjoy arguing.
    D It shows how easily the sexes disagree about things.

2 Grammar: gerunds 1

▶ Grammar reference p.214

Underline the verbs/phrase which must be followed by the *-ing* form of the verb. Then complete the exercise using an appropriate verb for each sentence.

1 Most people appreciate .... given a present on their birthday.

2 We'll have to postpone .... on a picnic if the weather is too cold.

3 She avoided .... on the motorway by using small country lanes.

4 I have considered .... for another job but I am unlikely to do so this year.

5 If I were you, I wouldn't risk .... so much money on a horse race.

6 Since leaving university, I miss .... a flat with my friends.

7 Did you mention .... the robbery to the police?

8 I've practised .... my lines for the play but still can't remember them.

9 It's worth .... the time to learn as much vocabulary as possible.

10 Ivan disliked .... lies, but sometimes it was necessary.

3 Grammar revision: articles

▶ Grammar reference p.214

Read the passage below and fill in the spaces using either: **the** (definite article) or **a(n)** (indefinite article); or leave the space blank (**zero** article).

Time for a feast

Picnics today often mean just sitting on [1] .... rug eating sandwiches. In [2] .... nineteenth century, however, wealthy people took them very seriously and picnics were often [3] .... elaborate affairs. [4] .... cooks prepared picnics for large groups of people, and servants went along to carry and serve [5] .... food. People would take their own furniture with them including [6] .... folding picnic tables and chairs, along with tablecloths and china cups and plates.

[7] .... word picnic was first used in England around 1800 and originally [8] .... picnic meant [9] .... occasion for fashionable people where each person brought something to eat. Later it meant [10] .... trip to [11] .... country where [12] .... food was eaten out of doors. [13] .... word is taken from [14] .... French *pique nique*, although [15] .... origin is unknown.

4 Vocabulary

Match the following words with their meanings:

1 a sum of money usually awarded for study by a government body

2 a place providing accommodation while you study

3 to owe money

4 a liking for something

5 dependent on one's own resources

6 to refuse to give in to temptation

7 a person in charge of an educational institution

8 to accept something is true

9 the money charged on a loan

10 people who are out of work

A self-reliant

B to admit

C the unemployed

D the interest

E a boarding school

F a principal

G a grant

H to be in debt

I to resist

J a taste

1 .... 2 .... 3 .... 4 .... 5 .... 6 .... 7 .... 8 .... 9 .... 10 ....

5 USE OF ENGLISH **PART 4**

For questions **1–10**, read the text below and look carefully at each line. Some of the lines are correct, and some have a word which should not be there.
If a line is correct, put a tick (✓) beside it. If a line has a word which should **not** be there, write the word beside it. There is an example at the beginning.

MYSTERIOUS HEALTHY DIET

1 ✓ If you want to live to a healthy old age and eat well along the way,

2 .... you should move to rural Greece or Crete. These are then the areas

3 .... of Europe whose inhabitants do live longest, thanks to their varied

4 .... diet. A surprising, common feature of diets in Crete and the three

5 .... villages studied around the Athens is their high fat content. The diet

6 .... of an average person included 40% fat, well over the recommended

7 .... limit. But the most of this fat comes from cheese and yoghurt and very

8 .... little from butter and milk, and this may be is the vital difference.

9 .... Researchers cannot yet explain why, given that all these products are

10 .... produced by the dairy cow, they should have such many different effects.

6 Grammar: reported speech 1
▶ Grammar reference p.213

George Maliatsos, 82, is a carpenter. He lives in a rural area near Athens. He has never dieted or taken special exercise and he is likely to live longer than most Europeans.
Look at the report written by a journalist who interviewed George Maliatsos. Then write down what the carpenter actually said in response to the journalist's questions.

George Maliatsos said he had enjoyed food and wine all his life and he had never

`I've enjoyed food and wine ....

worried about how good it was for him. He got up at 5.30, had some milk and bread

....

and walked a kilometre to his wood shop. At midday he went back for a large

....

lunch with lots of vegetables and cheese. He ate all kinds of meat but mostly

....

chicken; he loved fish but ate less as he grew older because it was so expensive. He cooked

....

in olive oil and put it on just about everything he ate – like salads and cooked

....

vegetables. He used to be a great wine drinker, about half a litre a day, but ten

....

years ago he cut back and decided to just drink a glass with his meals.

....

7 Grammar revision: present tenses

Grammar reference p.215

Look again at the article about Peter Quinn.

Underline all the examples of the present tenses you can find and write each one in the appropriate column in the table. Add more examples of your own to each column.

I am a typical Hispanophile. As a child I spent a lot of holidays on the *costas*, and at my school there were lots of Spanish students, so I developed a love for the place.

The social life is very easy. My Spanish has really improved in the year and a half I've been living here. I spoke textbook Spanish before I came, but now I speak much better colloquial Spanish. Watching TV is a great help. The people are very open and very warm – from the first day I was 'Peter', I wasn't a foreigner.

I was offered a place in Dublin to study arts, but I came to Spain to do a Spanish course at the University of Alcala. At the same time I was studying for *selectividad* – the Spanish university entrance exam. It was very hard but I passed, and I was accepted at two places. I chose Comillas.

I'm living in a rented room in a house out of the centre. I'd rather live centrally – if I want to go shopping at the moment, I have to take the metro. I don't know whether I'll have to pay the rent through the summer yet, though. Accommodation in Madrid is a problem – I'd like to have my own place one day, but it's very expensive. Getting grants isn't easy for foreign students.

present simple	present continuous	present perfect simple	present perfect continuous

LOVE MAKES THE WORLD GO ROUND

⚡ SPEAKING

Changing faces

1 What did you look like when you were younger?

Do you think you have changed a lot over the years?

Look at the photographs of some well-known people when they were children.
Can you match the faces of yesterday with the faces of today?

> Do some features of people's faces usually stay the same? Which ones?
> Do you look like your mother or your father?
> Or maybe you look more like a grandparent or another of your relatives?

2 Match the different adjectives describing people's character with each picture.

calm   friendly   thoughtful   extrovert   talkative   hot-tempered

3 Now match the short definitions with these adjectives.

1 very excitable and sensitive	cheerful
2 changeable and gloomy	patient
3 amusing and making people laugh	introvert
4 willing to give and share	nervous
5 behaving in a courteous manner	depressed
6 tolerant towards other people	efficient
7 easily annoyed	humorous
8 helpful and caring	moody
9 interested in oneself	generous
10 competent and organised	polite
11 mad and ridiculous	emotional
12 happy and good-tempered	kind
13 often in low spirits	crazy
14 easily worried	irritable

4 What kind of person are you?
Which of these words would you use to describe yourself?

Do you think we see ourselves as others see us?
What about your friends? How do you think they would describe you?

Do you like being by yourself? Do you like being with your family? Or do you prefer being with friends your own age?

Which **three words** would you choose to describe your best friend?
Which **three words** do you think she/he would choose to describe you?

1 Read questions 1–8 in the quiz and circle your answers a, b or c to find out whether you are a good friend!

What sort of friend are you?

QUIZ

1 One of your friends has had a terrible row with their parents. They ring you up to talk about it just as you're about to go out for the evening. Do you:
a say you can't talk now but you're sure everything will be all right by tomorrow?
b ring the person you are meeting to say you'll be late, and then ring your friend back?
c tell them that their parents are wrong, rush round and persuade them to pack a suitcase and move in with you?

2 Your best friend is worried about which university to attend – a local one or another one that's 300 kilometres away. Do you:
a read about the courses before giving any advice?
b tell them to go to the nearest one because you don't want them to move away?
c leave them to decide for themselves but see more of your other friends just in case your best friend moves away?

3 A friend has put on weight and needs to lose a few kilos. They decide to go on a diet. Do you:
a agree that it's a great idea?
b say you were worried because they were getting fat?
c go on the diet as well?

4 Your friend's new camera has broken and they want to take it back to the shop for a refund. The problem is that they are too afraid to make a fuss. Do you:
a take the camera back for them?
b tell them to take it back by themselves?
c agree to go to the shop with them for support?

5 You both go on holiday and, on the second day, you meet a very attractive member of the opposite sex. Do you:
a tell your friend that you'll see them on the return flight?
b buy them a guidebook so they can go sightseeing and leave you alone with your new friend?
c find someone else for your friend so that you can all go around together ?

6 Your best friend has spent a lot of money on buying some new clothes. Unfortunately you don't think the clothes suit them at all. Do you:
a tell your friend the clothes are really nice and they look fantastic in them?
b suggest they take the clothes back and buy something more suitable?
c ask whether you can try them on so your friend can see whether they suit you?

7 You have a completely free evening. Which of the following would you prefer to do:
a ask your best friend to come to your place so you can have a good chat?
b spend the evening out with a group of friends?
c go out by yourself to somewhere completely new?

8 Which of the following is most important for you in a friendship:
a loyalty?
b generosity?
c fun?

2 Now work out your score and talk about the result.

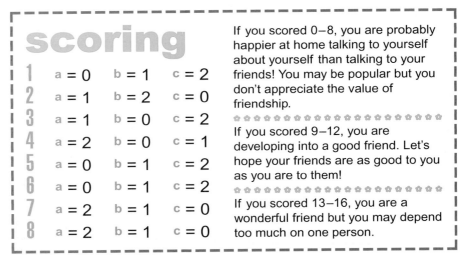

scoring

1	a = 0	b = 1	c = 2
2	a = 1	b = 2	c = 0
3	a = 1	b = 0	c = 2
4	a = 2	b = 0	c = 1
5	a = 0	b = 1	c = 2
6	a = 0	b = 1	c = 2
7	a = 2	b = 1	c = 0
8	a = 2	b = 1	c = 0

If you scored 0–8, you are probably happier at home talking to yourself about yourself than talking to your friends! You may be popular but you don't appreciate the value of friendship.

If you scored 9–12, you are developing into a good friend. Let's hope your friends are as good to you as you are to them!

If you scored 13–16, you are a wonderful friend but you may depend too much on one person.

LISTENING

Family life

1 Do you have any brothers or sisters or are you an only child?
Is there an ideal family size?
What are the advantages and disadvantages of being an only child?

2 You are going to hear part of an interview with a brother and sister called William and Frances who are in their twenties.

Before you listen, read the sentences below very carefully and see if you can guess the kind of word or phrase which may be missing.

As you listen, try to fill in the missing spaces using a word or a short phrase. Don't worry if you don't understand every word – try to pick out the key information and fill in the gaps by using the main words. Check that what you write makes sense – even if you're not completely sure that you have understood everything.

William and Frances used to (1) .... a lot when they were young.

Why did Frances dislike William? (2) ....

What is the age difference between Frances and William? (3) ....

What did William not help with? (4) ....

What is William ashamed of? (5) ....

What has Frances come to understand since growing up? (6) ....

3 Have you ever felt like Frances or William?
Discuss some of the things Frances complained about.
Do you think these are common problems in families?
What other difficulties can arise between brothers and sisters?
You may want to use your own experience of family life or you may know about other problems through your friends.

Talk about your ideas with another pair and write down a short list of the main points which you have just discussed.

Use **note form** – in other words you need not write in full sentences. Make sure you have written down enough information so that you have a record of everything that you discussed, as you will need to refer to these notes later in the unit.

Do some of the points occur more frequently than others?

Is it possible to divide the points into headings? For example: pocket money; helping around the house; freedom to stay out late; choice of friends, clothes, music and TV programmes; attitude to school work; use of free time, etc.

GRAMMAR ▸ p.216 / **Phrasal verbs**

1 What is a phrasal verb?

Look at these examples from the interview with Frances and William and match each phrasal verb with its meaning A–E.

1 we were always falling out

2 she always told me off

3 she'd go on at me

4 why I had to put up with being treated differently

5 I really do worry now about letting her down

A to scold or blame

B to disappoint

C to constantly annoy

D to tolerate

E to quarrel

2 How do you recognise a phrasal verb?
In the examples 1–5 above, underline the words that *make up* each phrasal verb.
What does *make up* in this context mean? Have you *come across* it with any other meanings?

3 In the following exercise complete the sentences by using one (or more if necessary) of the words in the box.
Then write down the meaning of the phrasal verb in each sentence. You can use Appendix 2 on pages 233–236 or your dictionary to help you.

through up out off to with down on of

1 If you feel too hot, take your coat ....

2 She's so irritable that people find her diffcult to get ....

3 Have you heard that Jo and Rob have broken .... their engagement?

4 If the weather is fine we'll set .... early tomorrow. (2 possible answers)

5 If you have a problem, it's best to face .... it.

6 If you hold the line, I'll put you .... to the manager.

7 Can you go to the shops for me? We've run .... bread.

8 In winter a lot of people go .... flu.

9 I would like to give .... smoking.

10 My plans for going on holiday have fallen ....

1 Look at the article *Relative Values*.
From the title what do you expect it will be about?

Find the answers to the following questions before you read the article in detail.

1 What is Martin Bell's job?

2 Where has he worked?

3 What happened to him in August 1993?

RELATIVE VALUES

Martin Bell, 58, is foreign correspondent for the BBC, having previously been their Washington correspondent for twelve years. He has also worked in Berlin, and in February 1993 he was named Journalist of the Year for his work in the former Yugoslavia. In August of the same year he was hit by shrapnel while filming in Sarajevo. He has been married twice and has two daughters, Melissa, 22, and Catherine, 19, from his first marriage. When he is in London, he stays with Catherine and his first wife, Helene. Catherine has finished her A-levels and, after travelling in Europe, plans to continue her studies.

Catherine Bell

1 When I was younger Dad tried to make us watch the news, but I never did. We lived in Washington and I never actually saw him on TV as he was reporting for the BBC.

2 I have some wonderful memories. He used to take me jogging or riding – though he wouldn't ride. And fishing in streams, though he had no inclination for fishing – he's too restless. We'd put the fish in jars and then let them out afterwards. He also used to take us on the most terrifying roller-coaster rides in the States. He was really petrified, but because we wanted to go, he went on every roller-coaster around.

3 He was always there for us, whether to cuddle me if I ran to his bed when I had nightmares and things, or in Washington having parties in my bath! I remember Dad bringing me half the kitchen for me to mix into concoctions and magic potions in the tub.

4 Now that I'm older we've become friends. He's very easy to live with. He's not strict at all and I respect him more now that I can understand what he's done. He spoils me, which is lovely. We discuss my boyfriends

– so far he seems to approve of them. I can't imagine him doing any other job. He simply couldn't become a banker and definitely not a comedian! So all I can do is let him know that I love him as much as possible. And that always makes him happy.

Martin Bell

1 Catherine is aware of how I earn my living. I have to pay the bills and no alternatives have been offered to me – other than being in the line of fire.

2 Because Catherine is dyslexic, and because I come from rather a literary family and books and words mean a lot to me, I used to read her lots of bedtime stories. Now I encourage her writing and poetry. I think there's a danger, if you are a busy parent with a heavy workload, that you become a secondary parent, which so many fathers become – a bit like the furniture. But if from time to time you look after the children, you have a more rewarding experience.

3 It was, and is, a warm and close relationship with both Catherine and Melissa. We had lots of holidays together and Catherine called me 'Disneyland Dad' because I used to take them to all the theme parks in America. They had a great time and there's no happier experience in a man's

life than seeing his kids enjoying themselves.

4 Now that the children are older, the relationship has changed. We go for long walks together. I'm not famous for saying a lot really, so we talk about her school work or her boyfriends. The relationship is less protective now that she can look after herself better. You have to know when to back off, to allow them to make their own mistakes, to a point, and allow certain freedoms.

5 She's responsible for her own life. But she knows that I am her safety net and that I will always be here for her, whatever happens.

2 Based on what **Catherine** says, find words in the text which mean:

1 constantly on the move (para. 2)

2 a ride – usually in a theme park – sometimes called a big dipper (para. 2)

3 extremely frightened (para. 2)

4 hold or hug a person (para. 3)

5 combine (para. 3)

6 an old-fashioned word for drinks (para. 3)

7 a bath (para. 3)

8 stern and severe (para. 4)

Based on what **Martin** says, find words or phrases in the text which mean:

9 leading a dangerous life (para. 1)

10 having difficulty in reading and spelling (para. 2)

11 enjoying literature (para. 2)

12 care for (para. 2)

13 giving personal satisfaction (para. 2)

14 acting to make sure a person does not get hurt (para. 4)

15 withdraw or retreat (para. 4)

3 ⟨I⟩ What do you think Catherine and her father have in common?

Think about their characters as well as as the activities they have shared in the past.

WRITING

Article

1 Look back at the notes you made about some of the problems connected with family life.

Now work with your partner and add to this list some of the positive aspects that you enjoy about family life.

In the FCE Paper 2 you will have a choice of writing tasks in Part 2. You may be asked to write a short article (between 120 and 180 words) which draws on your experience, perhaps aimed at the readers of a magazine for young people or a school newspaper, for example. Whatever the topic or the task, you will have to organise your ideas before writing.

Look at the way in which Catherine has written about her relationship with her father.

▶ in the first paragraph she looks back to a point in the past
▶ in the second paragraph she mentions some specific memories
▶ in the third paragraph she talks about their present relationship, and concludes her article with two sentences which express her feelings for her father

2 Imagine you have been asked to write a short article for an international magazine which is running a series of articles on what young people think about family life in different countries.

Organise the notes you have on family life into two paragraphs along the following lines:

Paragraph 1: postive aspects of family life + example(s) based on personal experience

Paragraph 2: negative aspects of family life + example(s) based on personal experience
Check your notes with another student's notes.

Paragraph 3: conclusion based on personal opinion(s)

Now write the complete article, using about 50 words for each paragraph.

3 When you have finished, compare your third paragraph with your partner's and help each other to correct any mistakes which you might have made in the article.

You may find it helpful to use some of the structures below to **introduce** your ideas, to **link** your ideas and to **conclude** your article.

Paragraph 1

Family life varies from one family to another ...
Family life is different all over the world. In my country ...
First of all ... To begin with ...
Firstly ... Secondly ...
One of the best things about family life is ...
Another postive aspect is ...
Moreover ... In addition ... Furthermore ...

Paragraph 2 (to link contrasting ideas)

However ... Although ... Nevertheless ...
In spite of the good things, there is/are ...
On the other hand, there is/are ...
Despite the advantages, there is/are ...

Paragraph 3

In conclusion ...
To conclude, I think .../my own personal opinion is ...
To sum up ...
Overall, I feel that ...

1 Look at the verb patterns in these sentences.

1A If you **feel** confident about yourself, **it's** easier to make friends.

1B If you **like** people, they usually **like** you.

1C If you **see** someone crying, **try** to help them.

2A If you **work** hard, **we'll go** out later.

2B **You'll need** a work permit if you **want** to work abroad.

2C **I'll cook** a special meal for you if you **come** to dinner.

What do you notice about the verbs in 1A, 1B and 1C?

What is different about the verbs in 2A, 2B and 2C?

Which example(s) refer to situations which could possibly happen in the future?

Which example(s) refer to situations which are generally always true?

In which example(s) could you replace *if* with *when*?

Which example(s) is giving an instruction?

2 Pick out the zero and first conditional patterns in the following sentences.

1 Will you lend me your camera if I go on holiday?

2 As long as you promise not to drive too fast, I'll lend you my car.

3 When you're feeling worried about something, talk to a friend.

4 I shall be really sorry if my friends decide to emigrate.

5 I can't relax unless I listen to music.

3 Now complete the following sentences using appropriate patterns.

1 .... your hair if it feels greasy.

2 Unless you book in advance, it .... difficult to get a seat on some trains.

3 If you're feeling tired, ...

4 When it's very cold, elderly people ....

5 As long as the weather .... fine, we'll spend tomorrow on the beach.

6 If you don't know the meaning of a word, ...

7 A dentist .... you without an appointment if you're in a lot of pain.

8 When autumn .... , deciduous trees lose their leaves.

9 If you practise regularly, one day you .... a good pianist.

10 There .... always be wars unless people learn to be tolerant of each other.

LISTENING

1 What do you do if you feel depressed?

Do you go out ? Do you talk about why you feel depressed? Do you keep quiet and hope the feeling will disappear?

What do you do if you feel angry about something?

Do you lose your temper? Do you bottle up your feelings inside?

2 Think of some things to ask your partner what they do if ...

If you can't get to sleep, what do you do? Do you count sheep?

3 You are going to hear five different people talking about what they do if or when ...
As you listen, choose the correct answer from A, B or C.

1 If Laura can't get to sleep, she

   A phones a friend.

   B reads a book.

   C learns her vocabulary.

2 If Lucien eats too much on one day, he

   A feels extremely greedy.

   B is sick shortly afterwards.

   C starves himself the next.

3 If Paula goes to university, her parents will

   A not give her much money.

   B send her money every month.

   C give her the money she needs.

4 According to Guy, when you get old it must be

   A nice to stay in bed all day.

   B hard to be dependent.

   C lonely to be by yourself.

5 Whenever Fay has a free evening, she prefers

   A staying at home.

   B seeing her friends.

   C going out somewhere.

VOCABULARY

4 Listen again and match the phrases in italics in 1–5 with their meanings A–H.

1 I *drop off*.

2 My mum says I'm *a bottomless pit*!

3 I reckon I *get the balance right*.

4 I *couldn't put up with it*.

5 *It just burns a hole in my pocket*.

A upsetting and irritating

B never full or satisfied

C fall asleep

D I spend money as fast as possible.

E perfect happiness

F evidence of having bought something

G feel that the situation is harmonious

H unable to tolerate something

6 I've got to send them *the receipts*.

7 It must be so *frustrating*.

8 It's *absolute bliss*.

1 What are the similarities and differences between these two photos?
What sort of life do you imagine these men lead?

2 In groups, discuss the ways in
which your own society looks
after the underprivileged, for
example the homeless.

> What happens if people
> fall ill?
>
> What do they do if they
> have nothing to eat?
>
> Do you agree that the
> 'poor get poorer while the
> rich get richer'?
>
> What sorts of changes
> would you like to see in
> your own country to help
> people?

Key vocabulary

Apart from the vocabulary practised within this unit, you also need to know the following words in connection with family and relationships.
Use your dictionary to look up any words you don't know.

How many of these words relate to you? For example, are *you* a brother or sister?
Put a tick (✓) against each word in column 1 that applies to you.
Then match the words in column 2 with their meanings.

1 People	2 Status	
aunt	bachelor	unmarried woman
brother	divorced	one of a pair
cousin	divorcee	married, living apart
first cousin	fiancé (m)	engaged woman
grandchild	fiancée (f)	divorced woman
granddaughter	engaged	unmarried
grandson	partner	state prior to marriage
grandparents	single	engaged man
husband	spinster	unmarried man
nephew	separated	once married, but
niece		not any more
parent		
sister		
triplets		
uncle		
widow		
widower		
wife		

Vocabulary in context

Fill in the missing words in the sentences below. Each word has been started for you, but you should use your dictionary if you need further help.

1 Are you going to Mark and Julia's w _ _ _ _ _ _ in July?

2 Did you know that Lucia is expecting tw _ _ _ in the spring?

3 Next year my parents will have been married for 25 years and the family is planning a party to celebrate their an _ _ _ _ _ _ _ _ _ .

4 Ma _ _ _ _ _ _ _ without your parents' consent varies from one country to another; if you are under 18 in England, you need your parents' permission.

5 Your next of k _ _ are your closest relatives.

6 My mother has remarried but I don't like my new st _ _ father very much.

7 I am lucky that my wife's parents are so kind to me – many people don't get on with their in-l _ _ _ _ .

8 Although we're divorced, my e _ -wife and I are still good friends.

Recycling: gerunds 1

Read the text and decide which word or phrase A, B, C or D best fits each space.

> Most people make up their minds how they feel about you in the first few minutes of contact. It is (1) .... learning some of the important signals of body language. For example, people who (2) .... meeting strangers will be able to look them in the eye, but others who feel shy will often (3) .... looking at people directly. People who are nervous sometimes (4) .... fidgeting with their hair or twisting their fingers as they speak. Sometimes body language can be misunderstood. When Americans (5) .... signalling that something is OK, they make a circle with their thumb and forefinger. For the Japanese, however, this signal means money. Similarly, tapping your nose in the UK can either (6) .... being secretive or be used to send a warning, but in Italy it is just a friendly warning to be careful of the people around you. If you plan on living abroad, most people would (7) .... finding out in advance about cultural signals, not to (8) .... asking which ones are those most likely to cause offence!

	A	B	C	D
1	time	worth	good	right
2	don't miss	don't object	don't want	don't mind
3	avoid	miss	consider	stop
4	risk	involve	keep	suggest
5	desire	consider	think	want
6	imagine	look	mean	say
7	resist	deny	argue	recommend
8	appreciate	prevent	prefer	mention

Learning record

When you have finished Unit 2, try filling in this record of what you have learnt.

1 How would you recognise a phrasal verb? What is important about the meaning of many phrasal verbs?

2 What do these words mean? *restless, strict* Write two sentences making it clear that you understand *how* they are used.

....

....

3 What does *rewarding* mean in the context of 'a rewarding experience'?

....

4 Write down some of the phrases which you can use in a piece of written English when

      introducing ideas ....

      linking ideas ....

      concluding ideas ....

Now write a sentence using each of the phrases which you have written.

....

....

....

5 What is the pattern of tenses for the first conditional?

FCE Checklist

Look back at the description of what the FCE examination comprises on pages 6–7 and then complete the checklist.

> I have practised:
> - speaking skills for Paper ......
> - reading skills for Paper ......
> - writing skills for Paper ...., Part .....
> - use of English skills for Paper ......
> - listening skills for Paper ...., Parts ..... and ......

EXAM ADVICE

3 Writing, Part 2

The Writing paper is in two parts. The task in Part 1 is compulsory – everyone has to answer this question. In Part 2, however, you have to answer one question out of a choice of four. (The fifth question is based on background reading texts – Exam Advice 21.)

In Part 2 of the Writing paper you may have the choice of writing an **article**.

- You will know the kind of writing you are being asked to produce because the instruction will tell you. In this case the instruction will read 'Write a short **article** ...'.

- Always identify the kind of writing that you are being asked to do.

- As you work through this course, you will practise using the grammar and vocabulary to help you write about a range of different subjects.

- It is worth learning how to tackle all the possible kinds of writing you may be asked to do, even if you have a 'favourite' type, as not all the different question types will appear on each examination paper.

- If you are going to write an article, make sure you clearly understand the topic, that you have something to say about it and that you know who or what you are writing the article for. It could be for a school magazine or newspaper, and you may be asked to draw on your own experience.

- You are not expected to have a sophisticated knowledge of what an article is, but you should be prepared to organise and plan your ideas before writing.

- The style in which you write should clearly express your views, opinions and ideas.

You should begin your article with an introductory paragraph. The next one or two paragraphs should attempt to answer the question, and your concluding paragraph should try to avoid repeating what you have written in the introduction.

Length

You will always be asked to write your answer in **120–180 words**.

Before the exam, you will have had sufficient practice to know what this *looks* like. If you write too few words, you will not have provided the examiner with a long enough sample of what you are capable of writing. In this case you will not be able to score as highly as you could. Similarly, if you write too much, you run the risk of making unnecessary mistakes and losing marks.

Don't waste time counting the number of words – learn to judge what approximately 150 words in your own handwriting look like on the page.

4 Reading, Part 3

Part 3 of the Reading paper consists of a passage which has 6 or 7 gaps in it. These gaps can vary from sentence length to (short) paragraph length. The missing sentences/paragraphs (including one extra) are printed in the wrong order, and you have to decide which sentence/paragraph fits each gap.

▸ The first gap will have been completed for you as an example. Make a note of which missing sentence has been used and don't use it again.

▸ There is one extra answer in the sentences/paragraphs which you will not need to use.

▸ The missing sentences/paragraphs will be lettered A–G (or H depending on the number of gaps). You will need to write only the letter on your separate answer sheet.

▸ Read through the text carefully and slowly. As you read try to focus on the main idea in each paragraph.

▸ Look at the list of what has been removed. Are there any key words in the missing sentences which refer to the main ideas which you noticed as you read the passage?

▸ Reread the text and look carefully at the grammatical structures which come **before** and **after** the gaps. The sentence links as well as the content of the sentences should help you decide what has been removed.

▸ Try reading back the paragraph to yourself (silently!), putting in the missing information. Does it make sense?

1 Writing: introducing, linking and concluding

Read the passage below and fill in the gaps with the correct answer A, B or C.

When we decided to go on a camping holiday last year we had little idea what to expect. We had looked at lots of brochures full of happy families at sunny campsites. ¹ .... , our experience proved rather different. ² .... we couldn't even find the site and when we ³ .... found it, it was in the middle of nowhere – miles from the nearest village shop. This meant that we had to buy everything from the very expensive shop on the campsite. ⁴ .... , we discovered that we had to pay extra for water and electricity. ⁵ .... all these disadvantages, we decided we would stay as the weather was fine and warm and the other campers seemed very friendly. We spent a few days exploring the surrounding area ⁶ .... deciding to move on. We packed up our tent and went to the camp office to collect the deposit which we had paid on arrival. The woman behind the desk looked puzzled. ⁷ .... we explained what we wanted, she simply shrugged her shoulders and shook her head. Apparently the deposit was not refundable – ⁸ .... there *was* no money to come back. We could hardly believe our ears. We had chosen to camp ⁹ .... it was the cheapest way of having a holiday, but ¹⁰ .... it turned out to be one of the most expensive holidays ever!

1	A	In addition	B	However	C Since
2	A	To begin with	B	Once	C After
3	A	lastly	B	finally	C at the end
4	A	Overall	B	Nevertheless	C Furthermore
5	A	Despite	B	Moreover	C But
6	A	and	B	before	C then
7	A	So	B	Because	C Although
8	A	on the other hand	B	on the whole	C in other words
9	A	as	B	therefore	C until
10	A	at last	B	in the end	C to conclude

2 WRITING   **PART 2**

An English language newspaper is offering a prize for the best article on the topic of friendship. You can write about friendship from any point of view.

Write an **article** in **120–180** words in an appropiate style.

3 READING PART 3

You are going to read a newspaper article about colour. Four word(s)/sentences have been removed from the article. Choose from the word(s)/sentences **A–E** the one which fits each gap (**1–4**). There is one extra item which you do not need to use.

DO YOU TURN RED, WHITE OR BLUE WITH ANGER?

Many languages use colours to create certain images, but a particular colour may not have the same associations in every language. Many Europeans turn green with envy, but the French go yellow while the Swedes use the compound word 'black-ill' for jealousy. **[1]** but the French also turn blue, and Italians and Germans go black, although really furious Germans turn white-hot with anger. **[2]** Germans in the same state become blue, and Spaniards encourage each other to enjoy their food by 'taking a green'. In Italy a detective story is 'yellow' and a romantic tale is 'a pink novel'.

Money matters also have their share of colour. When the Italians are short of cash they are green, but Swedes, **[3]**, are green when they are wealthy. The Turks have a colourful expression about savings: **[4]** However, there is one colour association that most languages share: when your bank account is in the red, you are in debt.

A   they talk about 'white money for a black day'.

B   To be black in French is to be very drunk.

C   by contrast

D   Red is popular for expressing anger,

E   similarly

4 Grammar revision: adjectival order

▶ Grammar reference p.217

Rearrange the following sentences putting the adjectives in the correct order.

1 My parents brought me back a .... bag from their holiday.

   leather   lovely   soft

2 I'm going to give away that .... sweater as it's too small for me now.

   red   tight   woolly

3 When Henry retired, his company presented him with a .... vase
   engraved with all the employees' initials.

   tall   glass   huge

4 I've just bought a .... sports car.

   blue   gorgeous   Italian   new

5 Write two or three sentences describing what you are wearing.

   ....

   ....

   ....

5 Grammar revision: adverbs

▶ Grammar reference p.217

When you were listening to people talking you heard
Laura say:

... and then I gradually get sleepy ... ;

Guy say:

... I feel really sorry for people who can't look after themselves ... ;

Fay say:

... I hardly ever get the opportunity ... .

Complete each of the sentences below about yourself by choosing an appropriate adverb from the box.

| usually   well   never   often   yesterday   probably   always |
| badly   normally   quite   sometimes   very   fairly   rarely |

1 I .... go to bed before midnight.

2 I will .... take my FCE in the next year.

3 I .... do my homework.

4 I saw some of my friends ....

5 I slept very .... last night.

6 I .... go out on Saturday evenings.

7 I try to do my homework .... carefully.

8 I think I speak English .... fluently already.

9 I like to keep in touch with my friends so I .... phone them.

10 When I come across a new English word, I .... look it up in the dictionary.

6 Vocabulary

Rearrange the words below to make three groups with six related words in each group. Make sure you know the meaning of each word.

divorced   cheerful   strict   daughter   separated   stepson   unmarried   unkind   patient
engaged   moody   emotional   widower   spinster   married   single   bachelor   partner

7 Grammar: phrasal verbs

⯈ Grammar reference p.216   Appendix 2 p.233

Rewrite the following sentences by replacing the word in italics with the correct form of one of the verbs from list **A** + a particle from list **B**.

A   set   go   fall   tell   look   put   break   take   make   get

B   through   down   in   off   up   out

Example

It's only a small factory, but it *produces* top quality furniture.

*It's only a small factory, but it **turns out** top quality furniture.*

1 If you don't know the answer to a question, you can always try *inventing* one!

   ....

2 Talks between the government and the union leaders have *failed*.

   ....

3 Although we *left* in plenty of time, we still arrived late for the meeting.

   ....

4 Don't drink that milk – I think it's *sour*.

   ....

5 What time does your train *arrive*?

   ....

6 Always *check* your work to see if you've made any mistakes.

   ....

7 Even though they're best friends, they're always *quarrelling*.

   ....

8 Mick asked the operator to *connect* him to directory enquiries.

   ....

9 You shouldn't have *scolded* Tara for spilling her drink – it was an accident.

   ....

10 I was completely *deceived* by his story about being penniless.

   ....

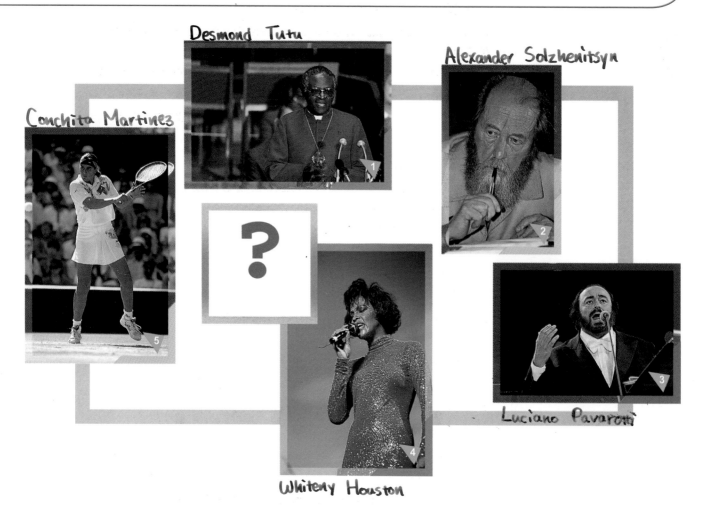

Desmond Tutu
Alexander Solzhenitsyn
Conchita Martinez
?
Whiteny Houston
Luciano Pavarotti

☒ SPEAKING

Birthdays

1 Do you recognise these famous people?
Even if you don't know them all, can you guess how old they are?

Below are some dates of birth. Can you guess who was born in which year?
Try matching the people with their dates; three dates will be left over.

    12th July 1973   August 26th 1960

December 13th 1915   May 1st 1918   3rd March 1940

    January 19th 1931   October 12th 1935

        11th September 1963

2 If you could choose to meet a famous living person, who would you choose? Why?

Example

I would choose ... because she/he ...

Write their name in the empty box above.

Do you know when they were born?
Do you think they will still be famous in 20 years' time?

42

1 You will hear a group of students discussing with their teacher the characteristics they most admire in these famous people.

You may hear specific words which you don't know, but if you listen carefully, you will hear other words and expressions which will help you understand the general meaning.

Before you listen, match these words which you will hear with their meanings.

1 stamina   A someone forced to live away from their own country

2 dissident   B strength, power to carry on with something

3 committed   C person who disagrees with the government

4 exile   D dedicated and determined

2 Look at the statements below.
As you listen, choose the statement A, B, or C which each person gives as a reason for their admiration.

1 The boy says that opera now is

 A less expensive.

 B more popular.

 C more imaginative.

2 The girl says that Whitney Houston's music makes her

 A tremble all over.

 B feel like crying.

 C want to scream.

3 The man admires Solzhenitsyn because he

 A travelled widely.

 B overcame hardships.

 C writes brilliantly.

4 The second girl expresses admiration for Martinez's

 A dedication.

 B speed.

 C success.

5 The teacher appreciates Bishop Tutu's stories because they are

 A very political.

 B so amusing.

 C very sensible.

What is your image of opera?
What do you think people mean by the *tingle factor* when they listen to music?
What do you think the man means when he talks about a 'flash magazine'? Do you know any magazines which might fit this description?
Do you know anyone who is committed enough to a sport to practise for hours each day?
Who can you think of who is a great story-teller?

1 Famous names are not necessarily famous worldwide. Some people may only be famous within their own country or continent. You can probably think of plenty of people who are really well known in your country but who are not international names.

You may not have heard of either of the people in the following articles, but in some countries they are well-known names.
Look quickly through the two texts to find the answers to the following questions.

1 What is the writer's main purpose in each text?

2 Where do you think these texts might come from?

3 Why do you think someone would read these texts?

> The controversial Argentinian film-maker Alejandro Agresti came to Europe in 1986 for the post-production of his first film and stayed. Now living near The Hague, at Zoetermeer, he misses some of the hardships of his native land

Why did you stay on in Europe?

At home I couldn't make the kind of films I wanted to make: there was no financing and no demand for art movies in Argentina at that time. The situation was completely different in Europe. I got my big break in the Netherlands at the age of 23. Most of my films are co-productions with other European countries, so I could probably have based myself somewhere else in Europe. I was lucky to arrive here at the right moment.

Do you still miss Argentina?

I miss everything: the culture, the explosion of temper and ideas, people being demonstrative, how couples work shoulder to shoulder to bring up their children – life is so hard but there is love. My grandfather came from Italy and my mother was Czech. Argentina has more than 30 races: we have a sense of our own identity without racism.

Has it been easier to express politically and economically sensitive ideas in Europe?

It used to be. But there is growing censorship, especially if you express anti-capitalist ideas. When I am looking for money to make my films, the backers say, 'Nothing red, nothing left, just soft pink.' I consider myself left-wing. It is more fashionable and even acceptable in film-making to be on the right and even far-right at this moment.

Have you become disillusioned about life in Europe?

At the moment, yes. People in the Netherlands are spoilt by the good social and economic environment. It's too cosy here: when it comes to developing ideas and writing scripts you do better when times are tough.

Are the ideas coming out of South America more exciting?

It's a micro-culture in the southern hemisphere. There are a lot of intelligent people and they have wonderful untold stories to tell. In Europe everything is getting quite dull.

Will you go back to Argentina?

I would like to. The possibilities have improved, but I am not so sure that the public is ready for the kind of films I make. Sardonic movies full of social criticism are low down on the entertainment scale.

Was it difficult to settle down in the Netherlands?

Yes, and after ten years it is still difficult. People still talk to me and start about the atrocities committed in Argentina. I say sure, the military government killed 50,000 ... but look at the junkies and young people in Europe addicted to drugs who will also die ... Isn't that appalling too?

What would you miss about Europe if you left?

The money to make my films; museums, the architecture – those kinds of reminders of the past. More than anything I would miss my friends if I left Europe: people matter most, not places.

What do you think of Dutch women?

My wife is Dutch. In general women in Holland are quite confused. They fight long and hard for what in the end they don't want. It's true they are exploited, and discrimination still exists. Men are to blame but that is only part of the story.

BRIEF LIVES

WHIGFIELD

**She appeared from nowhere to topple
Wet, Wet, Wet from the top of the charts with her single Saturday Night.
So who is the Danish singer with the silly name?**

*[handwritten margin notes:
Sarcastic
(形) 皮肉な、いやみを言う
cynical
(形) 皮肉な、世をすねた
innocent
(形) 無罪の (↔guilty)
(形) 単純の, 純真の
(=pure)]*

Age: 24
Full name: Sannie Charlotte Carlson
Appearance: an au pair who watches too much MTV
Occupation: overnight pop sensation *[handwritten: すぐに]*
Aren't they all? Her debut single went straight to Number 1. That has never been done before.
Who is buying it? British holidaymakers *[handwritten: 休日に入っている人]* fresh from Spain. They danced away those romantic sangria-soaked evenings to Saturday Night, which topped the charts there during the summer.
How does it go? normal sort of stuff: Saturday night ... I like the way you move ... be my baby ... I'll make you mine ... take you to the top ... driving me crazy ... da-da-da-da-di-di-di- ... pretty baby, etc. etc.
There's a dance as well: clap your hands, make a whooping noise, wiggle your arms to the left, wiggle to the right. Put your hands on your buttocks, jump backwards and forwards, jump to the right, clap hands, start again. Come Dancing it ain't.

Early life: Whigfield – she got the weird stage name from her singing teacher – went to boarding school in Denmark, but lived for four years in Africa, where her father was an engineer. 'It was wonderful to walk around without clothes,' she says.
Early career: after fashion college, she became a model. Even though models can go out with nothing on she didn't take to it. 'Being a model is an insult to women. It ignores intellect completely.'
Complete intellect: I'll make you mine ... take you to the top ... driving me crazy ... pretty baby ... (puts hands on bottom, jumps backwards and forwards).
Why she did it: 'There are so many things happening in the world. People are glad to hear a happy, innocent song.' Or she did it for a laugh, depending on which paper you believe.
Wild rock lifestyle: on Monday, she told reporters she didn't have a boyfriend because she was too busy. By Wednesday, she told them that her singer-boyfriend 'lived far away'. Whoop, whoop! Da-da-da! Probably not far enough.

---

2 Now read the texts more carefully to find the answers to the following questions. Decide whether you think the answer is Agresti, Whigfield or both of them.

1 Who thinks that people matter more than places?

2 Who went to a boarding school?

3 Who had their first taste of success in their twenties?

4 Who comes from a mixed marriage?

5 Who thinks that women are unclear about their desires?

6 Who is too busy to have a relationship?

1 Look back at the person's name which you wrote in the box on page 42. Imagine that this person is visiting your country. You are going to write a letter to her/him requesting an interview. You will then be able to write an article for your local newspaper based on this interview as part of your media studies course.

What kind of letter is appropriate?   In this case a formal letter is appropriate.

Why?   Perhaps the most obvious reason is that you probably don't know this person who you want to interview, so the tone of your letter and the style in which you write it, must not sound like spoken English.

What does that mean exactly?   ◗ write the verbs in full: e.g. *I am* not *I'm*
◗ no slang or colloquial expressions
◗ more formal language: e.g. *postpone* a meeting rather than the phrasal verb *put off*
◗ if you know the name of the person, begin with *Dear Mr, Ms, Miss* or *Mrs* (+ name), and end *Yours sincerely*, with your signature below
◗ if you don't know the person's name, begin with *Dear Sir or Madam*, and end *Yours faithfully*, with your signature below
◗ print or write your name clearly underneath your signature

fairly = quite

2 ⬚ Look at this letter and pick out some of the characteristics that make it fairly formal.

Rua Vitoria 759
10640 Buenos Aires
Argentina

April 10th 1997

Dear Ms Crawford,

An article about you in our local newspaper last month mentioned that you will be staying in Buenos Aires for a week at the beginning of May.

I am a nineteen-year-old student studying fashion and design and I am preparing a dissertation for my end-of-year portfolio entitled 'Supermodels'. I am writing to ask whether you would be willing to allow me to interview you when you are in Buenos Aires. I know you are very busy, but if you would like to suggest a time and day to suit you, I could come to your hotel. Alternatively, if it would be more convenient I could go to the TV studios where I read you will be doing a photographic session.

I would particularly like to ask you some questions about the early part of your career and what made you interested in modelling. However, I shall quite understand if you prefer not to answer all my questions.

I look forward to hearing from you and very much hope you will be able to see me.

Yours sincerely,

Jorge Mendoza

JORGE MENDOZA

In the FCE examination you will not be asked to produce any dates or addresses in a letter writing task, but you need to be able to recognise the **kind** of letter which you may be asked to write and to use a **style appropriate to the task**.

3 Make a list of the questions you would like to ask your famous interviewee. Look back at the reading texts on pages 44–45 to help you with your ideas. Now write a short letter in about 150 words. (The sample letter is approximately 170 words so this should give you an idea about how much you need to write.)
Use the guidelines and the examples below to help you.

▶ As you know the name of the famous person you are writing to, begin the letter with their name and make sure you follow it with a comma.

Dear .... *,*

▶ You need to introduce your reason for writing at the beginning of the letter. For example:

I am a student at City High School ...
I have been asked to write an article for our local newspaper ...
Everyone in our class has chosen to interview a famous person ...
I am writing to ask you whether ...
As part of my media studies course I have to write an article for our local newspaper ...

▶ Then you need to give some idea of the questions you would like to ask. For example:

I would like to ask you some questions about your childhood ...
I am interested to know whether you ...

▶ Finally you need to conclude your letter, politely and hopefully. For example:

I am enclosing a stamped, addressed envelope for your reply ...
I hope you will be able to see me. ...
Please let me know when it is convenient / when it would suit you ...
I look forward to hearing from you ...

Yours sincerely,

1 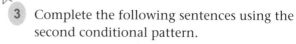 Look at this question and its answer from the text about Agresti on page 44.

*What **would you miss** about Europe **if you left**? More than anything **I would miss my friends if I left** Europe.*

Has Agresti already left Europe?
Is he planning to leave Europe?

Agresti does not think it is likely that he will leave Europe, but that does not stop him from speculating or hypothesising about it.
When we want to refer to something that is unreal or imaginary, we use the second conditional.

2 Think of three different answers to the following two questions and then practise the questions and answers with your partner.

A What would you miss about .... (the town/country you are in at the moment) if you left?

B What wouldn't you miss?

3 Complete the following sentences using the second conditional pattern.

1 Petra would not mind if you .... her camera; she never minds lending things to people.

2 If you .... enough money, you would be able to afford a holiday.

3 If his parents were not so poor, Felix .... be able to go to university.

4 I might lose weight if I .... on a diet, but I enjoy eating too much!

5 If I were an actress, I .... in Hollywood because life would be too competitive.

6 If I had the opportunity, I .... a job in another country.

7 If I won $1,000, ...

8 I wouldn't mind living alone if ....

9 If Marty lost his job, he ....

10 If my penfriend came to stay with me,
....

SPEAKING

⟨ **Who would you like to meet?** ⟩

1 Look at these photographs in groups.

The two students in the photographs were on holiday in the US when they came across these lifesize cardboard cutouts in a shopping mall!

The boy in the photo said, 'If I met President Clinton, I would ask him for his autograph.'
What do you think the girl said?
'If I met Hillary Clinton, I'd
....
...........................,'

If you had the chance to meet the Clintons, what would you like to ask them?

2 Now look at the pictures and talk about the things you would do if you were in each situation.

What would you do if ...?

1 🔲 Look at the article below. From the headline, what do you think the article is about?

What do you think children and young people can contribute to the running of companies? What are the disadvantages (from the adult point of view) of involving children in the running of a company?

VOCABULARY

2 Read through the article and find words or phrases which mean:

1 taking over (with the idea of force) (para. 1)

2 focusing on or aiming at (para. 2)

3 intervention (para. 2)

4 make something known (para. 2)

5 occurred to people (para. 2)

6 strange, unusual and excitingly different (para. 3)

7 draw and scribble without any real purpose (para. 3)

8 seeds or cereal (para. 3)

9 eagerly accepted (para. 3)

10 used or implemented (para. 3)

Kids in the boardroom

1 A new breed of director is invading the boardrooms of Britain. This one tends to have all his – or more often her – hair and to favour T-shirts over designer ties and chewing gum over cigars.

2 Children's boards are a new idea in business. If companies are targeting kids with their services or products, then it makes sense to have direct input from children themselves at the highest levels in the company. The children can comment on any aspects of the business, without the interference of external research companies; they may well bring to light ideas which would never have crossed the minds of adults; and of course, as well as benefiting the company, they may gain from the experience themselves.

3 A zoo park in the south of England has a junior board which meets three times a year. All its members are aged between eight and thirteen. They sit around a big table, with an agenda, minutes of the last meeting and jugs of water. They consider ideas for facilities, advertising and activities, vote their approval or otherwise and offer suggestions. 'I thought it would be a good idea if we had exotic drinks for children,' said ten-year-old Katie. 'And if we had paper tablecloths in the restaurant, children could doodle while waiting to be served. Also if we had a grain machine by the lagoon, we could feed the birds.' All her ideas were snapped up and put into practice!

3 How many examples of the second conditional can you find in the text? Write them down and check with your partner.

Imagine you can be like the children in the article and join the board of a company. In your group, decide on a company you are familiar with, not in any detailed way, but simply a company whose products or organisation you have heard of, e.g. Coca-Cola, McDonald's.

If you could make some suggestions in the way that Katie did, what would these suggestions be?

Would you like to see new products? Do you think existing products or services could be improved?

Talk about your ideas, write them down and then be ready to discuss them with the class.

READING 〉 **1**

Archbishop Tutu writes about how he usually spends his days.

Five sentences have been removed from the article and these are listed at the end.

Read the article carefully and then choose from the sentences A–E on page 51 the one which fits each gap.

A LIFE IN THE DAY OF

Usually I get up at 4 a.m. It's quiet and peaceful at that time, which I need to collect myself. It's a time when I try to engage with God. Many times this is a difficult thing to do.

Around 5 a.m. I shave and brush my teeth. I used to use a cordless razor but it left a rash on my face, so now I use the type that you find in the toilet bags you are given on the plane. I'll then go down to the office to read the Bible and I'll also have another book. I'm often asked to write forewords for books, or to read manuscripts. 1

I do my correspondence until about 6.45 a.m. and then I do some exercise. I used to walk in Cape Town, but I stopped because the winters are so dark and more recently there were security concerns. After that I have a shower and go to chapel

for 7.30. Up until this point I won't have spoken a word. 2 I talk far too much.

After the service I tell my staff where I'm going and what I've been doing. Then I go up to my apartment to read the newspapers.

I have breakfast at about 9 a.m. and from around 10 a.m. I have appointments. 3

I had always wanted to be a physician, and that seems to have rubbed off on my eldest daughter, who is studying medicine. But I have no regrets

about following the career I have.

I have lunch every day except Friday. 4 At 1p.m. I go to the chapel for 30 minutes. Then I eat, maybe fruit and cheese and yoghurt. I have a nap until 3 p.m., when I start up with the batteries recharged. More appointments follow until around 5p.m., when I go back to chapel. Evening prayers last until 6 p.m. and then I will spend an hour in the office.

My wife and I will have a drink before supper. 5 But when one is always talking, the thing one longs for is quiet. She's expecting to hear all that I have been up to and there can be tension. We watch the news and examine the day's events. At 9 or 10 p.m. I go to bed, and turn off the light by 11.

A Normally I have a three-hour lunch.

B That's important to me as I'm a noisy one.

C This is the time for that sort of thing.

D She complains I don't talk enough to her.

E There's a little corner of my heart that still wants to be a doctor.

2 Now read the article again and choose the best answer for the following questions.

1 Archbishop Tutu gets up early because he

   A can't sleep longer.

   B likes time to himself.

   C enjoys the dawn.

   D feels very energetic.

2 In the early hours of the day he

   A has a light breakfast.

   B talks to himself.

   C does some work.

   D goes for a walk.

3 What does Archbishop Tutu feel about the past?

   A He's glad he became a priest.

   B He wishes he had been a doctor.

   C He regrets not working harder.

   D He's glad his daughter is a doctor.

4 What does Archbishop Tutu's wife object to?

   A He works too hard.

   B He doesn't communicate.

   C He's always tired.

   D He's too talkative.

GRAMMAR / Word building 1: suffix *-ation*

1 Desmond Tutu's wife complained that her husband didn't *communicate*, and he admitted that his lack of *communication* could cause tension between them.

What happens to the spelling when the verb is changed into a noun?
Can you think of any other words that follow the same pattern?

The same suffix *-ation* can also be added to some verbs which end in *-fy*.

Example
modify → **modification**.

2 Match the following words with their meanings and then fill in the gaps in the text using the correct forms of the words.

1 clarify	devote oneself to
2 separation	inhabit
3 populate	understanding
4 realisation	division
5 dedicate	make something clear

Andy Warhol once remarked that everyone should be famous for fifteen minutes. Unfortunately, no one asked him for (1).................. of what he meant by famous. If it means getting your picture in the newspapers or your face on television, then a fair proportion of the (2)................ stands a chance of doing that in their lifetime. But few people have sufficient experience to (3)................ just how much (4)................ is required to enjoy the long-term status that (5)................ the truly famous from those who enjoy merely temporary fame.

Would you like to be famous – if only for fifteen minutes?
What are the disadvantages of being famous?

1 Desmond Tutu says he had always wanted to be a physician. What kind of job appeals to you, or are you already doing it?

2 ☒ Look at the list of jobs below.
Which of these occupations might lead to fame and fortune?
Pick out the two best paid jobs.
Are there any jobs listed which you wouldn't want to do? Why not?

3 You are going to hear five people talking about different aspects of their work and training. You have to identify each speaker's job from the list.

waiter   plumber   farmer   truck driver   lawyer   pilot
research scientist   shopkeeper   builder   chef   bank clerk
photographer   market trader

Before you listen, guess who does which job.
The first speaker is a woman and she could be a ....
The second speaker is a young man and he could be a ....
The third speaker is a woman – she could be a ....
The fourth speaker is a middle-aged man – he might be a ....
The fifth speaker is a woman and she might be a ....

4 Now listen and see if you can identify the job from what each person says. How many did you guess correctly?

5 Now listen again and this time write down some of the key words and phrases that helped you identify each person's occupation.
Speaker 1: ....
Speaker 2: ....
Speaker 3: ....
Speaker 4: ....
Speaker 5: ....

1　☒ Look at what you wrote down for Speaker 1 in the Listening exercise. What were the clues that told you she *must* be a chef? Before you heard the tape, what did you think she *might* be? When you first heard her speak, did you think she *could* be anything else?

2　The last speaker said:
*People ... look all surprised when they see me and ... you can see them thinking, 'That **can't** be a woman.'*
Look at what other people said to each other when they saw her:

Is that a woman?

1　It might be – slow down a bit!

2　It could be – let me have another look!

3　It can't be – women don't drive trucks!

4　It must be – that's why she's laughing at us!

Decide which statement(s) show(s) that the speaker is:

certain it's a woman.
not so sure whether it's a man or a woman.
fairly sure that it's a man.

3　Look at this photo and what two people said about it.

> Where do you think this photo was taken?

> But the words on the umbrella are French.

> I'm not sure. It could be Ireland. It can't be South America because the people look European.

> Oh right – then it can't be England ... it must be France!

Which modal verb(s) express(es) possibility and which express(es) certainty?

4 Match the dialogues with the degree of certainty or possibility that the people are expressing and underline the modal verbs.

1 Are you doing anything this evening?
I'm not sure. I may be going out.

2 I haven't been able to contact Lydia all evening.
She might be working late as she's very busy.

3 I hardly recognise Rula with long dark hair.
She must be wearing a wig.

present certainty
future possibility
present possibility

4 Is Sam coming on holiday with us?
He might come for the second week.

5 Look – the car's covered with ice.
It must be freezing outside.

6 The swimming pool's been closed for months.
They must still be repairing it.

5 ▌▌ Look at the pictures and ask each other what you think has happened.

Example
What do you think happened to that car?
I don't know – it **may/might/could have been** *damaged in a crash.*

Key vocabulary

Apart from the vocabulary practised within this unit, you also need to know the words related to jobs in exercises A and B.

Use your dictionary to look up any words you don't know.

A Wordsearch

There are ten jobs hidden in this puzzle. Read the clues to help you discover what they are.

Someone who:

1 designs buildings
2 specialises in animal health
3 works underground
4 hears cases in a law court
✓ 5 writes books, articles, etc.
6 carries luggage or acts as a doorman
7 looks after sick people
8 works in an office
9 cares for your teeth
10 makes cakes and bread

B Odd one out

Which job is the odd one out and why?

1 doctor chemist surgeon butcher
2 gardener refuse collector lecturer mechanic
3 artist musician designer fisherman

4 decorator prison officer painter graphic designer
5 solicitor caretaker barrister legal assistant
6 beautician hairdresser geologist jeweller
7 air steward/stewardess tailor travel agent tour operator
8 soldier newsreader TV presenter broadcaster
9 business executive sailor manager consultant
10 journalist printer caterer translator
11 receptionist engineer clerical assistant secretary
12 government official electrician politician police officer

Vocabulary in context

Fill in the missing words in the sentences below. Each word has been started for you, but you should use your dictionary if you need further help.

1 Xavier was sa _ _ _ _ _ from his job as a shop assistant at the supermarket for being rude and unhelpful towards the customers.
2 Do you think you need excellent eyesight in order to train as an opt _ _ _ _ _ _ ?
3 As the industry moves over to computerised technology so more and more telephone op _ _ _ _ _ _ _ _ are being made redu _ _ _ _ _ _ .
4 Many sales rep _ _ _ _ _ _ _ _ _ _ _ _ _ _ are paid on commission – in other words the more they sell, the more they earn.
5 If you enjoy meeting people, a job as a bar atte _ _ _ _ _ _ would probably suit you.
6 Unem _ _ _ _ _ _ _ _ _ is a problem which faces most governments in the developed world.
7 Most people expect an annual sal _ _ _ _ increase to maintain their living standards.
8 I have applied for the po _ _ _ _ _ _ _ of head caretaker at my old school.
9 Many phot _ _ _ _ _ _ _ _ _ _ work on a freelance basis selling their pictures to newspapers and magazines.
10 You need a good head for figures if you want to be an acc _ _ _ _ _ _ _ _ _ .

Recycling: phrasal verbs

Read the text and decide which phrasal verb A, B, C or D best fits each space.

In the past, actors, politicians, sports personalities and so on confined themselves to their memoirs: now any celebrity seems prepared to write a novel in order to (1) .... the times. Why do they do it? The reasons are not necessarily financial although some celebrities certainly make money. One celebrity confessed to having to (2) .... large debts, but most of them seem to be pursuing a very ancient human inclination: the wish to be taken seriously. They (3) .... as feeling inferior and are terrified of being thought to live frivolous or worthless lives. A certain abstract dignity still attaches to the novel, and anyone who (4) .... a book – whatever its literary merits – is thought to have achieved something worthwhile. In the future it looks as if the celebrity novel is going to mean big business as more and more people (5) .... writing.

1 A keep in with   B keep on at   C keep up with
   D keep away from
2 A pay in   B pay into   C pay for
   D pay off
3 A come up   B come round   C come out
   D come across
4 A brings out   B brings up   C brings round
   D brings in
5 A turn to   B turn up   C turn down
   D turn over

Learning record

When you have finished Unit 3, try filling in this record of what you have learnt.

1 How do you form the nouns from the verbs *separate* and *specify*?

2 If a letter begins *Dear Sir/Madam*, how would you end it?

3 What is the basic verb pattern for the second conditional?

4 *Her ideas were snapped up.* What does this expression mean?

5 Which modal verb do you use when you want to express certainty?

6 Can you complete the following table of irregular verbs?

Verb base	Simple past	Past participle
bite	....	....
....	flew	....
....	....	let
run	....	....
....	wore	....

FCE Checklist

Look back at the description of what the FCE examination comprises on pages 6–7 and then complete the checklist.

I have practised:
- ❯ speaking skills for Paper .....
- ❯ .... skills for Paper 4
- ❯ word building skills for Paper ....., Part 5
- ❯ .... skills for Paper 1
- ❯ writing skills for Paper .....

EXAM ADVICE

5 Writing, Part 2

In Part 2 of the Writing paper you may have the opportunity to write a non-transactional letter which could be formal or informal, in response to a variety of different tasks such as asking for information, applying for a job, replying to an advertisement or complaining about something you have bought.

▶ You will **not** be asked to write any addresses.

▶ Look carefully at the **bold type** which will usually tell you the kind of letter you are being asked to write. For example: 'Write your **letter of application** ...' . Is the letter you are being asked to write formal or informal? Do you know the person to whom you are writing?

▶ Once you are clear about the kind of letter you are going to write, decide on the appropriate way to begin. You may be given the name of the person to whom you are writing or you may have to decide whether you need to use *Sir/Madam*. (Look back at page 46 of this unit if you need to check.) At the same time, think about how you will need to end the letter.

▶ Highlight the key words in the question which will provide the content points of your letter.

▶ Check whether you need to include any personal information.

▶ Don't choose this option if you are not comfortable with the topic.

▶ Don't start writing until you have made a few notes on how you are going to organise your ideas, paragraph by paragraph, and make sure that you can think of enough to write.

▶ Try to include as wide a range of vocabulary and grammatical structure as you can. Show the examiner how much you know!

▶ Divide your writing time sensibly between planning, writing and checking.

6 Use of English, Part 2

Part 2 of the Use of English paper requires you to fill in the 15 missing words in a text based on a topic which will be described in the title.

▶ Look at the title. What is the passage going to be about? If you don't recognise the word(s) in the title, don't panic but look at the opening few lines of the passage for the answer.

▶ Without trying to fill in any of the words, read through the complete passage quite quickly to get an idea of the content.

▶ The answer will always be **one** word. You won't lose marks for putting a wrong answer, but you will lose marks if you try and fit two words into the space even if they both seem correct.

▶ The missing words are going to focus more on grammar and less on vocabulary, so pay particular attention to the structure of what you are reading. How are the sentences linked to develop the writer's ideas?

▶ The chances are that you will find some gaps easier to fill than others.

▶ On a second, slower reading, fill in the missing words which you are confident of by writing them in the appropriate numbered spaces on your separate answer sheet. In the actual exam be very careful that you write the word in its correct space if, for example, the first word you are certain of is the answer to the fourth gap.

▶ If there are some gaps which you can't immediately fill, first of all try and decide on the kind of word which you think is missing.

▶ Be a language detective and use all the clues available: do you need a noun, an adverb, a preposition, a linking word, part of a phrasal verb, etc. to complete the sentence? If it is a verb, which tense is it likely to be in? If you can identify the kind of word (and even if you can't), then make a sensible guess – don't leave your answer sheet incomplete as there is always a chance you may be right!

▶ Finally, when you have filled in all the missing words, check that you have **spelt each word correctly**.

▶ Now read the passage through again. Does it make sense and read correctly?

1   USE OF ENGLISH   PART 4

For questions **1–15**, read the text below and look carefully at each line. Some of the lines are correct, and some have a word which should not be there.
If a line is correct, put a tick (✓) beside it. If a line has a word which should **not** be there, write the word beside it. There is an example at the beginning.

A DEGREE IN GIPSY?

1	✓	Have you ever wondered what to study at university?
2	....	If you are looking for an unusual language to learn,
3	....	the Bucharest university could be interesting. Romania,
4	....	home is to one of the largest populations of Gipsies in
5	....	Europe, is to offer courses to study Gipsy as a foreign
6	....	language. It is so thought that Gipsy has oriental roots,
7	....	and it will be taught alongside to Sanskrit and Hindu as
8	....	part of a three-year course. However, it may be difficult
9	....	to get funding to study Gipsy as it is not an established
10	....	academic subject. But this should not yet prevent you
11	....	from applying as more and more universities will offer
12	....	courses in subjects which, until recently, were unheard
13	....	of. For one example, a British university is offering a
14	....	degree course in soap opera based on such popular TV
15	....	programmes from the US, Australia and the UK itself.

2 Grammar: second conditional

▶ Grammar reference p.218

Complete the following sentences using the correct verb patterns.

1 If I lived by myself, ...

2 I wouldn't lend Nick any money unless ....

3 If I knew where they lived, ...

4 I would love to stay longer ....

5 If Norbert took more exercise, ...

6 If you found a child wandering alone at night, ... ?

7 .... , she wouldn't marry him.

8 Sue wouldn't ask for help unless ....

9 If had more time, ...

10 If I had the power to change things, ...

3 WRITING **PART 2**

You would like to apply for the holiday job advertised below. You have to write to the manager of City Hall explaining why you think you are suitable for the job.

Holiday Job

City Hall is offering free playgroup facilites for children aged 2-8.
Parents may leave their children for up to 2 hours while shopping.

We need supervisors to help with the playgroup.
No special qualifications necessary, but you must enjoy being with children.

Write a **letter** in **120–180** words in an appropriate style. Do not include addresses.

4 Grammar: modal verbs 1

▶ Grammar reference p.218

Rewrite the following sentences using an appropriate modal verb to replace the part of each sentence in italics.

Example
The rain is coming through the roof – *there's definitely* a leak.
The rain is coming through the roof – **there must be** *a leak.*

1 They're digging up the road near our house so *there's a chance I shall arrive* late as the traffic is terrible.

    ....

2 That *certainly isn't* my coat you've found as it doesn't have any pockets.

    ....

3 It *often gets* very hot around midday so make sure you don't sit around in the sun for too long.

    ....

4 Eating too many sweets *possibly damages* your teeth.

    ....

5 *Perhaps you'll see* Carla when you're in town, but I doubt it as I think she's still away on holiday.

    ....

6 The light is on in Max's bedroom so *he's still working.*

    ....

7 *Perhaps Jamie wasn't lying* but he wasn't telling the whole truth either!

    ....

8 *I'm sure Sandra's got* a new car because I saw her driving a really smart sports model today.

    ....

9 I don't know how they can afford to go on another luxury cruise – *maybe they've won* the national lottery!

    ....

10 *Ally apparently failed* his exams because he's staying on at school for another year to retake them.

    ....

5 Word building 1

Fill in the missing words in these columns. Don't forget the spelling rule.
If you don't know the meaning of a word, look it up in your dictionary. Then use the correct form of the words to complete sentences 1–10.

	verb	noun		verb	noun
1	agitate	....	14	....	magnification
2	beautify*	....	15	....	meditation
3	....	celebration	16	....	moderation
4	congratulate	....	17	negate	....
5	....	duplication	18	notify	....
6	....	elaboration	19	qualify	....
7	estimate	....	20	quantify*	....
8	exemplify	....	21	reserve	....
9	fluctuate	....	22	satisfy*	....
10	....	gratification	23	starve	....
11	hibernate	....	24	terrify*	....
12	horrify*	....	25	vegetate	....
13	....	illumination	26	verify	....

* These words do not follow the same pattern as the others – be careful!

1 .... on passing your driving test!

2 Many people are .... by spiders – even really tiny ones.

3 There are very few jobs for which you don't need some kind of ....

4 Many animals .... during the winter months and emerge when it's spring.

5 It's a good idea to .... a seat on busy flights.

6 Some elderly people use a .... glass in order to read small print.

7 World prices for coffee beans have .... quite a lot in recent years.

8 Police found large .... of stolen fruit on sale in the supermarket.

9 Before you can enter university, the admissions officer must be .... that you have passed the appropriate examinations.

10 The tramp was found to have died of ...., having not eaten for more than three weeks.

6 Grammar revision: past tenses 1

 Grammar reference p.218

On the following page is part of an article about the actress and model, Isabella Rossellini.
Fill in the gaps by putting each verb in brackets into its correct form using either the **past simple** or the **past continuous** tense.

Isabella Rossellini is the daughter of the actress Ingrid Bergman and the director Roberto Rossellini. Her parents [1] .... (divorce) when she [2] .... (be) four years old and thereafter she [3] .... (live) sometimes with her Swedish mother in France and sometimes with her father in Rome. 'I [4] .... (always move) around,' she says, 'so I never [5] .... (have) much stability in my life.'

Rossellini [6] .... (start) work in the cinema, the family business, as a costume designer for her father and [7] .... (follow) this with modelling assignments. At the age of twenty-eight, however, she [8] .... (make) her modest debut in a movie. 'As I [9] .... (grow up) I [10] .... (realise) there wasn't much difference between being a model and an actress. The basic body language is the same. I [11] .... (work) as a model without realising that I [12] .... (act) at the same time. There is the sense of rhythm needed to maintain the audience's interest, learning how to grab people's attention.'

---

7   USE OF ENGLISH   PART 2

For questions **1–15**, read the text below and think of the word which best fits each space. Use only **one** word in each space.

PICTURE POSTCARDS

Few people realise that during the golden age of the picture postcard, **(1)** .... lasted from the beginning of the century until the end of the First World War in 1918, **(2)** .... amazing 860 million postcards were **(3)** .... every year in Britain alone.

There were several reasons **(4)** .... the popularity of postcards in the early 1900s. **(5)** .... , the cost of sending a card **(6)** .... much cheaper **(7)** .... a letter, and secondly postcard manufacturers **(8)** .... a vast and infinitely varied number of illustrations. As well **(9)** .... being posted, the cards were **(10)** .... collected – usually in albums – and treasured for years **(11)** .... come.

Postcards **(12)** .... a sporting or recreational theme were particularly popular, **(13)** .... some sports more than others seemed to appeal to artists and cartoonists. Cycling was all the rage. Many cyclists wore colourful caps and jackets, and social cyclists **(14)** .... part in mass night-time cycling rallies, lit by Chinese lanterns.

One sport which doesn't appear very much in humorous postcards is cricket. Perhaps the national game was considered far **(15)** .... serious a business for postcard cartoons.

OUT AND ABOUT

SPEAKING

Who eats what?

1 Which countries are these meals associated with?
Do you know what they are called?

2 Think of some food or dishes typically associated with your own country.
Are there any dishes which are typically eaten to celebrate a festive
occasion? In the UK, for example, turkey is traditionally eaten in December
at Christmas.

3 What do you notice about the groups of words below?
Which of these words would you use to describe the food or dishes you thought of?

bitter	creamy	heavy	hot	tender	fresh
sour	fatty	light	spicy	tough	raw
sweet	greasy		mild		ripe
savoury			salty		
			nutty		

4 Is the area where you live famous for any speciality? In Brittany, in northern France, savoury pancakes – sometimes filled with cheese or ham and called *galettes* – are very popular. In Greece, a wide range of snacks called *meze* (usually served with drinks) are very popular.

5 Do you have a favourite food or dish? What is it called? What are the ingredients? How is it made?
Which of these words do you need in order to explain how it is made?

bake	chop	grate	melt	peel	steam
beat	cut	grill	microwave	roast	stir/stir fry
boil	fry	heat	mix	slice	stew

READING

Chinese festivals

1 Read the article overleaf about Chinese festivals and the part that food plays in their celebration. There will probably be some words which you don't recognise, but try to guess the general meaning from their context as you read.
When you have read the passage once, answer questions 1 and 2.

A popular Chinese event in Hong Kong is the Festival of the Hungry Ghosts. This is when the spirits of the dead are allowed to wander the earth for a whole month.

5 Those with living relatives will go to their homes, to share the comforts there, but the rest will roam the streets, hungry and envious. Unless placated by food and entertainment, the homeless ghosts might

10 begin hating people and cause mischief. Therefore, feasts and Chinese operas are staged for them in public places.

Then there is the delightful Mooncake Festival, which, according to one legend,

15 traces its origins to the fourteenth century. At that time China was in revolt against the Mongols*. Patriots sent messages up and down the country hidden inside pastry cases, and lanterns

20 signalled the start of the rebellion. Vast quantities of mooncakes are eaten during the celebrations. They actually look more like pies, round in shape to symbolise the moon and stuffed with sweet bean paste

25 or a mixture of melon and lotus seeds.

One of the top festivals in the Chinese calendar is the Dragon Boat Festival. This festival is traditionally associated with poet-statesman Chu Yuan, who was a prominent Court official in the fourth century BC. He campaigned against corruption in the government and was

30 eventually ordered into exile. He decided to drown himself instead and jumped into a river. Fishermen raced out in boats and tried, in vain, to save him. For years afterwards, people walking along the riverbank stopped to throw rice into the river to feed his spirit. One day, so the story goes, it appeared on the river bank and thanked

35 them for the offerings but said that the fish and turtles were eating all the rice; could they please wrap it up in little packets? Today a sticky rice concoction, wrapped in little packets, is sold during the festival.

* people who lived in Mongolia in central Asia

1 Where do you think this passage comes from?

A a novel about China
B a history textbook
C a travel magazine
D a tourist leaflet

2 Why do you think someone would read this passage?

A to learn how to make mooncakes
B to find out about Hong Kong
C to understand about foreign customs
D to discover how festivals develop

2 Now look carefully at the first paragraph.

   3 What does *Those* (line 5) refer to?

   4 Which word in this paragraph means the same as *roam* (line 7)?

   5 What does *envious* (line 8) mean?

     A greedy for more food and drink

     B wanting what other spirits get

   6 Which word best fits the meaning of *placated* (line 8)?

     A satisfied

     B rewarded

   7 Why do the Chinese put on operas and feasts for the spirits?

Now look carefully at the second paragraph.

   8 What does *its* (line 15) refer to?

   9 What does *in revolt* (line 16) mean?

     A at war with

     B to negotiate with

  10 Which word in this paragraph has a similar meaning to *revolt*?

  11 Which of these pictures best decribes the legend about mooncakes?

Now look carefully at the third paragraph.

  12 What does *prominent* (line 28) mean?

     A wicked

     B important

     c cruel

  13 What does *into exile* (line 30) mean?

     A to be locked up in prison

     B to have to leave one's country

  14 Which word best fits the meaning of *in vain* (line 31/2)?

     A hopefully

     B unsuccessfully

  15 What does *it* (line 34) refer to?

  16 Why are the rice offerings now wrapped up?

If you could visit one of these festivals, which one would you choose? Why? Is there a festival in your country that you would recommend visiting?	What is the festival called? What time of year does it take place? What does it celebrate? What happens during the festival? What do you like best about the festival?

1 ☒ Look at sentence A from the text and compare it with sentence B. Do you think there is any difference in meaning between the two sentences?

A Unless placated by food and entertainment, the homeless ghosts might begin hating people and cause mischief.

B Unless placated by food and entertainment, the homeless ghosts might begin to hate people and cause mischief.

2 Now compare these pairs of sentences and decide which of the following applies to each pair.

▶ slight difference in meaning
▶ significant difference in meaning
▶ no difference in meaning

1 A I started going to festivals when I was a child.
  B I started to go to festivals when I was a child.

2 A I love watching street entertainers.
  B I love to watch street entertainers.

3 A People stopped to throw rice into the river.
  B People stopped throwing rice into the river.

4 A I prefer staying at home when it's very cold.
  B I prefer to stay at home when it's very cold.

5 A I don't remember visiting the caves at Guilin.
  B I didn't remember to visit the caves at Guilin.

6 A I regret cancelling my holiday.
  B I regret to say I must cancel my holiday.

3 Put the verb in brackets in each sentence into either the infinitive or the gerund. The intended meaning for each sentence is explained in red.

1 After leaving school Gregoris went on .... (study) medicine.
  start something

2 Please stop .... (worry) about the exam – I'm sure you'll pass.
  discontinue an action

3 Can you remember .... (buy) some fruit on your way home, please?
  you mustn't forget

4 I live in London, which means .... (use) public transport as I can't afford a car.
  involve

5 I regret .... (miss) the carnival in Rio when I was there last year.
  be sorry about something that happened in the past

6 Car alarms sometimes go on .... (ring) for ages before anyone takes any notice.
  continue

7 Don't forget .... (get) a ticket for the pop festival before they all sell out.
  do something in the future

8 My watch needs .... (mend) as I dropped it on the pavement.
  something needs to be done – passive use

9 I like .... (go) on holiday with friends.
  generally speaking for enjoyment

10 She tried .... (count) sheep, but she still couldn't get to sleep.
  as an experiment

LISTENING

Something to celebrate

1 Look back at the map on page 64. You are going to hear part of a radio programme in which the presenter is talking about Asian festivals in Japan, Thailand and Singapore.
Before you listen, look at the notes below which are incomplete. Read them carefully as they will help you to focus on what you are going to hear.
Listen and complete the notes using a word or a short phrase.

Asian festivals

Some festivals in Asia are connected with harvests or

(1) ....

Festivals offer people an opportunity to (2) ....

The Japanese throw (3) .... to frighten away evil

spirits.

The festival in Sapporo has sculptures made out of

(4) ....

Young people who are (5) .... are congratulated

on Adults' Day.

On Children's Day people fly banners painted with pictures of

(6) ....

During the Loy Krathong festival in Thailand, people put four

things into a small boat: (7) .... , incense,

(8) .... and a small coin.

The Monkey God was originally (9) ....

Chinese parents want their children to have the Monkey God as

their godfather because he is (10) ....

> Which of the Asian festivals do you find most interesting?
> Which one would you like to see?
> How do festivals help people to escape the cares of everyday life?

VOCABULARY

2 Look at the adjectives in the box which are used to describe the Monkey God. Fill in the gaps in each sentence by making other words from these adjectives.

> energetic   tough   crafty   courageous
> strong   temperamental   wise

1 The pickpocket behaved so .... that by the time everyone realised what had happened, it was too late to catch him.

2 Socrates was renowned for his

....

3 Regular weightlifting develops your muscles and builds up your ....

4 Small children seem to have unlimited

....

5 She has a very easygoing .... , and is always calm and pleasant.

6 The .... of the meat suggested it had been undercooked.

7 Learning how to parachute requires a certain amount of ....

3 Listen to part of the recording again and write down the words which the speaker uses to describe other aspects of Asian festivals.

Asia has (1) .... festivals.
They are (2) .... , exotic and very much part of local tradition.
Japan has (3) .... gods, and hardly a day goes by without a festival somewhere. In February each year, people throughout the country hold a bean-throwing festival. They scatter roasted beans to drive away (4) .... devils, shouting: 'Fortune in, devils out.'

Now listen to the rest of the recording for words which are similar in meaning to those below; as you hear them, write them down.

5 once a year ....

6 magical ....

7 to show respect to ....

8 able to live forever ....

READING

1 Most festivals and celebrations are associated with food and drink; sometimes very special food is reserved for such occasions and it may involve elaborate preparations. But what about the food you eat every day? In groups, write down some of the things that you eat and drink almost every day and compare them with other people's eating habits.

2 Quickly scan the short article on eating out in Russia which is taken from a magazine for tourists, and note down some of the food you can expect to eat if you go to Russia.
Compare lists in your group. Have you written down anything that you have never tasted?
Would you miss any of the things you normally eat every day if you were a tourist in Russia?

3 Now read the article more thoroughly to check you have written down all the items of food.

1 THERE IS SOME good food to be had in Russia, but don't expect it at every meal. Breakfast normally consists of sweet fruit juice, tea, bread, eggs, jam, butter and possibly porridge. Lunch and dinner are fairly similar, the buffet style meal being popular, very good value for money, and also a good chance to try out lots of different things. Even in a poor winter the Muscovites will manage to provide a salad of sorts, but generally fruit and vegetables are in short supply unless they have been preserved. Meat, poultry and fish are cooked plainly, but well.

2 Russia is, however, a snacker's paradise, as the cakes and ice cream are both first-rate. In the traditional tea bars you can get rid of a few roubles by buying a pot of tea and a cake, and at the same time participate in something quite typically Russian. You take your pot of tea to the table, where a huge silver samovar sits, full of hot water. Gradually you water down the tea, which is a sort of concentrate, and drunk black. Finish off with an excellent Russian brandy, or splash out on a bottle of Russian champagne!

VOCABULARY

4 Find words and phrases from the text which mean:

Paragraph 1

1 a meal where you help yourself from a number of dishes, often eaten standing up

....

2 worth what you pay ....

3 sample ....

4 in limited quantities ....

5 food which has been treated (salted, bottled, dried, etc.) so that it can be kept

....

6 cooked without adding a lot of extra ingredients ....

Paragraph 2

7 ideal places for people who like eating between meals ....

8 spend a large sum of money very freely

....

5 Now read a short article about South America, which has been written to give European readers some information about traditional food. However, the paragraphs are in the wrong order. Work with your partner to rearrange them so that you produce a coherent article.

The correct order for the paragraphs is:

_3_ ....

1 Yet it is all too obvious that many visitors to the continent are quite unprepared for its effect, which turns up in food when they least expect it, and makes tears trickle down their cheeks at mealtimes!

2 Over the centuries these chillies have brought life to a relatively mundane diet of corn and potatoes. But Europeans have a lot to learn about this bringer of heat. After hundreds of years Europeans still barely understand the subtleties of the chilli.

3 First impressions of South American food may dazzle the eye and the tongue, but the markets and the cooking glow with red chillies, yellow corn and green herbs; there is purple corn too, blue-black lobsters and brilliant orange sweet peppers.

4 When the Spanish arrived in South America they did not find the gold they had originally come for; instead they discovered golden pumpkins, corn and peppers, and the buried treasure they took back was potatoes – more than 100 varieties. The ancient Andeans even worshipped the potato as a god, but the influence of red chillies in cooking is everywhere.

6 Underline the clues in the text that helped you put the paragraphs in the right order.

Look at the article on Russia and the way the writer has organised the information; the article consists of two paragraphs and is approximately 200 words long.

Paragraph 1
introductory sentence → description of some meals, typical ingredients → general comment(s) on style of food available

Paragraph 2
more detailed information on popular places to eat and drink → one or two examples of food/drink which are typically Russian

Now look back at the vocabulary which you used at the beginning of this unit and the ideas you discussed with your partner.
Write a short article about traditional food in your country for readers who have not visited your country before.
Plan your ideas in two paragraphs and write between 120 and 180 words.

[ ] SPEAKING

Shopping around

1   If you are going to buy food and drink for a party or a special celebration, do you have a favourite place, store or shop?
Would you go to a market or a department store to buy what you needed?
Do you like to serve yourself or do you prefer to be served?
Are you prepared to bargain?
What other things do you shop for?
What do you spend your money on?
How do you like to pay:

with cash?

by cheque?

with your credit card?

2   In groups, look at the picture opposite of a shopping mall. Match the names of the shops/goods below with the windows A–X.

..... clothes boutique	..... sweaters	..... trainers and sports shoes	..... discs and tapes
..... computers	..... videos	..... stationery	..... books
..... flowers	..... kitchenware	..... toys	..... office furniture
..... newsagent	..... health foods	..... posters and prints	..... rugs and carpets
..... confectionery	..... ice cream parlour	..... china and glass	..... jewellery
..... souvenir and gift shop	..... furniture	..... musical instruments	..... mountain bikes

3 Imagine you have an hour to spend in the mall. Decide which shop(s) you want to visit and why.

Write down what each person in your group says.

Example

Nesta: *I want to go to the flower shop to get some flowers for my parents.*

I Work with a new partner from another group. What did Nesta say?
She said she ....
....

Look at the notes you have written and report to your partner what the students in your group said when they were deciding which shops to visit.

◻◻ **LISTENING**

1 Listen to a conversation between a boy and two other people.
What is the relationship between the boy and the two people?
What are the three of them doing?

2 Now listen again and fill in the gaps in the passage below. Make all the necessary changes to the verbs and pronouns. There is also one adverb that needs changing.
Your teacher will pause the tape as you listen so you will have plenty of time.

Nick *told* his grandmother that it (1) ....
.... a great meal. She *asked* him whether he
(2) .... like some more. He *replied* that he   ·
(3) .... far too much and he
always (4) .... when he (5) ....
supper with (6) .... He told his grandmother
that she (7) .... a brilliant cook and his
grandfather *remarked* that that (8) .... why he
(9) .... married her. Nick (10) .... he could cook like his grandmother but his
grandfather *commented* that Nick (11) .... need to cook and that (12) ....
.... even know how to make a cup of coffee. His wife said that times (13) ....
changed and if he (14) .... Nick's age, he would have to learn how to look after
(15) .... His grandfather *answered* that he (16) .... see why and that he
(17) .... find himself a nice young – but Nick *interrupted* and *explained* that everyone
(18) .... nowadays and (19) .... things like the cooking and cleaning. His
grandfather *snorted* and *replied* that it wouldn't suit (20) .... His grandmother said that Nick
(21) .... right and that it (22) .... time he learnt to cook. She said she
(23) .... his mother and father (24) .... always busy, so the
(25) .... day when he (26) .... round to supper she (27) .... show
him how to make – chocolate cake! Nick said that he loved (28) .... chocolate cake and that
perhaps he (29) .... just have another slice ...

3 What do you notice about the verbs in italics?

4 Complete the sentences below using a different reporting verb in each sentence without using *say* or *tell*. Look up the list of reporting verbs on page 220 if you need to before you begin the exercise.

1 'I shall leave home if you don't let me have a motorbike,' Jack
.... his parents.

2 'Let's go out for dinner this evening,' Fay .... to her sister.

3 'Don't worry about coming home late from the party; I'll be there to pick you up,' .... Hella's mother.

4 'If you carry on driving so fast, sooner or later you're going to have an accident,' Pinella's father .... her.

5 'You should cut down on the number of cigarettes you smoke each day,' the doctor .... his patient.

6 'Yes, I'm the one who stole the money,' Theo .... to the police.

7 'Your son has just kicked his football into my garden and damaged the roses,' the elderly lady ....

8 'I'm very sorry that I lost that book you lent me,' the student .... to her teacher.

READING

Smart shopping

1 When you were talking about the places where you shop, did anyone mention the possibility of shopping from a plane? Although it's not yet very common, one or two airlines already offer the possibility of shopping – not just buying duty-free items – while you are sitting in a plane. Can you imagine what shopping will be like in future?

2 Read the texts which illustrate the various ways in which we will be shopping in future and match them with the titles below.

1 Department stores will be competing with home shopping services by attracting customers with devices such as the 'virtual mirror' that lets clothes shoppers view themselves in any outfit they choose.

2 A bar-code reading dustbin will keep track of used goods and order replacements. An 'intelligent' fridge can display contents on screen.

3 Video shopping will be possible at 35,000 feet as airlines offer a multimedia duty-free service that connects with home delivery networks so goods can be waiting at home on arrival.

A   IN THE AIR .....

B   IN THE HOME .....

C   IN THE STORE .....

3 What do you think of these new shopping methods?
Is there anything you will miss about shopping in the future which you enjoy today?

4 Now read the following article carefully. When you have finished, choose the headings which you think are the most suitable for each paragraph.

No more waiting   Shopping in the sky   What lies ahead?   Staying put   Electronic fantasy

A

In years to come shopping is likely to be a very different experience from what we know at present. British retailers are shaping a future for shopping which, within ten years, is set to change the habits of a nation.

B

The first is home shopping – the comfort of your own living room rather than the hassle of the high street. The other, for those who like going out to buy, is a new type of 'smart' department store that will put an end to queues and even be an entertaining experience. Making purchases from home (or the workplace) is already being tested, as cable channels, satellite television and telephone companies begin to offer interactive video services, which, in a few years' time, will compete with the high street retailer and out of town superstore.

C

In the 'smart' shopping malls there will be no queues at the tills. In supermarkets, for example, shoppers will be able to scan products using a remote-control device. Instead of pushing a trolley round a store, customers will point at the display model of the item they want, see all the details on the small screen and press a button to buy it.

D

Shopping malls will also offer attractions such as the 'virtual mirror', to be sited in the fitting rooms of a clothes shop. You stand in front of the mirror and choose from a range of clothes displayed on a screen. The mirror then superimposes images of the clothes, allowing you to see how they would look on you, even if you did a 3D twirl.

E

Shopping at 35,000 feet will become commonplace. On long-distance services some airlines will provide a screen which will allow passengers to order duty-free goods to be delivered straight to their homes.

VOCABULARY

5 Now look at the following vocabulary from the passage.

For numbers 1–12, pick out the word from each list which corresponds with the way in which each word is used in the passage.

1 retailers
  A traders B buyers C shopkeepers

2 habits
  A costumes B traditions C characteristics

3 hassle
  A quarrels B difficulties C obstacles

4 making purchases
  A buying goods B choosing things
  C getting information

5 compete with
  A control B rival C offer

6 tills
  A money machines B cash registers
  C service desks

7 scan
  A examine B read C make

8 range
  A limit B stock C selection

9 superimposes
  A adds B overlays C matches

10 twirl
  A dance B roll C spin

11 commonplace
  A boring B ordinary C routine

12 straight
  A direct B fast C simply

1 Do you remember what Nick said about wanting to cook like his grandmother?

I wish I could cook like that.

He could also have said:

If only I could cook like that.

Which of the two structures seems more emphatic?
What do you notice about the tense of the verbs which follow _wish_ and _if only_?
Compare these tenses with the ones used in sentences 1–6 below.

2 Match the beginning of sentences 1–6 with their endings A–F; then decide whether each sentence refers to past, present or future time. Which sentence expresses a complaint?

1 I wish I could afford to go on holiday,

2 If only I hadn't lost my wallet,

3 I wish our neighbours didn't make so much noise,

4 If only our friends weren't coming this weekend,

5 I wish he would do his homework,

6 I wish I hadn't washed that sweater,

A I would still have my credit cards.

B then it wouldn't have shrunk.

C but he's too lazy.

D then I would be able to sleep at night.

E but I'm saving up for a new CD player.

F but it's too late to contact them now.

3 The exercise below describes various situations which refer to the past, present and future. Write down what you would say in each situation using _wish_ or _if only_ followed by the correct form of the past tense.

1 You told your parents a lie and now you regret it.

2 You are at the airport, your flight number has been called and you can't find your passport.

3 You went out to dinner last night and ate too much; this morning you feel ill.

4 Your classmate keeps tapping a pencil on the desk.

5 You left your student notebook on the bus and now you need it for your lesson.

6 You lent some of your favourite tapes to a friend who has since lost them.

7 You have been invited to a party tomorrow but you can't go.

8 You missed your appointment at the dentist's last week and now you have bad toothache.

9 You can't meet your friend this evening because you have too much work.

10 Your friend keeps interrupting as you are trying to explain something.

4 Look at the pictures below and the different situations they illustrate.
Decide what you think the various people in each picture might be wishing, regretting or complaining about and how they would express these feelings.
How many different sentences can you think of for each situation?
For example, in the first picture the girl might be thinking: 'I wish I looked like that.'

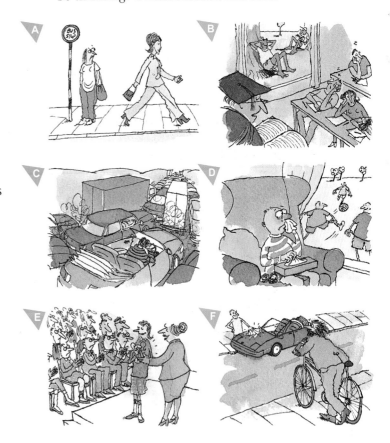

Key vocabulary

Apart from the vocabulary you have practised within this unit, you also need to know the following words in connection with food and drink. Use your dictionary to look up any words you don't know.

Rearrange the words below under the three headings:

drink	savoury (snack) food	sweet (snack) food

crisps   spirits   cider   toasted sandwich   chips
biscuits   fruit juice   wine   fruit tart   beer   bun
hot dog   alcohol   roll   peanuts   milkshake

Vocabulary in context

Fill in the missing words in the sentences below. Each word has been started for you, but you should use your dictionary if you need further help.

1 Toothpaste is generally sold in tu _ _ _ _ .

2 People's ta _ _ _ s in food vary all over the world.

3 If food is undercooked, it can be difficult to swa _ _ _ _ _ .

4 Most food is sold with a sell-by-d _ _ _ _ stamped on it so you know how long it will keep.

5 Food which has gone bad is ined _ _ _ _ _ .

6 Most bread goes st _ _ _ _ very quickly if it is not kept in an airtight container.

7 Some people find a traditional English breakfast much too fi _ _ _ _ _ _ and prefer something like fruit or cereal instead.

8 Vegetables which have gone ro _ _ _ _ _ have to be thrown away.

9 Some people avoid eating too many pu _ _ _ _ _ _ _ as they are usually very sweet and can be quite fattening.

10 Strict veg _ _ _ _ _ _ _ _ refuse to eat any meat.

Recycling: conditionals

Complete the conditional sentences below. If you need to, look back at pages 32 in Unit 2 and 48 in Unit 3 to remind yourself of the patterns.

1 If you .... to Cannes during the Film Festival in May, you will find lots of well-known actors staying there.

2 I wouldn't go on a rollercoaster unless I .... a friend with me.

3 If you smell burning, ... the fire brigade.

4 People may get headaches if they .... TV for too long.

5 It .... be wonderful if we had a world without poverty.

6 If you chose to eat at a favourite restaurant, which one .... you pick?

7 If .... food which is dirty, it can give you food poisoning.

8 If you .... lies, nobody will believe you when you tell the truth.

9 .... you write to me if I give you my address while I'm abroad?

10 .... home late, let me know and I won't lock the door.

Learning record

When you have finished Unit 4, try filling in this record of what you have learnt.

1 What does the word *envious* mean?

2 Does the word *try* change its meaning if you follow it with the infinitive or the gerund?

3 What would you expect if somebody offered you plain food?

4 Rewrite the following sentences using reported speech:

A 'I hope it won't rain when we have our barbecue this evening,' Sally said.
Sally said that ....
....

B 'Congratulations on passing your exams,' Molly said to her brother.
Molly congratulated ....
....

5 Rewrite the following sentence using *wish* so that it means the same as the original one:
You're really lucky to have won $100.

....

Look back at the description of what the FCE examination comprises on pages 6–7 and then complete the checklist.

I have practised:

> reading skills for Paper .....
> grammar skills for Paper .....
> listening skills for Paper ....., Part 2
> .... skills for Paper 2
> .... skills for Paper 5

EXAM ADVICE

7 Writing, Part 2

You should remember to identify the kind of writing that you are being asked to do, especially if there is no bold type which identifies it for you.

> **Who are you writing for?** In the task which you are going to do in the FCE Plus section on page 80, you will see that you are being asked to write an entry for a competition.

> This kind of task is asking for your own personal reasons for making a choice of country/countries which you would like to visit. The chances are that it will be read by a number of different people who will decide on the winning entry.

> Don't choose this kind of topic unless you have enough ideas to support your choice(s).

> This kind of writing is fairly open-ended as you have to create your own framework for what you want to say.

> Once you have decided on the country/countries where you would like to go, note down some of the reasons for your choice(s).

> Try to avoid repeating the same structure – in this case *I would like to ...* too frequently. Try to vary the way you introduce each paragraph and each sentence, for example:

> > *My main reason for wanting to visit ...*
> > *One of the main things that attracts me to this country is ...*
> > *I have always wanted to visit ... because I have heard/read about ...*

> Don't be afraid to give honest reasons even if you think they may be rather obvious. If you choose to write about something personal, then your own reasons are what the examiner wants to read about; try to make these reasons as interesting as possible.

8 Use of English, Part 5

In this part of the Use of English paper, your vocabulary is tested by your ability to form words to fill gaps in a text. The base form of the word is printed beside the line in which the word is missing.

> The passage will have a title, so first of all look at this and then read the passage through once very carefully to make sure you understand the content.

> The word which you have to build must fit the grammar of the sentence, so look at the structure either side of the gap for clues as to whether you need to form a noun from a verb base, an adverb from a noun, an adjective from a verb base, etc.

> If you don't immediately recognise a word, use what you know about word building. For example, most adverbs will need -*ly* added, but if the printed base word ends in -*y* (e.g. *beauty*), you will also need to make spelling changes (e.g. *beautifully*).

> Before the exam, make sure you have revised the word building sections in this course so that you are familiar with the common ways in which we form nouns, e.g. using -*ment*, -*ence*, -*tion*, etc.

> Does the word need a prefix like *un*- or *im*- to make it negative? Or maybe it needs a suffix like -*less* to make the meaning negative as in care → *careful/careless*.

> Check whether the word needs to be singular or plural if you are required to fill the gap with a noun.

> When you have decided what the word is, write it on your separate answer sheet, making sure that you transfer the correct word into its numbered space and that you have spelt it correctly.

1 READING PART 2

You are going to read an article about how a man likes to spend his holidays. For questions **1–8**, choose the answer (**A, B, C** or **D**) which you think fits best according to the text.

My wife is a teacher, which means we suffer from the tyranny of the school holidays. It's hard to think how twelve weeks is unreasonable, but there we are. We always go away for the last two weeks, which is fine because I like going late. The thought of having to come back after a summer holiday to more summer seems to me spiritually wrong.

I have two sorts of holidays: one is work-related, the other absolutely self-indulgent and pure pleasure. It's flop, eat and sleep. If somebody offers to lend me their house in the south of France, I just haven't got the strength to say: 'No, I think I'll do something more bold.'

Recently we've been borrowing a house near Toulouse. Whenever I meet people who've been going to the same place every year, I feel terribly jealous because they seem to know everyone and they're so massively integrated. But really it's just so dull and unimaginative. Even worse, I've been going to the same place for years and I've never even become part of it. I still can't remember the name of the woman in the bakery; we just grin stupidly at each other year after year in an 'it's you again' sort of way.

We tend to go away with family and friends, as many as sixteen of us one year. I love meeting round the supper table in the evening, getting silly and catching up on what happened during the day. The only disadvantage to going away with other people is that the holiday seems to go faster.

I never, ever want to leave. I'm very slow-witted in that way. I don't look forward to holidays particularly, but once I'm there I've forgotten all about work and I have no desire to return home. Suddenly, I can't believe we could be so stupid as to take only three weeks' holiday a year.

I love that feeling of being completely exhausted by heat; when nature just defeats you and you have to give in and do very little. I'm afraid I haven't got the patience or the character to have a wet summer holiday and think it's fun. The worst disaster I remember is one year when we were in a house on the west coast of Ireland, which was damp and our clothes got wetter and wetter; it was just so awful, I was unhappy all the time. The fantastically green and wildly beautiful countryside left me absolutely cold. When you're so wet you don't even want to get out of the car, let alone into the sea, somehow the beauty seems to slip away.

1 Why does the writer like taking a late holiday?

    A He prefers being away during the school terms.
    B He thinks the weather is usually much better then.
    C He feels that late summer suits his own mood.
    D He knows his wife prefers the end of summer.

2 Why does the writer accept the offer of someone else's house?

    A It makes it easier to organise a holiday.
    B He is unable to resist the attraction.
    C He likes sharing it with his friends.
    D It makes it easier for him to work there.

3 The writer feels jealous of people who

    A are more adventurous than he is.
    B own a beautiful house abroad.

C appear friends with local people.

D lead more interesting lives.

4 Why does the writer seem slightly annoyed when he is in his friend's house?

A He realises he has a bad memory for names.

B He feels awkward when shopping for bread.

C He dislikes meeting people who recognise him.

D He knows he is unlikely to ever belong there.

5 What does the writer find unattractive about being away with lots of people?

A The time passes too quickly.

B People behave in a silly way.

C Meals take too long to prepare.

D People spend hours gossiping.

6 Once he is on holiday, the writer is surprised

A that he hasn't looked forward to it more.

B that he hasn't planned a longer holiday.

C by how slowly the three weeks pass.

D that he forgets about his work so easily.

7 How does the hot weather make the writer feel?

A lifeless but hopeful

B happy and energetic

C tired and annoyed

D worn out but contented

8 How did the writer react to his surroundings in Ireland?

A He appreciated the coastal scenery.

B The constant rain made driving difficult.

C The bad weather spoilt everything for him.

D He liked the greenery of the countryside.

2 Grammar: gerunds 2

▶ Grammar reference p.219

Read the text below and fill in the missing verbs with the correct form of the word in brackets.

When Sian woke up, she remembered ¹............ .... (speak) to someone who had been holding her hand at the scene of the crash. If only she could remember who it was. It all seemed a very long time ago now. She struggled to sit up and immediately began ²...................... (feel) extremely sick. She tried ³..................... (recall) what had happened but without success. She needed ⁴..................... (ask) someone for help, but she felt as if she were floating in and out of a

dream and had forgotten ⁵...................... (tell) anyone where she was. She stopped ⁶................. (move) her head and that seemed to help; at least it meant ⁷................. (be) able to focus on the room in which she realised she was lying. At the far end was a plain wooden door and above it a red light. Her eyes continued ⁸................. (travel) round the room until they came to rest and she suddenly saw two faces smiling at her through a window. The faces went on ⁹............ (smile) and Sian opened her mouth to speak; she wanted ¹⁰................. (let) them know she was all right, but as suddenly as the faces had appeared, they disappeared.

3 WRITING PART 2

You are going to enter this writing competition:

Win an Inter-Rail pass for 26 countries!

Every year thousands of students explore Europe with an Inter-Rail pass which offers a month's unrestricted rail travel.

You now have a chance to win a pass for two people.

All you have to do is write and tell us where you would most like to go in Europe and why.

Write a **composition** in **120–180** words in an appropriate style.

4 Grammar: reported speech 2

▶ Grammar reference p.220

Rewrite the following sentences in reported speech, changing the verbs, pronouns, and time and place references as necessary. Use the reporting verbs which are given in brackets.

1 'Why don't we go out for a meal this evening?' Terry said. (suggest)

....

2 'The first train for London will leave from platform 3,' said the guard. (announce)

....

3 'Ernst is always late for English lessons,' said his teacher. (complain)

....

4 'I'll be free to come out tomorrow evening, Katie,' her father said. (promise)

....

5 'I never said I wanted to share a flat with Jo,' Gerd said. (deny)

....

6 'Are you hoping to catch the last bus home?' the driver said to the man. (enquire)

....

7 'Put your gun down and come out of the building with your hands up,' the policeman said to the gunman. (order)

....

8 'Gina still loves me and wants to marry me,' Matt said. (say)

....

9 'Have you any idea where I can buy an Albanian dictionary?' the man asked me. (ask)

....

10 'Don't touch that live wire with wet hands,' the electrician told the child. (warn)

....

5   USE OF ENGLISH   PART 5

For questions **1–10**, read the text below. Use the word given in capitals at the end of each line to form a word that fits in the space in the same line. There is an example at the beginning (**0**).

EXOTIC HOLIDAYS

For most people holidays offer an escape from (**0**) .... *boring* .... lives   **BORE**

which are routine and lack (**1**) .... These people attach   **EXCITE**

great (**2**) .... to their annual holiday and spend many happy   **IMPORTANT**

hours in what may appear to others as pointless (**3**) ....   **ORGANISE**

It is easy to mock such characters. For many of them the (**4**) ....   **FLY**

alone holds many (**5**) .... , and they need courage and   **TERRIFY**

plenty of (**6**) .... to fulfil their dreams of a holiday in a   **DETERMINE**

(**7**) .... country which they may know little about.   **DISTANCE**

On their return, however, they are in a position of strength.

Family and friends will receive (**8**) .... to supper and will be   **INVITE**

expected to listen to (**9**) .... descriptions of various adventures.   **END**

Moreover, the evening would be considered (**10**) .... without   **COMPLETE**

admiring hundreds of photographs and other souvenirs!

---

6 Grammar revision: past tenses 2

▶ Grammar reference p.220

Below is the beginning of a well-known story called *Swiss Family Robinson* by Johann Wyss, retold in simple language for young children. Fill in the missing verbs using the past perfect simple or continuous tense.

The storm [1] .... (last) for almost a week and it was getting worse. Our ship [2] .... (blow) far off course and we were lost. Suddenly there came a cry that someone [3] .... (see) land, but at that moment the ship struck a rock and began to sink. From up on deck we could hear the sound of shouts and running footsteps. I made my way up to the deck only to see, through the spray, the last of the ship's boats disappearing.

They [4] .... (forget) us. I rushed to the side and shouted but the sailors could not hear my voice above the storm.

By now the ship was stuck fast on the rocks. It was no longer in danger of sinking, so I returned to my family to calm their fears. Next morning all was quiet; the wind [5] .... (drop) away.

Since all the boats [6] .... (go), we would have to make one. After we [7] .... (search) the ship for a few hours we found tools and wooden planks and my sons and I started work. While we [8] .... (look) for these things, however, my wife [9] .... (find) some food and [10] .... (prepare) a very welcome meal.

SPEAKING

A breath of fresh air

This is an advertisement on behalf of an organisation called Friends of the Earth. It campaigns for an awareness of our environment.

Discuss the following questions; try to support your opinions with reasons.

Is this the future you want for your children?

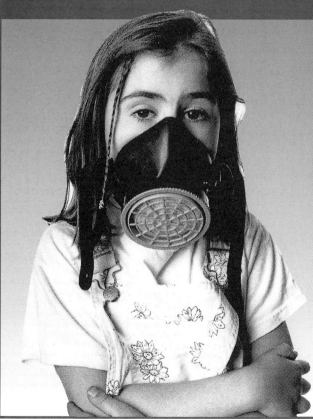

With the backing of people like you, Friends of the Earth is fighting for your right to clean air. Your support will help everyone breathe easier.

Do you think this is an effective advertisement?
Would it encourage you to find out more about the organisation?
Would it persuade you to join the campaign?
Would it persuade you to send the organisation some money?

1 Look at these logos used by an international organisation called Greenpeace.

Read the short texts and then match each one with its logo by picking out the key word(s) or phrase(s) which make the connection clear.

1 We need to prevent the destruction of vital habitats – particularly rainforests and wetlands – and to protect species of wildlife which are in danger.

2 We are working out a policy with fishermen in order to protect the decreasing stocks of fish in our oceans.

3 We care about the poisonous waste which enters our rivers and seas, and want to introduce cleaner methods of production in our industries.

4 We want to campaign for a future which is free of nuclear weapons.

5 We are campaigning for an international agreement to reduce harmful gases in the atmosphere, which expose us to harmful radiation from the sun.

2 Here are the headlines which go with the texts.
Match each headline with its appropriate text and logo; two will be left over.

The nuclear threat   **Toxics**   **Noise pollution**

Endangered species   **Ozone**   **Food additives**

Over-fishing

3 Look back at the texts and pick out the words and phrases that you would find useful if you had to write or talk about conservation and the environment.

Compare lists with another pair. You may not agree on all the vocabulary, but in your group decide on the ten most useful words.

1 Many people belong to environmental pressure groups and campaign on behalf of various organisations by raising money, distributing leaflets and taking part in demonstrations.

You are going to hear a conversation between Anička and two of her schoolfriends, Sara and Luke.

As you listen, answer questions 1–7 by writing A (for Anička), S (for Sara) or L (for Luke).

1 Who has already planned something for the weekend? .....

2 Who thinks conservation is a waste of effort? .....

3 Who suggests that people come before animals? .....

4 Whose views seem uncertain? .....

5 Who is the least keen on zoos? .....

6 Who thinks the disappearance of pandas may be nature's intention? .....

7 Who is considering supporting the campaign? .....

2 Do you support any particular charity?
Have you taken part in raising money for any organisations as Anička has?

TREES of the WORLD

PRUNED BY Steven Appleby.

A FOREST OF JAPANESE BONSAI

A SHOE TREE.

3 SIAMESE TREES

A TREE STUMP IS FITTED WITH AN ARTIFICIAL TREE.

Only the whole forest still to fix.

A RAIN FOREST TREE.

A FAMILY TREE.

GRAMMAR ▸ p.221 Linking conditional sentences

1 ▢ You heard Anička say:

... and if we don't act now, it will be too late to save rare species ...

Which of the following sentences could she have used to express the same idea?

A Because we act now, it won't be too late to save rare species.

B Whenever we act, it will be in time to save rare species.

C Unless we act now, it will be too late to save rare species.

Which word in the correct sentence means the same as *if not*?

2 These words and phrases are also used to link conditional sentences:

as long as/provided (that) = if and only if
  OR on condition that
suppose = imagine

Complete the following sentences using one of the four links: *unless, as long as, provided (that), suppose.*

1 Many scientists think global warming is inevitable .... we reduce the amount of CFCs (chlorofluorocarbons) in the atmosphere.

2 When the world runs out of oil and coal, there will be further supplies of energy .... we make use of the wind and the sun.

3 .... we preserve the world's rainforests, climate patterns are likely to change.

4 .... people continue to support international charities, we can help developing contries to improve their living standards.

5 Some people think that .... we reduce pollution levels from motor vehicles, health problems like asthma will continue to increase.

6 .... you sponsored me on the panda walk, how much would you be willing to pay?

7 I don't mind if you protest against unpopular developments .... you keep within the law.

8 Most people are not interested in joining environmental campaigns .... they are directly affected by the issues.

9 .... there is money to be made from industrial developments, there will always be people willing to invest in such businesses.

10 .... you could choose to support a particular pressure group, which one would you choose?

1 When we talk about our environment, we are usually thinking of our natural surroundings. What about our immediate environment – the places where we go to school or college, our homes or the places where we work? Look around the room where you are now, and discuss these questions.

Is it comfortable? Is it noisy? Is it decorated in sympathetic colours?
Where do you study best? Do you have a favourite room?
If you do, tell your partner about the room and why you like it.
Is there one particular place where you feel very uncomfortable?

2 Look at the list of symptoms which people who work in a poor environment may suffer from, and the conditions which can cause these symptoms.

In groups, match the symptoms with the conditions; obviously, some conditions may have more than one symptom, and you could argue that all these conditions can cause headaches. Discuss what you think with the other people in your group.

Symptoms	Conditions
1 tiredness	A poor lighting, bright or flickering lights
2 blocked/runny nose	B noisy phones, keyboards, air-conditioning
3 sore throat	C too cold or too hot
4 difficulty in breathing	D too moist or too dry
5 dry, itching eyes	E lack of fresh air
6 headaches	F poor ventilation
7 coughs	G dusty atmosphere
8 colds	H smoky atmosphere

3 Some people, especially those who spend their working day in offices, suffer from the effects of a poor working environment. This problem is known as 'Sick Building Syndrome'.

Look at the picture of a modern office. Can you spot seven potential problems for people working in this office environment?

1 Look at the picture of a new library which has just opened in your town.

You use this library for studying each day but you think that there are a number of improvements which could be made so that it is more comfortable for everyone.

You decide to write a letter to the manager of the library with some suggestions.

2 Before you begin writing, look at this letter which was written by a student. Underline the words/phrases in the letter which you think are particularly unsuitable in the way they are expressed, and be ready to explain why you think so. If you had received this letter, how would you have felt and why?

Dear Manager of the Library,

I am writing to tell you that the new library is awful. I think you should know that my friends and I think the library is a total waste of money. It's really stupid to put the tables by equipment like the photocopier. I can't concentrate when everyone is moving around and making a noise.

I think you should stop children coming into the library so that students like me can get on with their work. Next week I am coming to the library to tell you what I think personally, so you should be in your office on Tuesday.

From

A very angry student

3 **Plan your letter.** (See page 46 in Unit 3 to remind yourself of some of the things you need to think about when writing a formal letter.)

▶ As this is a formal letter, you will need to introduce yourself and explain why you are writing.

▶ You are more likely to get a positive reaction to your letter if you include a few comments about some of the good things in the library.

▶ Make two or three constructive suggestions based on your own experience.

▶ Finish your letter with a polite request for a reply.

Try to use conditional patterns with the linking words which you have just practised.

4 Now write your letter in 120–180 words in an appropriate style.

1 Look at the example letter on page 87 again. How would you turn the verb *concentrate* into a noun? (See Unit 3 if you need to remind yourself.) Does the same suffix apply to the verb *equip*?

Look at these words: agree, agreement; appear, appearance; differ, difference.

The verb base *agree* can be changed into a noun by adding the suffix *-ment*; *-ance* and *-ence* are also common suffixes which can turn verbs into nouns.

2 Look at the words that follow these patterns and complete the columns; take care with your spelling and use your dictionary to help you.

verb	noun	verb	noun	verb	noun	verb	noun
1 advertise	....	7	dependence	13 fulfil	....	19 perform	....
2 amuse	....	8	disappearance	14	ignorance	20 prefer	....
3	appointment	9 disappoint	....	15 insist	....	21 refer	....
4 argue	....	10	disturbance	16 interfere	....	22	resentment
5 arrange	....	11 enjoy	....	17 manage	....	23	statement
6 assist	....	12	excitement	18	payment	24 treat	....

3 Now fill in the gaps in the following text. Use the word given in capitals at the end of each line to form a word that fits the space in the same line.

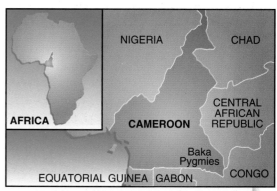

The Baka Pygmies live in the south-eastern corner of Cameroon, an area which is covered in dense, moist rainforest. They are just one of several groups of Pygmies scattered throughout the rainforests of equatorial Africa, although there are many (1) .... between the various groups. **DIFFER**
The Baka's (2) .... on the forest is almost total in terms of **DEPEND**
what they need to survive. Any (3) .... of the forest area **DEVELOP**
would therefore destroy their very (4) .... : it is their lifeblood. **EXIST**
In many ways the Baka's most remarkable skill is their ability to lead a life of
(5) .... based on their ability to exploit their forest environment. **CONTENT**
The rest of the world could learn a great deal by observing the Baka people and the ways in which they treat their environment.

4 Now read the text again and this time match the verbs 6–10 with the phrasal verbs A–E. Then turn the verbs 6–10 into nouns.

6 survive   7 destroy   8 learn   9 observe   10 treat

A care for   B look at   C break up   D get by   E pick up

1 A few years ago a British film company made a film called *Baka People of the Rainforest*. The three members of the film crew stayed for two years with the villagers, but for the first six months they did not attempt to film them. They tried to learn the language of the Baka and to integrate themselves gradually into the life of the community.
The film was shown on television and a booklet was published to accompany the programmes. The extract below is taken from the booklet.

Look at the picture of the Baka and read the extract carefully. Then, in pairs, discuss the questions that follow.

A DAY IN THE LIFE OF A BAKA VILLAGE

It is dawn. Mist shrouds the trees which tower around the village clearing and the air feels damp and chilly. A few birds are calling. An old woman, slight but strong and upright, emerges from one of the huts scattered around the clearing. She begins to talk to the still sleeping village. There has been an argument within the group: she accuses those involved of disturbing the peace of the community, calls on them to behave as Baka should and forget their differences. People are listening and murmurs of agreement are heard.

Two women come out of their huts with large pots and set off down the hill to collect water. The rest of the village is waking up too. The women clear the ashes from yesterday's fires and light fresh ones in front of the huts, peel enormous bunches of plantain* bananas for breakfast, comfort irritable children. The men wander to the meeting hut in the centre of the village and warm themselves at the fire. Soon, in front of every hut, pots are bubbling, surrounded by groups of women. On her mother's instructions a young girl takes a mound of the cooked plantains to the men in the meeting hut. The women and children eat separately, laughing and chatting. The day has begun.

As the sun rises and burns through the mist, people begin to leave the village. Lines of women carrying baskets and machetes* set off for the plantations, or the forest to fish and gather. The men follow them to the plantations or take their spears* to hunt and check their snares*. The children disappear for the day to play, leaving only the tiny ones in the care of the elders who are no longer strong enough to join the hunters and gatherers. A baby cries for its mother. An old woman rocks it in her arms and under her breath sings a lullaby until it is quiet.

The heat of the midday sun is intense. The few people who are left rest in the shade of their huts. Only the insects call, incessantly*.

As the air cools in the late afternoon, men and women drift back to the village in twos and threes. One of the men has a dead antelope* slung over his shoulder, or better still some honey: the children go wild with excitement. Some of the women carry small, perfect leaf packages containing forest mushrooms, fruits or fish.

The men gather in the meeting hut to discuss the day's events. The women once more collect firewood with which to cook the evening meal.

The sun sets rapidly in the tropics – about 6.30 every day of the year. The people sit around the glow of the fires outside their huts sharing food with their neighbours. Everyone relaxes, tells stories, exchanges gossip. Then the children begin to fall asleep in their mothers' arms. Gradually people retire to their huts. For a while the conversation continues to be exchanged from hut to hut, until finally everything is quiet and the village sleeps.

*plantain - banana-like fruit with a green skin
machete - a broad, heavy knife
spear - a weapon with a long handle and a sharp, pointed end
snare - a trap for small birds/animals
incessantly - continually
antelope - an animal with long legs and horns

What do you think the advantages and disadvantages of Baka village life are?

If you could visit the Baka people, would you like to do so?

Do you think we have anything to learn from societies like the Baka?

Do we have anything to offer such societies?

2 Read the text again and choose the correct answer A, B, C or D for questions 1–5.

1 Why is the old woman talking to the villagers?
   A She wants them to change their views.
   B She feels cross with some of them.
   C She has quarrelled with one of them.
   D She hopes they will stop being noisy.

2 What do we learn about Baka customs?
   A The men are responsible for lighting fires.
   B The women eat before their children do.
   C The men wait for food to be brought to them.
   D The women look after the elderly people.

3 What do we learn about Baka children?
   A The older ones look after the babies.
   B Their mothers take them everywhere.
   C Babies are not picked up when they cry.
   D Older children go off by themselves.

4 What makes the children excited?
   A the idea of killing wild animals
   B seeing their parents return safely
   C helping to cook the meat and fish
   D looking forward to good things to eat

5 Which of these phrases best describes the evening atmosphere?
   A talkative and noisy
   B quiet and exhausted
   C calm and sociable
   D busy and friendly

1 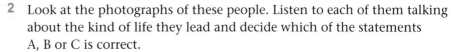 Look at these photographs of a city environment.

How would you describe the pattern of your daily life? Do you feel your life has a rhythm to it like that of the Baka people?
Do you find a routine reassuring or frustrating?
Do you have a favourite day of the week? Some people love the weekends and other people prefer weekdays.

2 Look at the photographs of these people. Listen to each of them talking about the kind of life they lead and decide which of the statements A, B or C is correct.

1 Most of my time is spent waiting

  A for buses.
  B in queues.
  C for news.

2 I spend most of the day

  A on my feet.
  B with my mother.
  C behind a counter.

3 I've always been used to

  A staying in bed quite late.
  B being up bright and early.
  C leading a very quiet life.

4 My day ends with checking

  A on the weather.
  B the farmhouse.
  C my animals.

5 My day begins with

  A a hot drink.
  B some fruit.
  C breakfast.

3 Who do you think leads the hardest/easiest life? Why?

4   Look at the list of adjectives that describe people.
    Check the meanings in a dictionary if necessary.
    Now listen to the recording again, this time
    concentrating on the tone of voice each speaker
    uses.
    Decide which word best matches how they feel
    about the life they lead; there will be three words
    left over.

Speaker 1	contented
Speaker 2	bored
Speaker 3	determined
Speaker 4	casual
Speaker 5	eager
	weary
	considerate
	complaining

GRAMMAR ▶ p.221   (Verbs followed by the infinitive)

1   🗓 Look at what these speakers said:

*... sometimes I can **afford** to buy meat ...*
*I've **offered** to help my children but they don't seem
interested.*
*... rain or shine, you've **got** to look after them.*

Is it possible to use the *-ing* form of the verb
after the verbs in bold type?
What is the pattern after these particular verbs?

2   Now read the passage and underline the verbs
    which are followed by a verb in the infinitive;
    there are eight altogether, including the title!

The Earth is under threat, but could we manage to live on another planet?

Beyond the orbit of our planet Earth lies the red world of Mars. If you look at Mars through a
telescope, the planet appears to have patches of a blue-green colour which scientists think may
be some kind of plant life. Beyond Mars are Jupiter and Saturn, which are both very cold worlds
and surrounded by thick atmospheres of poisonous gases. We need to learn more about both
these planets, but neither of them is a likely environment for living creatures. As for life on other
planets, Mercury is too hot on one side and too cold on the other, and it has no atmosphere. So
Mercury would not seem to provide any alternative. If in the next century we send a spacecraft
to the stars, we may well find another planet with life like that of our own world. Before that,
however, we may decide to build huge space colonies where people could choose to live. They
might be shaped like wheels and filled with air, and the climate would be controlled so people
could walk around as freely as on Earth. Scientists are hoping to develop these ideas once they
have the money, but no government has yet promised to make so much money available!

---

3   Now think of your own sentences using each of
    the underlined verbs.
    Write your sentences **leaving out the key verb
    before** each infinitive and exchange them with
    your partner.

Complete your partner's sentences.
Example
*Have you **managed** to write down nine sentences?*

don't leave Earth without us!

The space scientists of today are already looking for the people who will lead space research into the 21st century. An organisation called Space School offers students holiday courses, competitions and opportunities to take part in space projects and have work experience in the space industry.

Imagine you were on a panel of judges at Space School and had chosen the winning entry (below) in a student project competition.
Discuss why this entry won the prize.
Be ready to explain your decisions to other students.

Would a holiday course at the Space School interest you?

Key vocabulary

Apart from the vocabulary practised within this unit, you also need to know the following words in connection with the environment and space.
Use your dictionary to look up any words you don't know and to help you with the incomplete words.

environmentally friendly   green _ _ _ _ _   effect
illegal dumping   ferti _ _ _ _ _ _   astron _ _ _
gr _ _ ity   rockets   satel _ _ _ _ _   household waste
power stations   ex _ _ _ _ _ _   fumes   oil slick

Vocabulary in context

Complete sentences 1–12 using the appropriate words from the list above.

1 Very few people have had the chance to become an .... and journey into space.

2 On the moon the pull of .... is only one sixth of that of the earth.

3 More than two thirds of the earth's surface is covered by water so people are right to be concerned about the .... of toxic waste in the oceans.

4 The first .... were made by the Chinese over seven hundred years ago.

5 The Russians launched the first space .... in 1957.

6 Many manufacturers are concerned to make products that they consider to be
.... ,
like aerosol sprays and washing powders.

7 Farmers who do not use chemical .... on their crops sell their fruit and vegetables under an organic label.

8 Over the past few years there have been a number of accidents at nuclear ....
.... , but the worst one was probably at Chernobyl in 1986.

9 Catalytic converters fitted to cars are intended to reduce harmful .... escaping into the atmosphere.

10 Whenever there is an accident at sea involving an oil tanker, thousands of fish and seabirds risk being killed by the ....

11 Some countries have very efficient policies for dealing with .... ,
and people are encouraged to put bottles, tins, paper, etc. in special banks.

12 The effect of temperature increases in the earth's surface is sometimes referred to as the

....

Recycling: direct and reported speech

Rewrite the sentences turning 1–5 into direct speech and 6–10 into reported speech.

1 The customer complained to the waiter that her soup was greasy.
The customer said, '.....................................
.... ,'

2 The children were warned by their teacher not to accept lifts from strangers.
....

3 The coach driver told the tourists to be outside their hotel by 8 a.m.
....

4 The manager announced that some employees would lose their jobs.
....

5 The newsagent told me that the magazines had all been sold.
....

6 'I think you should go to bed now,' Tony's father said.
Tony's father said that ....
....

7 'All today's lectures are cancelled,' announced the professor.
....

8 'If you don't give me back my book, I shall never lend you another,' Ella said to her friend.
....

9 'I wish I had bought that coat I saw yesterday,' remarked Mrs Wood.
....

10 'I promise to be home before midnight,' Maya said to her parents.
....

Learning record

When you have finished Unit 5, try filling in this record of what you have learnt.

1 What words can we use to link ideas in conditional sentences other than the word *if*? Use one of them in a sentence.

2 How would you make the verb *insist* into a noun?

3 How would you make *argue* into a noun?

4 What is the verb from the noun *disappearance*?

5 List five verbs which must be followed by the infinitive.

FCE Checklist

Look back at the description of what the FCE examination comprises on pages 6–7 and then complete the checklist.

I have practised:

> reading skills for Paper ....., Part 2
> grammar skills for Part 5 of Paper .....
> listening skills for Parts ..... and ..... of Paper 4
> writing skills for Paper .....
> speaking skills for Paper ....., Parts ..... and .....

EXAM ADVICE

9 Use of English, Part 1

Part 1 of the Use of English paper consists of a passage with 15 gaps. The passage is followed by 15 multiple choice questions; each question has four options A, B, C and D.

> This exercise focuses on vocabulary. Therefore more of the questions will require you to decide on the right noun, adjective or a word which relates to the content of the passage in order to fill a gap.

> The title of the passage tells you what you are going to read about.

> Read the passage fairly quickly in order to understand the context, and look at the example which will have been completed for you.

> You may even recognise what some of the missing words are likely to be before you look at the multiple choice questions.

> Concentrate on answering the questions which you are fairly sure of before you spend time on those which you find more difficult.

> If there are words which you don't know, try *hearing* the various alternatives in your head. Although it's not a reliable technique for answering examination questions, sometimes your feel for the language may help you eliminate the wrong answers.

> The topic-based vocabulary in this course will help you prepare for questions which ask you to choose from options which seem very similar, but where in fact only one answer is correct.

10 Writing, Part 1

Part 1 of the Writing paper is a compulsory question so you have to answer it. It carries the same number of marks as the written task that you choose in Part 2 of the paper. In this question you will have to write a letter which may be formal or informal.

> This letter is called a **transactional letter**. It is like a guided writing task and puts you in a situation where you have to write a letter in order to achieve something. For example, you may have to write to a language school for information about their holiday courses.

> In addition to the instructions, there will be **extra information** which you have to read carefully so that you understand the situation which is being explained. The extra information may be in the form of an advertisement, some hand-written notes, part of another letter, someone's questions, etc.

> You have to identify the situation, the task and who you are writing to.

> You don't need to include any dates or addresses, but what you write should look like a letter in the way in which it is laid out on the page.

> The instruction for writing the letter will include the phrase **in an appropriate style**. This means you must decide whether the letter is formal or informal, as that will affect the tone of your letter as well as the way you begin and end the letter.

> Make sure you cover all the points which will need to be included to complete the task as fully as possible.

1 USE OF ENGLISH PART 1

For questions **1–15**, read the text below and decide which word **A, B, C** or **D** best fits each space.

WORK TILL YOU DROP

I am sitting in a room with a view. I can see a jumbled (**1**).... of postcards on a notice-board, a plant with crinkled leaves and a faint ray of daylight between drawn blinds. Rows of desks, screens, fax machines and photocopiers (**2**).... into the distance. All around there is a (**3**).... of paperwork: books piled high, notebooks filled and (**4**).... to one side, magazines half read and covered in a fine (**5**).... of dust. Air-conditioning hums in the (**6**).... . Telephones ring. A colleague is shouting (**7**).... the phone. Another strikes his keyboard as a child bangs a piano. A (**8**).... chatters to herself as she writes like an excited songbird.

It is (**9**).... another day in the office, and I'm feeling fine. My nose is (**10**).... , my back aches, I can't feel my leg muscles and my brain feels as if it has been (**11**).... in brown paper.

If you think that sounds bad, (**12**).... and reflect on your own working conditions. Sit back in your chair and look around. Listen to the noise. (**13**).... you still feel happy, you are lucky. The (**14**).... world of work, it seems, is making many of us feel (**15**).... out.

1	**A** gathering	**B** collection	**C** confusion	**D** mixture
2	**A** stretch	**B** bend	**C** travel	**D** develop
3	**A** stock	**B** mass	**C** amount	**D** number
4	**A** passed	**B** set	**C** fallen	**D** thrown
5	**A** line	**B** thickness	**C** layer	**D** piece
6	**A** setting	**B** scene	**C** background	**D** rear
7	**A** along	**B** through	**C** with	**D** down
8	**A** single	**B** more	**C** third	**D** similar
9	**A** just	**B** still	**C** yet	**D** exactly
10	**A** stuck	**B** blocked	**C** stopped	**D** cleared
11	**A** tied	**B** held	**C** done	**D** wrapped
12	**A** halt	**B** hold	**C** pause	**D** leave
13	**A** Unless	**B** Suppose	**C** Provided	**D** If
14	**A** mental	**B** emotional	**C** physical	**D** material
15	**A** exhausted	**B** worn	**C** put	**D** left

2 Grammar revision: future tenses 1

 ▶ Grammar reference p.221

Complete the following sentences by using an appropriate tense based on the verb in brackets; more than one answer may be possible, in which case you should note down the alternatives with a brief explanation why.

1 'What .... (do) when you leave school?' the teacher asked.

2 The forecast for tomorrow .... (say) it will be sunny.

3 I think Brad .... (take) my advice and work harder next term.

4 I .... (play) snooker this evening – would you like to come?

5 I'm afraid I .... (be) late for the party as I have to work late that night.

6 I .... (not walk) all that way – it's more than twenty kilometres!

7 The baby's crying – .... I .... (go) and see what the matter is?

8 The shops .... (open) early on a Saturday morning.

9 We .... (move) house next month.

10 Don't keep playing with that glass vase – you .... (break) it.

3 Grammar: verbs followed by the infinitive

 ▶ Grammar reference p.221

Fill in the spaces using the correct form of the verbs in the box. Each verb can only be used once, so read through the whole exercise carefully before you begin.

| threaten | fail | refuse | agree | mean |
| expect | hope | arrange | pretend | ask |

1 He .... to be honest and many people were taken in by him.

2 I didn't .... to disturb you but I thought this would be a good time to ring.

3 I had .... to catch the last train but unfortunately it was cancelled.

4 Joely .... to drive on icy roads in case she had an accident.

5 The politicians .... to meet again the next day to discuss their differences.

6 If you .... to see my brother, tell him I've been trying to ring him.

7 Unless the ransom money was paid, the gunman .... to shoot his hostages.

8 In the fog the driver .... to see the car in front and crashed into it.

9 Could you .... to meet me outside the station at 7 p.m.?

10 You should have .... to use the phone before making such a long call.

4 Grammar revision: *too/enough* (+ *for*) + infinitive; *so* + *that*

▸ Grammar reference p.221

A Rearrange the following sentences so that the words are in the right order.

1 dirty me for water in the too swim is to

....

2 stars close are see to telescope some enough without not a

....

3 Mars breathe the on too atmosphere to is poisonous

....

4 Sun's too for develop the hot temperature surface form any is of to life

....

5 be are fish able polluted to some for too survive rivers to

....

B Now rewrite each sentence in two different ways, remembering to make all the necessary changes, especially when choosing new adjectives.
The first one has been done for you as an example.

1 *The water is **so** dirty **that** I can't swim in it.*

*The water is not **clean enough for** me to swim in it.*

2 ....

....

3 ....

....

4 ....

....

5 ....

....

5 Vocabulary

Before you do this exercise, you might want to listen again to the recording with Anička, Sara and Luke.
Then in the context of what you have listened to, match the words and phrases below with their meanings.

1 a nuisance		**A** wait a minute	
2 choke to death		**B** sense of what is most important	
3 rare		**C** kept in cages	
4 sponsor		**D** some money	
5 in captivity		**E** to die from coughing	
6 priorities		**F** support with money	
7 hang on		**G** an annoying person	
8 contribution		**H** very unusual	

1 .... **2** .... **3** .... **4** .... **5** .... **6** .... **7** .... **8** ....

6 WRITING [PART 1]

You are studying at a language school in the UK. Your principal has told you about the town council's plans to build a bypass which will affect the local park opposite the school as the land will be needed for the bypass.

Below is part of the council's advertising campaign.

> ➠ **The new bypass is for everyone!**
> *In future:*
> ➠ heavy traffic will be directed around the town centre
> ➠ no more traffic jams
> ➠ parking zones will be provided outside the centre
> ➠ traffic free shopping precincts
>
> Support your local council working for *your* future!

You are not in favour of losing the local park as it's the only recreation area in the town. The college principal has asked for support from all the students.

Write a **letter** to the town council in **120–180** words in an appropriate style, objecting to the development of the bypass. Do not include addresses.

THE BODY BEAUTIFUL

READING

Look at the text on reflexology. As quickly as you can, underline nine different words connected with parts of your body and six different words connected with health.

Reflexology was first practised by the Chinese 5,000 years ago. It is the healing art of foot massage and is based on the principle that there are ten energy zones running through the body. These zones are accessible through the soles of your feet. Each foot represents the left or right side of your body and the soles of your feet are divided up into 'reflex' areas which correspond to parts of your body.

Imagine the sole of your foot as a map of your body: think of your big toe as your head, the top third of the foot as your chest, the middle section as your stomach and your heel as the area around your hips.

Reflexologists use pressure at various points on the sole of the foot to stimulate energy, reduce stress and improve the circulation of the blood.

SPEAKING

Look at the reflexologist's map of the right and left soles of the foot. Check you know the words for the different parts of the body.

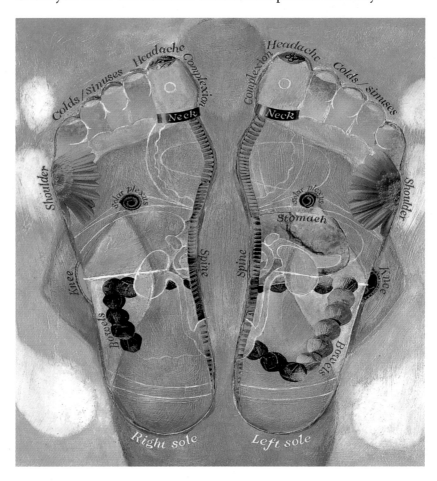

Discuss with each other which part of the foot you think you would massage to help the following symptoms:
headaches back pain head cold stiff neck knee problems stress stomach-ache

1 Reflexology is sometimes referred to as 'complementary' medical treatment. Some people accept complementary or alternative treatments like acupuncture and homoeopathy more readily than other people.

In the article below Michael Keating describes an alternative approach to medicine, which is called *feng shui* (pronounced 'fong shoy'). Read it carefully and then decide whether the statements that follow are true or false.

1 I was raised in Birmingham by Irish parents who ran a social club. I trained as a sound engineer, then I got into alternatives – meditation, massage, Chinese medicine – and came across a book about *feng shui*.

2 I've been studying *feng shui* for about seven years, but I'm still very much a student. I started at the age of 27, but *feng shui* masters have been practising since the age of five.

3 *Feng shui* means 'wind-water', and is the Chinese art of creating a harmonious environment, based on *chi,* or life force. It's about 7,000 years old, and in the early days the *feng shui* man was called in to look at where crops would survive best, where the house wouldn't be affected by negative *chi.* Nowadays, in Hong Kong for example, major banks are designed on *feng shui* principles.

4 In *feng shui* diagnosis I use an 8-sided shape; each section represents a life area, such as relationships, career, wealth, health, which I mentally superimpose* onto a person's space. Any missing section in the space points to a possible problem in the corresponding life area. The ideal space is rectangular or round. L-shaped homes create problems; apart from having a missing section, they are symbolic of boots, so people tend to trip up in life. Sharp corners create cutting *chi.* This may all sound very superstitious and weird*, but the effect can be profound*.

5 It is not necessarily difficult to put things right. You don't have to move fixed things or knock out walls. You just need to help the *chi* flow, or to recreate a missing space you might use a mirror.

6 The Chinese say working with your back towards a door is bad for business and concentration; facing the door gives strength. Your house should embrace* you, so when you walk in from a hard day, your *chi's* uplifted, you're inspired and you can relax. An entrance is the first thing that hits us, and should be bright and welcoming. Recently I went to a house where the entrance opened directly onto a wall. The owner was unwell and could hardly get out of bed. She hung up a mirror and after a few days she felt much better.

7 The success rate of *feng shui* is very high. I feel really lucky to have found it – even though I don't make a fortune from it – and it's a good way of helping people to help themselves.

*
superimpose – put or set one thing over another
weird – strange, peculiar
profound – very deep or intense
embrace – (usually) put your arms warmly around another person; in this context it suggests that the house should have this warm effect on you

1 Michael Keating found out about *feng shui* through a friend.

2 It takes seven years to train as a *feng shui* master.

3 *Feng shui* focuses on the areas surrounding you.

4 It is important for architects in Hong Kong to know about *feng shui*.

5 *Feng shui* masters believe every problem has eight sides.

6 The best shape is usually a complete shape.

7 Michael thinks that *feng shui* may seem unbelievable.

8 You have to rebuild certain walls to improve *chi* flow.

9 If you don't face a door, your business may suffer.

10 *Feng shui* enables Michael to make a lot of money.

2 Find these words in the passage and match them with their correct meanings:

1 raised (para. 1) **2** got into (para. 1) **3** came across (para. 1) **4** called in (para. 3) **5** trip up (para. 4)

summoned make mistakes became involved in discovered brought up

✗ SPEAKING

1 Work in groups and discuss the following questions.

Do you think alternative medicine can really work?

Have you any personal experience of complementary medicine?

If you haven't, would you be prepared to try it?

2 Now match the name of the therapy A–H with its definition 1–8 and its picture I–P.

1 a method of diagnosing, treating and managing conditions which can be traced to your joints

5 an ancient system of healing using very fine needles to relieve pain and balance the physical, emotional and spiritual aspects of the individual

6 based on the principle that only nature heals and that the body has the ability to heal itself through its own internal 'vital force'

2 the treatment of common health problems using strong-smelling, concentrated oils extracted from petals, leaves and roots of plants

A Homoeopathy **E** Aromatherapy
B Acupuncture **F** Herbal medicine
C Hypnosis **G** Naturopathy
D Osteopathy **H** Chinese medicine

7 works on the principle of treating the whole body by using small amounts of a drug that, in healthy people, produces symptoms similar to those of the disease being treated; in that way the body's own healing mechanism is stimulated

3 a complete health system using herbs, acupuncture, exercise and nutrition to keep the body balanced

4 a trance-like state of complete relaxation and concentration used to treat emotional problems

8 aims to treat the whole body and uses plant remedies instead of synthetic drugs

I   J   K   L   M   N   O   P

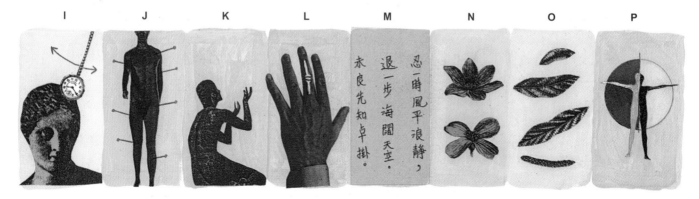

3 After reading these texts, have you changed your mind about alternative/complementary medicine?

1 Look back at the opening sentence of the article on page 101:

*I **was raised** ... by Irish parents ...*

and at these examples from paragraph 3:

*... the feng shui man **was called in** ...*
*... major banks **are designed** ...*

What is the subject of the sentence in each of these examples?
Do we know who called in the *feng shui* man?
Does it matter if we don't know? Why not?
Who is likely to design a bank?
Why is the person who designs a bank not mentioned?

Based on your answers to these questions, what can you say about sentences which use the passive form?

2 Now underline the passive structures in the following text.

As a homoeopath I am sometimes asked whether homoeopathy can be used alongside other forms of therapy. I value mixing therapies that complement each other, for example homoeopathy and osteopathy, which can be used to treat back injuries. People come to me for advice all the time, but ultimately the decision is theirs. If someone wants to try a combination of treatments, they are recommended to find out all they can about the treatment beforehand. If things don't get better, most people rely on conventional medicine. In certain cases people only make a full recovery if an operation is performed by a qualified surgeon.

What is the tense of the passive structures which you have underlined?

What tenses are used in the examples from the article on page 101?

*I **was raised** ...*
*... the feng shui man **was called in** ...*
*... major banks **are designed** ...*

3 Fill in the gaps in the text below using the verbs in the box in their correct passive form.

believe	replace	release
raise	understand	

Shape up!

Exercise isn't only good for the body; it can make you feel happier and more relaxed.

Physical exercise is not only good for your body. Some people find their energy levels
(1) .... when they take exercise. Their sense of frustration, irritability or anger (2) .... by feelings of calm or contentment.
The cause of these changes (3) ....
not yet .... , but it may be due to increased oxygen supply reaching the brain. It seems that certain chemicals
(4) .... into the
bloodstream during exercise. This may be one of the reasons why it (5) ....
that people who take regular exercise live longer.

1 Do you do anything special to stay fit? Or does a busy life keep you fit and healthy?

Do you exercise? Daily, weekly, or when the mood takes you?

Do you watch what you eat and drink?

You are going to hear an interview with a boy called Joby Mason.
As you listen, fill in the missing information in his weekly schedule. You don't need to write full sentences, just two or three key words in each space.

Joby Mason (1) .... for his country in the Olympic Games.

WEEKLY SCHEDULE

time	activity	place
5.30 a.m.	(2)	(3) .... (with trainer)
7.00 a.m.	(4)	(5) ....
3.00 p.m.	(6)	(7) .... (alone)
5.00 p.m.	(8)	at home
7.00 p.m.	(9)	(10) ....

Saturday: (11) usually takes part in ....

Sunday: (12) .... with sister

2 Rewrite the following sentences making each one passive.

1 *Sport Slot* invited Joby Mason onto the programme to talk about his fitness routine.

Joby Mason ....

2 The interviewer asked him whether he had always been keen on sport.

He ....

3 Joby Mason builds his whole week around his swimming schedule.

Joby Mason's ....

4 His trainer picks him up at 5.30 a.m. every weekday.

He ....

5 Joby does his homework before he leaves for more training.

Joby's ....

VOCABULARY

3 Look at these expressions the interviewer used. Do you think any of them are insulting?

1 *curled up with a good book*   3 *glued to your TV*

2 *a fitness freak*   4 *a couch potato*

Match them with their pictures.

4 During the interview the speakers used the following phrasal verbs:

> take over   drop off   build up   give up   pick up

Complete sentences 1–5 using a phrasal verb from the box in its correct form.

1 I'm not usually late for school because my mother .... me .... on her way to work.

2 Pam could have been a successful athlete but she .... too easily when the training got difficult.

3 I enjoy sport but I don't like the way it .... some people's lives and they can't talk about anything else.

4 Roy's been ill for over a year and it's going to take him some time to .... his strength again before he can go back to work.

5 He waited ages for his friend to .... him .... and then he found out he'd been waiting in the wrong place.

You have been asked to help plan an activity weekend for a group of teenagers aged between 14 and 16 years old. You need to work out a daily programme of varied activities as well as make suggestions for a suitable menu.

First of all, choose the activities and food from the charts and information opposite. The statistics are there for background information only; you do not have to include them in any way but you might find them interesting for discussion purposes. Decide what you think would provide an enjoyable and varied day with the right kind of diet, and jot down your suggestions.

Food provides the energy your body needs to keep going. Different foods contain body-building substances known as nutrients. These are proteins, carbohydrates, fats, vitamins and minerals. Your body needs all these nutrients to work properly.

The energy in food is measured in kilojoules or calories. On average, adolescents between the ages of 12 and 16 need between 2,100 and 2,800 calories a day.

Exercise uses different amounts of calories; if you do the sports listed here, each hour you'll burn up:

175 calories
table tennis
snooker
cricket
sailing

270 calories
badminton
10-pin bowling
canoeing
dancing
rowing
diving

355 calories
basketball
cycling
hockey
judo
skating
tennis
walking

435 calories
climbing
running slowly
football
skiing
swimming

740 calories
normal running
rugby
squash
water polo

A balanced daily diet should contain about 50–60% carbohydrate, 20–30% fat and 12–15% protein, with vitamins and minerals in addition.

		cals per 100 gms
carbohydrates	bananas	50
	potatoes	65
	bread	60
	rice	130
	pasta	107
fat-rich foods	butter	721
	oil	883
	cheese	401
	cream	209
proteins	chicken	148
	sardines	216
	boiled egg	73
	cheese	301
	green beans	7
	peas	53
	peanuts	564
vitamins & minerals	oranges	27

WRITING

Write three short paragraphs (about 50 words each) outlining your plans for the activity weekend.

In paragraph 1 describe the various activities you have chosen and explain why you think your programme will appeal to the teenagers.

In paragraph 2 write about the kinds of food you have chosen, explaining why you think these foods will provide a good menu. (You don't need to include any figures or statistics.)

In paragraph 3 write about whether you think there would be any complaints from the teenagers about the activity weekend, with your resaons. For example, do you think they would miss junk food, fizzy drinks, TV, etc?

Look at the statements and decide in groups whether each one is true or false.

Body knowledge quiz

1 You can make yourself relax by holding your breath.

2 You should exercise for 20 minutes, three times a week to keep healthy.

3 Weightlifting is good exercise for young people.

4 Always try to eat a good meal before exercising.

5 You can build up stamina by eating fresh fruit.

6 It is dangerous for people with disabilities to exercise.

7 Exercise helps people cope with stress.

8 Let your food digest before going for a swim.

9 To encourage your bones to grow you must take regular exercise.

10 Walking barefoot is bad for you.

GRAMMAR ▶ p.223 Verb + direct object + infinitive without *to*

Look at the following examples from the Body knowledge quiz:

*You can **make** yourself **relax** ...*
*Exercise **helps** people **cope** with stress.*

Can you find one other verb in the quiz which follows this pattern?

How does this pattern differ from:
Always try to eat a good meal before exercising.

Now complete the exercise using a suitable verb in each sentence.

1 If you think you're overweight, why not .... some exercise?

2 The teacher made the child .... the homework more neatly.

3 I think I'd better .... home as it's getting late.

4 The crowd roared as the ball .... the goalpost and rolled away.

5 You can take a horse to water but you can't .... it drink!

6 Paula noticed the light .... out in the room opposite.

7 Could you let me .... your new phone number?

8 Sheena watched her son .... the other runners to the finishing line.

9 'You must .... as you're told or you'll get into trouble,' warned the guard.

10 I'd rather .... my free time watching TV than doing sport.

Answers to quiz: 1F 2T 3F 4F 5F 6F 7T 8T 9T 10F

Look back at the list of sports on page 107.
Do you take part in any of these? Do you have a favourite sport?
Is there a sport you do that isn't included in this list?
Is there a sport you would like to take up in the future?

You are going to hear five different people talking about different sports.
As you listen, write down one or two words which sum up how each person feels about the sport.

1 How does she feel about horse riding?

....

2 What does he feel about running long distances?

....

3 What did she feel about playing football?

....

4 What does she feel about aerobics?

....

5 What does he feel about table tennis?

....

GRAMMAR ▶ p.223   **Gerunds 3: after adjectives/verbs + prepositions**

◻◻ Listen again to the people talking about different sports; in particular listen out for the following phrases and fill in the missing prepositions.

1 I *insisted* .... learning…

2 I was so *frightened* .... going…

3 I was really *good* .... running…

4 I started to *look forward* .... running…

5 Most of us were really *fed up* .... playing netball…

6 I was never *interested* .... doing sport…

7 I spent the entire time *apologising* .... missing the ball…

8 I really *objected* .... waiting around…

9 You've got to be *capable* .... moving at top speed…

⬛ SPEAKING

Use the examples above to ask each other generally what you are *good at doing*, what you *object to doing*, etc.

1 Look at these examples of adverbs or adjectives which take -ness when they are changed into nouns.

cheerful	cheerfulness
thoughtful	thoughtfulness
naughty	naughtiness
pretty	prettiness

Now read the passage and underline the adverbs and adjectives which take -ness as nouns.
The numbers in brackets at the end of each paragraph tell you how many words you need to search for in that paragraph.

Life improves with sport

What sort of person makes a good sportsman or woman? Are there any particular characteristics which we recognise in early childhood? Do people need a lot of self-discipline? It's not likely that a lazy person will be prepared to put in hours of practice in the way that Joby Mason does each day. Equally if you want to become a professional sports person in the public eye, you are unlikely to be very shy. (3)

According to Joanna Newton, who won an Olympic silver medal for swimming, no one ever looked at her when she was young and bright and said that she was going to be Olympic standard. She did sport for fun and was happy to ride horses, swim, do ballet and other sports simply because she enjoyed them. One of the things that has made her sad in recent years is the decline in school sports in the UK, as she feels a lot of her talent developed while she was at school. She looks back thoughtfully on those years at school w i t h distinct feelings of gratitude.(4)

Sport develops self-discipline and gives you the chance to test yourself. It is crazy to think it's not a competitive world. Anything worth having takes effort and a lot of hard work. An American golfer was once told how lucky he was after winning a tournament. 'Funny,' he said, 'the more I practise the luckier I get.' (2)

2 Now use the noun form of five of the words you have underlined to complete the sentences.

1 She suffers from such acute .... that she never accepts invitations to parties.

2 Although he was looking forward to his new job, he couldn't help feeling a certain .... as he said goodbye to the people he'd worked with for years.

3 The .... of the car headlights was so dazzling that for a moment I couldn't see anything.

4 His .... combined with his lack of qualifications meant he was likely to remain unemployed.

5 It is generally agreed that money does not guarantee .... – although it helps!

Key vocabulary

Apart from the vocabulary practised within this unit you also need to know the words related to sport and health in exercises A and B.
Use your dictionary to look up any words you don't know.

A Wordsearch

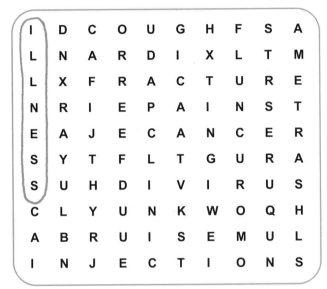

I	D	C	O	U	G	H	F	S	A
L	N	A	R	D	I	X	L	T	M
L	X	F	R	A	C	T	U	R	E
N	R	I	E	P	A	I	N	S	T
E	A	J	E	C	A	N	C	E	R
S	Y	T	F	L	T	G	U	R	A
S	U	H	D	I	V	I	R	U	S
C	L	Y	U	N	K	W	O	Q	H
A	B	R	U	I	S	E	M	U	L
I	N	J	E	C	T	I	O	N	S

There are fourteen words connected with health hidden in this puzzle.
Read the clues to help you discover what they are.

✓ 1 state of being unwell
  2 not as bad as a break
  3 can cause disease
  4 .... and cold
  5 she came out in a ....
  6 not always curable
  7 given with a needle
  8 short for 'influenza'
  9 a place to go for medical treatment
 10 aches and ....
 11 a bluish black mark on the skin
 12 it may make you bleed
 13 capable of being spread
 14 photographs the body

B Groupings

Rearrange the words below under the four headings:

equipment (10); **people** (7); **place/venue** (7); **sport** (6). The numbers in brackets show you how many words there are in each group.

weights driver ring boxing surfing net rider court gym(nasium) saddle athletics circuit trainers F1 racing car player boxer track volleyball horse-racing stadium surfboard weightlifter athlete kit racecourse boxing gloves whip motor racing surfer weightlifting

Vocabulary in context

Fill in the missing words in the sentences below. Each word has been started for you, but you should use your dictionary if you need further help.

1 If you live in the UK and you need an amb _ _ _ _ _ _ _ in an eme _ _ _ _ _ _ _ , you should ring 999.
2 The only g _ _ _ _ was scored by the home team, so they won one-nil.
3 People who are emotionally disturbed may be treated with tran _ _ _ _ _ _ _ _ _ _ _ .
4 The ca _ _ _ _ _ _ of a team is usually the best player.
5 Broken arms or legs are usually put in pla _ _ _ _ _ to help them mend.
6 People who watch sports events are called spec _ _ _ _ _ _ _ .
7 People can be all _ _ _ _ _ _ to insect bites, food or virtually anything, and in severe cases may need treatment at an all _ _ _ _ _ clinic.
8 Certain drugs can only be obtained with a doctor's pre _ _ _ _ _ _ _ _ _ _ .
9 A docotor's wait _ _ _ _ r _ _ _ _ is just the kind of place to c _ _ _ _ _ a cold!
10 Heart attack patients are initially cared for in an intensive w _ _ _ .
11 Sports injuries may require treatment by a special _ _ _ _ .
12 Some people's fears of being oper _ _ _ _ _ on may lead them to depend on pills and tablets in the hope of avoiding the oper _ _ _ _ _ _ the _ _ _ _ _ .

Fill in the missing words using the vocabulary in the box, making any changes you think necessary.

insure   treat   equip   arrange   appoint   vaccinate

Health Centre Advice Sheet

All (1) .... must be made with Reception on 33 91 07.

Are you up-to-date with your tetanus (2) .... ? In order to have maximum protection you should be vaccinated every 10 years.

Dr Plank is planning to walk 50 kilometres to raise money to buy (3) .... for the Health Centre. Please support her!

If you are planning to go abroad, make your (4) .... well in advance if you need to take any medicines with you. Make sure you have a health (5) .... policy as the cost of medical (6) .... abroad can be very expensive.

Learning record

When you have finished Unit 6, try filling in this record of what you have leant.

1 Rewrite the sentences making each one passive.

A My mother called the doctor after I had fainted.

....
....

B Ray broke his racket during the tennis match.

....
....

C Within minutes of the accident, ambulances were taking the injured to hospital.

....
....

D A different country stages the Olympic Games every four years.

....
....

2 Complete the sentence with a suitable phrase.

They had better ....
if they want to stay fit.

3 Correct the following sentences by crossing out the wrong word(s) and writing in the correct one(s).

Example

I insist ~~to pay~~ for my own ticket.
on paying ......

A Peter is not used to cook his own meals.

....

B I am very sorry to waking you up so early.

....

C Not many people are capable to run a marathon.

....

FCE Checklist

Look back at the description of what the FCE examination comprises on pages 6–7 and then complete the checklist.

I have practised:

▶ reading skills for Paper .....
▶ grammar skills for Paper .....
▶ listening skills for Part ..... of Paper 4
▶ writing skills for Paper 2, Part .....
▶ speaking skills for Paper .....

11 Reading, Part 4

The last part of the Reading paper, Part 4, consists of a multiple matching reading task. The questions come **before** the reading text(s) and vary from 13 to 15 in total; some questions may have two answers, but the order in which you put these two answers does not matter. The questions may also include one or two multiple choice questions (Exam Advice 2).

▶ You are not expected to know all the vocabulary in the texts.

▶ Learn to scan through the material which is redundant (not relevant), until you come to the specific information which you *do* need in order to answer the questions.

▶ The questions will not be in the same order as the information in the text, so be prepared to scan the text a number of times before you find the specific information you need.

▶ As the same information can be used more than once, the amount of information to choose from remains the same throughout the exercise.

12 Use of English, Part 3

Part 3 of the Use of English paper asks you to transform sentences by changing one grammatical structure to another using a **key word**. The key word is printed in **bold type** below the first sentence, and the rewritten sentence is incomplete. Using this key word, you have to fill in the gap in the incomplete sentence using no more than 4 more words, so that the new sentence has a similar meaning to the original one.

▶ You must **not make any changes to the key word** or you will lose marks.

▶ You must use between 2 and 5 words to complete the sentence.

▶ If you use a contraction, for example *he's*, this counts as 2 words.

▶ The beginning and the end of the new sentence will be printed on your question paper, but you only need to transfer the missing words onto your answer sheet.

▶ Make sure that the new sentence includes all the points from the original sentence.

▶ Check that you have spelt the missing words correctly.

1 Grammar revision: future tenses 2

▶ Grammar reference p.223

Complete the following sentences using an appropriate tense based on the verb in brackets.

1 Don't ring my father at 6 o'clock; he .... (watch) the news on TV.

2 I hope the garage .... (mend) my parents' car by the time they get back from abroad.

3 By the end of the century more astronauts .... (land) on the moon.

4 You may not recognise Mimi when you see her because she .... (colour) her hair blonde by next week.

5 I .... (wait) for you outside the cinema so make sure you get off at the right bus stop.

6 Andrew .... (learn) to drive for almost a year soon, and he still isn't ready to take his driving test.

7 This time next week I .... (lie) on a beach beside the Indian Ocean.

8 I haven't quite finished my essay but I .... (do) by late this afternoon.

9 The weather forecast for tomorrow says it .... (be) wet and windy.

10 By the end of this year I .... (learn) English for five years.

---

2   READING   PART 4

You are going to read three articles about how three men cope with stress. For questions **1–15**, choose from the articles **A–C**. Some of the articles may be chosen more than once. When more than one answer is required, these may be given in either order.

Which person or persons:

emphasises the amount of stress in their early training?	**1**	
says that discussions with colleagues is a benefit?	**2**	**3**
comments on the virtual absence of stress?	**4**	
is only allowed to work for short periods of time?	**5**	
turns to sport for relaxation?	**6**	**7**
may be told to stop work by other colleagues?	**8**	
comments that job satisfaction cancels out stress?	**9**	
accepts that they are affected by stress?	**10**	**11**
finds their colleagues more demanding than their job?	**12**	
may be emotionally affected by their work?	**13**	
extends their working day by exercising?	**14**	
has felt physically threatened in their job?	**15**	

Air Traffic Controller   A

I stop planes from hitting each other. With that comes a certain amount of stress. At any one time you are responsible for eight to nine planes, and you have to keep each of them five kilometres apart, with a distance of 400 metres of vertical space between them. We're helped by computers and strict procedures, but the thought of a plane crash is always on your mind. By law we can only work a maximum of two hours and then we have to take half an hour break in between. It helps us relax – there aren't many jobs where you can take time out to think about what you are doing.

Air traffic controllers have to sound very calm when talking to pilots – outwardly that's the case, but your mind is always working, planning where your planes need to go. Ultimately, I suppose, this is a great strain. Talking with other controllers helps. I work out, play hockey and cricket – this all relieves it in some way.

I also train other controllers. I sit behind them and listen to every command they give to the pilots. It's more stressful than my job – and if they make a mistake, it's down to me. When you see a controller who you've trained doing well, it makes all the stress worthwhile.

Accident and Emergency Unit Doctor   B

Throughout your training, you are constantly put under pressure to perform. The idea is that the stress you experience as a student will be far greater than that experienced on the wards. And to a certain extent this is true. There are always colleagues around who will cover for you and make sure you don't make any mistakes, but as a junior doctor you have to learn how to cope.

Obviously, when there are life and death decisions to be made, there is stress involved. But because of the depth of the training you receive, and because you are so confident you can deal with anything that comes into the Unit, then stress is almost removed. You often feel as though you are dealing with just the condition. Unfortunately, because you are so focused, you rarely treat the patient as a human being.

Colleagues pick up the signs of stress very quickly and will tell you to take a break, but I enjoy the work. It is physically and mentally exhausting, but if you stick with it, it doesn't affect you. The way I handle stress is to make myself so overtired that all I want to do is sleep. After a 12-hour shift I'll go for a run and then spend an hour in the gym. I can work out any anger or problems and sleep well afterwards.

Firefighter   C

If I do suffer from stress, I don't recognise it. We rarely see that many serious jobs – by serious I mean fires with people involved. But if I'm honest, if you suspect that people are involved, stress increases. And however much information you get about the job, it's never straightforward. Fatalities, particularly children, probably affect me the worst.

My life has been in serious danger once. A staircase I'd been standing on collapsed. But even then, my day wasn't ruined by it. I felt very tense for about 24 hours afterwards and that was it.

Talking about a job with the rest of the team undoubtedly helps relieve any stress. It's not a formal discussion, just a light-hearted talk about how everyone performed. Everyone in the job accepts that it's serious, but you can't afford to let it bother you because you will have to do it again and again. A different kind of stress that affects me more than when I'm on a job is managing the team of firefighters. It's hard managing twelve different personalities in a shift. Dealing with a fire is far easier, believe me.

3 Grammar: using the passive

▶ Grammar reference p.222

Fill in the gaps in the text below using one of the verbs in the box in an appropriate passive form.

employ   produce   surround   bring up   say
list   supply   choose   born   design

Ingvar Kamprad is the founder and chairman of the giant furniture organisation IKEA. He

1 .... and 2 .... in Sweden and according to him he

received a poor education. His first business involved mail order sales of small items like pens.

He lived in a small town called Almhult near a lake which 3 .... by a number of

small furniture factories. He says that his home was not well-to-do and that he was aware of ugly and poorly-

made furniture. It 4 .... that he put together his first furniture catalogue when he

was twenty-three, and that the items 5 .... by him.

Today only a small percentage of the products sold by IKEA 6 .... by the

company. However, most of their products 7 .... by their own team of designers

and then these products 8 .... by firms in other countries.

Altogether about 11,400 articles 9 .... in an IKEA catalogue. The company now

has 125 stores in 26 countries with 30,500 people who 10 .... on either a full or

part-time basis.

---

4   WRITING   PART 2

Your teacher has asked you to write a composition based on your own experience in reponse to the following criticism: *Most young people lead very unhealthy lives.*

Write a **composition** in **120–180** words in an appropriate style.

---

5 Grammar: gerunds 3

▶ Grammar reference p.223

Write ten separate sentences using your own ideas. Each sentence must include one word from list 1 and one from list 2 followed by the *-ing* form of the verb. Some of the words in list 2 will need to be used more than once.

Example
*I was **afraid of travelling** by train when I was younger.*

1		2
1 afraid	6 sorry	in
2 bad	7 bored	on
3 responsible	8 clever	for
4 succeed	9 apologise	with
5 terrified	10 insist	at
		of

6 USE OF ENGLISH PART 3

For questions **1–10**, complete the second sentence so that it has a similar meaning to the first sentence. Use the word given and other words to complete each sentence. You must use between two and five words. **Do not change the word given**.

Example
The piano is not small enough to get through the door.
too

The piano *is too large to* get through the door.

---

1 'Let's go out,' Harry said to his wife.
   should
   Harry suggested to his wife .... out.

2 Please could you speak more quietly.
   so
   I wish .... loudly.

3 Nic and Marianne are always quarrelling with each other.
   out
   Nic and Marianne .... with each other.

4 I've never seen a better cartoon than *The Jungle Book*.
   best
   The Jungle Book is .... ever seen.

5 Hundreds of new books are advertised by various publishers each week.
   advertise
   Various .... hundreds of new books each week.

6 It's ages since I read a good book.
   long
   I haven't read a good .... time.

7 I won't be able to stay longer if I don't renew my visa.
   unless
   I won't be able to stay longer .... visa.

8 It's possible that the letter has got lost in the post.
   may
   The letter .... in the post.

9 I would prefer to go by bus than walk.
   rather
   I .... by bus than walk.

10 When she heard the joke, Tilda burst out laughing.
    on
    Tilda burst out .... joke.

HAVE YOU GOT DRIVE?

SPEAKING

Making money

This man is one of the richest men on earth, worth around $18 billion.
How do you think he became so wealthy?
Look at the list of possible jobs he might have which make him so wealthy.
Decide on one of these possibilities and be ready to explain your choice.

He owns a number of oil wells.
He is an international banker.
He owns a chain of fast-food restaurants.
He buys and sells works of art.
He has a computer software company.
He publishes comic books.

(Turn to page 133 to see if you were right.)

1 Read the article carefully and then do the vocabulary exercise which follows.

Bill Gates is god of the microchip. The Henry Ford of our day, he is the force behind the most explosive technology on earth. Bryan Appleyard talks to a supreme technocrat.

1 Bill Gates is both the most brilliant computer programmer in the world and one of the most ruthlessly competitive businessmen. 'He is,' says one of his senior associates, 'incredibly important, one of the smartest people of the 20th century.'

2 Gates's speed of thought is unparallelled, his range of reference breathtaking; he has, according to another employee, 'the biggest bandwidth of any person I've ever met.' (Bandwidth is electronic jargon best understood as scope.) He is the supreme technocrat, the gatekeeper of the future, certainly one of the most fascinating and possibly one of the most important men on earth.

3 He grew up in Seattle in the US, and his early brilliance seemed to be leading him into a career as a pure mathematician. At Harvard*, with the help of a friend, Paul Allen, he had a vision. In 1975 a small home computer, the Altair, was put on the market. It was a primitive box with switches and lights. Gates and Allen realised two things – first the Altair needed software to make it work and, secondly, this was the future. Computing power was to move from the big mainframes and down into the home and office in the form of PCs, personal computers. He dropped out of Harvard without finishing his degree.

4 The mistake Gates did not make – and, if there is one key to his success, this is it – was to think that this meant he should build computers. Computers were just chunks of hardware that could be considered as an effectively free commodity; any fool could make them. What counted was the software, a product that needed high intelligence, meticulous accuracy and an intuitive grasp of what might be possible. The wealth of the Information Age lay not in manufacturing, but in the painstaking compilation of millions of lines of code that turned silicon chips* into devices of unbelievable complexity and power.

5 The rest is history. Combining his programming genius with an awesome business sense and a high percentage of luck, Gates and Microsoft have dominated the software market. Most spectacularly he wrote and maintained control of MS-DOS, an operating system that is installed on millions of computers around the world. Microsoft Windows, a very sophisticated system that makes computers easier to use, is installed on millions more and Windows 95 provides on-line electronic services for further millions of computer users. Gates and his company are now the leaders in the most potent and explosive technology on earth.

*
Harvard – famous American university
silicon chips – tiny pieces of hard material used in electronic circuits

VOCABULARY

Paragraph 1

1 What does *ruthlessly* mean?
 A hardheartedly
 B unkindly
 C meanly

Paragraph 2

2 What does *unparallelled* mean?
 A the best
 B without equal
 C most famous

3 Which word (other than *bandwidth*) has a similar meaning to *scope*?

4 What does *jargon* mean?
 A private language
 B technical language
 C difficult language

Paragraph 3

5 Which phrase means *he was able to see future developments*?

6 Which phrase means *went on sale*?

7 What does *primitive* mean?
 A original
 B traditional
 C basic

8 Which phrasal verb means *withdrew from a course*?

Paragraph 4

9 Which phrase means *vital explanation of*?

10 What are *chunks*?

    A small thin pieces

    B thick solid pieces

11 Which two adjectives are associated with the idea of *paying very careful attention to detail*?

12 Which phrase means an *intuitive grasp*?

    A automatic understanding

    B clear understanding

    C instinctive understanding

13 *Compilation* means putting or collecting things together. What do you think the infinitive of the verb is?

14 What does the noun *complexity* mean?

    A something very fast

    B something very complicated

    C something very special

Paragraph 5

15 What does *awesome* mean?

    A good

    B careful

    C amazing

16 What noun can you form from the verb *maintain*?

    Which word means *maintained*?

    A made

    B kept

    C used

17 What noun can you form from the verb *install*?

    Which phrase means *installed*?

    A in place

    B connected to

    C developed

18 What does *potent* mean?

    A forceful

    B powerful

    C influential

---

2 Now choose the best answer A, B, C or D to the following questions.

1 How does Bill Gates treat his business rivals?

    A with cruelty

    B without mercy

    C with tolerance

    D without nastiness

2 Bill Gates is highly thought of because he

    A has made so much money.

    B can see into the future.

    C is so good at mathematics.

    D is such a computer genius.

3 What is at the root of Gates's success?

    A He recognised the importance of computer hardware.

    B He knew there would be a demand for personal computers.

    C He concentrated on writing computer programmes.

    D He produced more computers than any other company.

4 Why do so many computers use Microsoft products?

    A Microsoft systems are the most popular.

    B There are no other alternatives.

    C Microsoft controls the market.

    D Microsoft products are the easiest to use.

1 🔲 At the beginning of this unit you had to guess Bill Gates' *possible*
occupation from a list of *possibilities*. Bill Gates is obviously a very *able*
person with brilliant mathematical *ability*.
What is the pattern for turning these adjectives into nouns?
Look at the words below that follow similar patterns and complete the
columns.

	adjective	noun		adjective	noun
1	able	....	10	horrible	.....................*
2	....	adaptability	11	intelligible	....
3	....	advisability	12	....	irritability
4	available	....	13	....	legibility
5	....	capability	14	mobile	....
6	credible	....	15	probable	....
7	....	desirability	16	....	respectability
8	eligible	....	17	responsible	....
9	flexible	....	18	terrible	.....................*

*These words do not follow the same pattern as the others – be careful!

2 Now choose the correct words from the columns to complete sentences
1–10. You may need to make certain words negative.

1 Taking parties of young foreign students
abroad places a great ....
on the organisers of such trips.

2 You have to have worked for an employer for
a number of years before you become
.... for a pension.

3 I hate this humid weather – it makes me feel
very .... and short-
tempered.

4 Old people can remain ....
well into old age, provided they stay fit and
healthy.

5 The .... of exotic fruit
and vegetables throughout the year in most
supermarkets means that things like fresh
dates and mangoes are no longer considered
luxuries in northern Europe.

6 Pete mumbles so badly when he speaks that
he is virtually ....

7 In this day and age it is not really
.... for young people to
backpack alone; travelling with others is
considered safer.

8 Could you rewrite this address so that it's
..........................., please.

9 Benna is quite .... of
sitting still for more than five minutes – she's
the most restless girl I've ever met.

10 The .... of being able to
arrange one's own hours to suit oneself makes
working from home a very attractive option.

1 The developments in electronic technology are making it possible for more people to work from home.

Computer users can communicate with others by typing a message and sending it electronically using e-mail and a modem link, which connect the computer to the outside world using the telephone network.

You are going to listen to a woman called Carol Butcher talking about the computer technology which enables her to work from her own home.
Do you expect her to feel positive or negative about working from home?
What do you think are the advantages and disadvantages of working from home?

2 Read the questions below **before** you listen to make sure that you understand all the vocabulary.
Choose the best answer from A, B or C as you listen.

1 Carol Butcher used to work
   A in a government office.
   B in an information technology centre.
   C in a university library.

2 What does Carol say about e-mail?
   A It makes people feel rather isolated.
   B It provides immediate contact with others.
   C It is still rather expensive to use.

3 According to Carol, computer technology makes people seem
   A more liberated.
   B less friendly.
   C more interesting.

4 What does Carol feel about communicating with her friend in New York?
   A Phone calls are the easiest way.
   B E-mail would be more convenient.
   C Using the postal system is the cheapest.

5 Why does Carol sound so surprised?
   A Because she never again wants to work in an office.
   B Because all their friends are now working from home.
   C Because there are still not that many e-mail users.

3 Listen again to Carol Butcher. This time your teacher will pause the tape so that you can jot down some of the words and phrases Carol uses when she talks about her work. The first one has been done for you as an example; the others are connected with personal relationships.

1 *has been in on* .... has been involved with
2 .... in touch with
3 .... by yourself
4 .... tied to
5 .... being isolated
6 .... mix with others
7 .... exchange ideas
8 .... form a relationship with
9 ....
10 .... } close, warm and friendly

GRAMMAR ▶ p.224 ⟮ *would rather; it's time* ⟯

1 🔲 When talking about her friend in New York phoning so early in the morning, Carol Butcher said:

I'd much rather she e-mailed me ...

What is Carol expressing?
    a regret about what has happened in the past
    a wish that her friend would do something differently

Which of these statements expresses the same idea?
A I wished she wouldn't phone so early.
B I wish she would use e-mail, not the phone.

2 When talking about the users of e-mail, Carol went on to say:

It's high time more companies encouraged their employees ...

What is Carol saying?
    It's too late for many employees to use e-mail.
    It's very important that employees use e-mail as the technology has been available for ages.

Which of the following statements expresses the same idea?

A I really wish companies would encourage their employees to use e-mail.
B I would prefer companies to encourage their employees to use e-mail.

3 Complete the sentences below so that the second sentence is similar in meaning to the original.

Example
I wish you would learn how to use a word processor.
It's about time you learnt how to use a word processor.

I wish you would set up an office at home.
I'd much rather you set up an office at home.

1 I wish you would ring me instead of writing.
  I'd ....
  instead of writing.
2 I wish we had access to the Internet.
  It's ....
  access to the Internet.
3 I wish you would buy a computer.
  It's ....
  a computer.
4 I wish we had our own fax machine.
  I'd ....
  fax machine.

Look at the pictures below and take it in turns to practise using either *would (much) rather* or *it's (about/high) time* for each situation. Imagine what you would say depending on which person you are in each situation.

Example
It's about time you turned that off!

1 ▥ Look at this photograph. What do you think the man is doing with the laptop computer? (Turn to page 133 for the answer.)

In the future cars may be controlled by computers which decide your route for you, control the speed at which you drive and do not need steering with a conventional steering wheel. The driver will simply programme the car's computer, sit back and be driven to the destination!

Does the idea of the computerised car appeal to you. Why/why not?

Until the day when these cars are on the market, however, most young people want to learn to drive and have a car of their own.

2 Read quickly what the four young people on page 126 say about their experiences of learning to drive.

Who do you think owns which car?

Rebecca (18 years old)

The most negative thing about driving is that it's made me lazy – I don't walk anywhere any more. But it has made me more independent, is safer and more convenient than using public transport, and is good for socialising.

My mum has more patience in traffic than me; I'm probably a more aggressive driver than my parents. I drive a bit slower if I have friends in the car, and try to make their journey as smooth as possible.

I haven't had any accidents or near misses yet – the worst happened during a driving lesson when I broke a wing mirror after hitting a traffic cone. A near miss is probably a good thing, because it makes you more careful. Safe driving has a lot to do  with attitude. I think 17 is too young to learn: perhaps 20 would be a better age.

Martin (22 years old)

Dave (18 years old)

My age group is more safety conscious than my parents' generation. No matter how good a driver you are, it's impossible to predict what might be around the corner. I've never felt that being a young driver has made other road users act aggressively towards me, although I was recently stopped by the police for no apparent reason.

I sometimes worry that I won't react fast enough in certain situations, for example if a car suddenly pulled out in front of me. I've had a couple of small accidents, when I've driven too close to parked cars. I always carry a mobile phone which makes me feel more secure in a car.

Hayley (18 years old)

Learning to drive has changed my life – I am far more independent. It's also a benefit to my parents, as they don't have to worry about me taking public transport at night or giving me lifts to places.

---

3 Now read the texts again and answer questions 1–8.

1 Which driver seems the most nervous?

2 Which driver seems the most aggressive?

3 Which drivers now feel more independent?

4 Which driver feels safer with a mobile phone?

5 Which driver drives more slowly with passengers?

6 Which driver thinks they might have been unfairly treated?

7 Which driver thinks they have caused minor damage?

8 Which driver thinks their parents are not concerned enough about danger?

Look at the text and the questions. In groups, discuss your views of young drivers.

> Putting an independent teenager behind the wheel of their first car can be one of the most stressful and expensive stages of being a parent.
>
> In the UK young people can learn to drive when they are 17 years old, but the car must be supervised by someone at least 21 years old who has held a full British licence for at least three years.
>
> In the UK, drivers under 21 are involved in 1,000 of the 4,000 fatal road accidents every year, and it is not just their safety that is the concern, but also the risk of them harming other road users. Although 17–25-year-olds only make up 10% of all drivers, they are involved in 20% of accidents.

How old do you have to be in your country before you can learn to drive?

Do you think young drivers in your country are more dangerous than older drivers?

What is your experience of being driven by your friends?

What is your experience of being a driver?

WRITING

Formal letter 3

A motoring magazine wants young people to write in with their views on young drivers.

Write a letter to the editor of the magazine giving your views on the following points:

▶ speed

▶ age

▶ attitude to safety

▶ accident rate

Choose one of the openings below for your letter and write about 120 words.

> Dear Editor,
> I am .... years old and have been driving for .... years.

OR

> Dear Editor,
> I am .... years old and I haven't learnt to drive.

1 🔲 Look at this sentence again:

> In the UK young people can learn to drive when they are 17 years old, but the car must be supervised by someone at least 21 years old who has held a full British licence for at least three years.

A Pick out the modal verb which means that you are allowed to do something.

How would you make this modal negative?

B Pick out the modal verb which means that you are obliged by law to do something.

How would you make this modal negative?

Look at these examples from the regulations called *The Highway Code*, published in the UK for motorists, pedestrians, cyclists and horse riders. Are they examples of laws which must be obeyed or are they expressing something else?

1 If you have to step into the road, watch out for traffic.

2 At night you should either wear or carry light-coloured, bright or fluorescent items which will help you be seen in the dark.

3 You need to give elderly people or people with disabilities plenty of time to cross the road.

2 Which word(s) convey(s) the most authority in the list below?

must   have to   should   need to

Here is another extract from *The Highway Code*. Fill in the gaps with a suitable modal verb, using the negative if necessary.

> You (1) _____ make sure your vehicle is roadworthy and in a good condition. Any loads carried or towed (2) _____ be secure and (3) _____ stick out dangerously. You (4) _____ drive under the influence of drugs or medicines. You (5) _____ be able to read a vehicle number plate from a distance of 20.5 metres. If you need glasses (or contact lenses) to do this, you (6) _____ wear them when driving.

3 Which of the following examples A–D expresses:

1 no need or necessity

2 no obligation

3 strong advice or recommendation

4 advice or recommendation

(You occasionally see this sticker in offices or small shops in the UK.)

4 ⊠ Look at this sentence again:

> In the UK young people can learn to drive when they are 17 years old ...

In other words, people are *not allowed* to drive until they are 17.

Think of the things which you can and can't do before a certain age in your own country. For example, leaving school, getting married or watching certain categories of film which may contain explicit sex or violence. Make a list and be ready to tell the class.

Do you think the things on your list are reasonable rules? Do you think it's time any of them were changed? Do we need more laws to protect children, for example?

Is it true that children *need to* be protected against violence and bad language on television? Some people think parents *needn't* worry about what their children watch.

5 In the following exercise, fill in the gaps using *needn't, needn't have* or *didn't need to* (adding the correct pronouns where necessary) and putting the verbs in brackets in their correct form.

1 I .... (take) a taxi as I was given a lift home.

2 You .... (do) the washing up, but it was very thoughtful of you.

3 We .... (pack) umbrellas as the weather forecast for the week was completely wrong.

4 You .... (worry) about your exam results – you've come top!

5 How nice of you to bring some flowers, but .... (bother)!

6 You .... (do) this homework if you're too busy.

📖 **LISTENING**

Favourite cars

1 You are going to hear a boy interview one of his teachers for an article in the school magazine. The questions he asks her are on page 130.

Read the questions carefully and underline the key words in each question. This will help you to focus on picking out the important information during the interview.

If possible, interview someone in your class who is a driver before you listen. Use questions 1–10 on page 130.

1 How did you learn to drive?

2 What was your first car?

3 What do you drive now, and why?

4 Do you like driving?

5 What is your most hated car, and why?

6 What is your dream car?

7 What is your worst habit in the car?

8 What makes you most angry about other drivers?

9 What is the most unusual thing you have done in your car?

10 What do you listen to in the car?

2 As you listen to the interview, write down the main point the teacher makes in each of her answers.

If you interviewed someone in your class, did they or did you give similar replies to any of the questions?

SPEAKING

In the future cars may be powered by battery or made of plastic.
In a competition to design a car for the future, many students saw a future in which increasingly crowded cities would require smaller, more environmentally friendly vehicles.

If you could have the car of your choice, what would it be like?
Do you like any of the futuristic cars pictured here?
Would you choose a sporty open-air model?
A mini-car for city use only?
Is colour important?

Key vocabulary

Apart from the vocabulary practised within this unit, you also need to know the following words in connection with science, technology and motoring. Use your dictionary to look up any words you don't know.

Rearrange the words opposite under the two headings. Then use the words to label the numbered parts of the pictures.

Science/Technology	Motoring

boot   CD Rom   mouse   microchip   bonnet   disk   clutch   gear lever   accelerator   brake   keyboard   engine   fax machine   answerphone   petrol tank   windscreen   tyre   laser printer

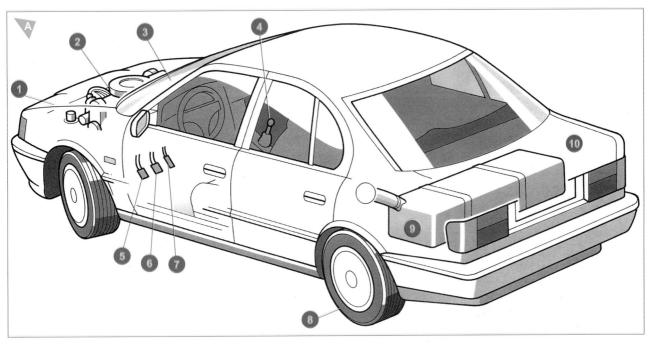

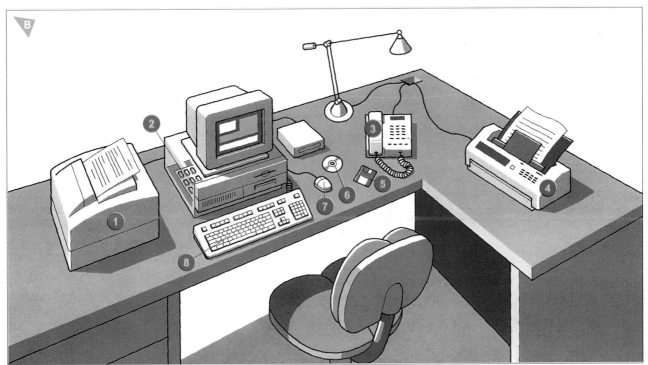

Fill in the missing words in the sentences below. Each word has been started for you, but you should use your dictionary if you need further help.

1 The inve _ _ _ _ _ _ of the motor car dramatically changed travel for most people.

2 As I was parking my car I scraped the bu _ _ _ _ _ against the wall – but then I suppose that's why it's called a bu _ _ _ _ _ !

3 Some electrical soc _ _ _ _ _ have safety covers to prevent children from putting their fingers inside.

4 It is important to keep car headl _ _ _ _ _ _ free from dirt so that they give maximum brightness at night.

5 In the twenty-first century we shall be able to shop by remote co _ _ _ _ _ _ and order things directly from our TV screens.

6 Scientists are researching alternative fu _ _ _ _ , and when the world's supplies of oil run out one possible energy source may be sugar.

7 There are hundreds of different labour-saving gad _ _ _ _ _ designed for use in the kitchen, one of the most recent is the mic _ _ _ _ _ _ _ oven.

8 Road accidents are often caused by people overt _ _ _ _ _ _ in dangerous circumstances, especially on blind corners.

9 The scien _ _ _ _ _ _ advances in personal computers have been amazing in the last few years, and the benefits of high-tech equipment are available to everybody.

10 In some countries passengers in the back seat of cars have to wear safety b _ _ _ _ _ _ .

Read the text and fill in the missing words.

When Jon was a student, he insisted (1) .... cycling everywhere. Most of his friends had cars, but Jon was afraid (2) .... getting into debt and decided not to buy a car until he could really afford one. He preferred cycling (3) .... using public transport, but his girlfriends got fed up (4) .... having to cycle everywhere as well whenever they went out together. When it rained, his girlfriends objected (5) .... getting cold and wet, and although Jon apologised (6) .... not having a car it didn't make any difference. Girls got bored (7) .... waiting for buses and were impatient with his excuses. So he decided to look for a girlfriend who had her own car and succeeded (8) .... finding one who had a smart little sports car. The only problem was that she also had a very large dog and as she used to worry (9) .... leaving the dog in the house on its own, there wasn't any room for Jon in her car. She felt sorry (10) .... making Jon cycle everywhere while she went by car – but it couldn't be helped!

When you have finished unit 7, try filling in this record of what you have learnt.

1 Complete the following sentence with a phrasal verb:
   He found his university course so difficult that he decided to ....

2 What is the adjective from the noun *intuition*?

3 Turn the following adjectives into nouns:
   available ....
   capable ....
   irritable ....
   terrible ....

4 Complete the second sentence so that it means the same as the first.

   A I wish you would have your hair cut.
      It's .... you had your hair cut.

   B Please don't phone me after midnight as I shall be asleep.
      I'd .... you .... me after midnight as I shall be asleep.

5 Write two sentences of you own which make it clear that you know how to use *must* and *should*.

Look back at pages 6–7 and complete the checklist.

I have practised:
  ▶ reading skills for Paper ....., Part .....
  ▶ word building for Paper ....., Part .....
  ▶ listening skills for Paper 4, Part .....
  ▶ writing skills for Paper .....
  ▶ spcaking skills for Paper ....., Part 4

EXAM ADVICE

7 Reading, Part 1

Part 1 of the Reading paper is a multiple matching exercise in which you have to match headings or summary sentences to different parts of the text. You can expect either 6 or 7 questions, and the list of headings will always include one extra heading which will be left over.

▶ The list of headings (or summary sentences) comes before the text.

▶ The headings will not be in the correct order, but jumbled up.

▶ Read through the headings and make sure you understand them **before** you look at the passage.

▶ Then read through the first section of the text, which needs to be matched with its corresponding heading. Make sure you have understood the main focus or ideas in each section of the text before you look back to the list of possibilities for the answer. If you have understood the text correctly, there will only be one correct matching heading or summary sentence.

▶ The headings will be lettered A–G (or H depending on the number of questions). You will need to write only the letter on your answer sheet.

8 Listening, Part 1

The Listening paper consists of 4 parts and 30 questions. You hear the recordings on a cassette, and they last about 45 minutes, which includes 5 minutes at the end for you to transfer your answers onto the separate answer sheet. You hear everything twice and the instructions are both spoken on the tape and printed on your question paper.

Part 1 consists of 8 short extracts and 8 three-option multiple choice questions.

▶ Before the tape begins, you will be allowed time to read through the questions. It is really important that you use this time to prepare yourself for what you are going to hear, and at the same time try to identify the situation or the context for what you will hear.

▶ Each three-option answer is preceded by a question which you will also hear spoken on the tape. If you miss it or don't hear it properly, don't panic because it's on the page for you to read.

▶ The fact that each short extract is different means that if you fail to understand one of the situations there is plenty of opportunity to have another go and to get all the others right. So don't panic and allow one 'problem' to affect everything else.

▶ The extracts are short – about half a minute each – and may be either one speaker (monologue) or two speakers (dialogue). Each extract is repeated.

▶ On the first listening try to pick out the correct option, and use the second listening to check your answer.

(See page 118.) Bill Gates is the founder and boss of Microsoft, the world's largest and most profitable computer software company.

(See page 125.) This photograph was taken during a Grand Prix race. A laptop computer can be plugged into a car's gearbox control unit and immediately diagnoses any faults. Racing cars are now equipped with electronic systems which allow laptop computers to read a car's performance.

1 Grammar revision: comparatives and superlatives

▶ Grammar reference p.225

1 Look back at the pictures of the four second-hand cars on page 125 and then look at the table which gives some details about these cars.

	Citroën 2CV	Volkswagen Beetle	Rover 100	Fiat 500
price	£2,000	£3,500	£4,700	£4,000
mpg*	55	45	43	52
max. speed (mph)*	77	85	95	80

* miles per gallon – 1 gallon = approx. 4.5 litres; 1 mile = approx. 1.6 kilometres
miles per hour

A Which car is the cheapest?

B Which car is the most expensive?

C Which car does the most miles per gallon?

D Which car does the fewest miles per gallon?

E Which car is the fastest?

F Which car is the slowest?

2 Look back at what the four drivers said on page 126. Underline the examples of comparatives and superlatives. There are twelve examples altogether, and Rebecca uses the most.

3 Complete the patterns below.

good	....	....
....	worse	....
hard	....	....
....	....	largest
comfortable	....	....

For questions **1–15**, read the text below and think of the word which best fits each space. Use only **one** word in each space.

ELECTRICITY FOR THE 21st CENTURY

Spacecraft are power-hungry. Without electricity, life in space (**1**) .... impossible: there would be no navigation system, no communications (**2**) .... Earth and no scientific experiments. Cosmonauts (**3**) .... on electricity for cooking, lighting, ventilation and even entertainment, and without fans to circulate the air cosmonauts (**4**) .... eventually die.

Fast, reliable communications are vital. Huge amounts of information on (**5**) .... state of both spacecraft and crew are automatically sent (**6**) .... mission control. Radio, telex and television links help crew members stay up-to-date with (**7**) .... is happening down below and (**8**) .... them in touch with their families.

The (**9**) .... popular leisure activity is simply to (**10**) .... out of the window at the world passing (**11**) .... , but equipment (**12**) .... as cassette tapes, TV and videos need electrical power.

One way to provide extra sources of power for spacecraft and space stations is to generate electricity in space by using what scientists (**13**) .... a 'tethered satellite'. The satellite is, in (**14**) .... , an electrical generator which is flown like a kite at the end of a 20 kilometre-long cable attached to a space shuttle. As the satellite sweeps through the Earth's magnetic field, it (**15**) .... produce electricity using the free electrons from its surroundings.

3 Grammar revision: *used to, be used to, get used to*

▶ Grammar reference p.226

Complete the following sentences with *used to*/an appropriate verb pattern.

1 When I was a child I used .... every holiday with my grandparents.

2 My sister is not used .... to bed early as she runs a restaurant.

3 I didn't like English food very much when I first tried it but I've got .... eating it over the years.

4 My brother was .... having his own way when he was little as he was the youngest.

5 I used .... a lot of strong black coffee but I don't any more.

6 My father isn't used .... for himself as my mother generally prepares all the meals.

7 Are you .... working on a word processor?

8 When I went abroad for the first time I wasn't .... many of the customs.

9 You will have to get .... on your feet all day if you want to be a hairdresser.

10 Professional musicians are .... practising for hours each day.

---

4   WRITING   PART 1

Your class is interested in organising a holiday at a Youth Hostel. You have seen the advertisement below but you need some more information and you have been asked to write to the Youth Hostel Association.

Read carefully the advertisement and the notes which the class has made. Then write your letter including the points in the notes and any other information you think necessary.

Write a **letter** in **120–180** words in an appropriate style. Do not include addresses.

Rent-a-Hostel

How do you fancy having a whole Youth Hostel for your own use, together with friends, family or group – with freedom to come and go as you please? You can do just that with YHA's Rent-a-Hostel scheme which runs for most of the year with the exception of a few months.

HOSTELLING
INTERNATIONAL

number of beds?
when are they available?
where are they? mountains? coast?
how much?
meals? shops?

5 Grammar: modal verbs 2

Grammar reference p.224

Complete the following sentences with a modal verb in its correct form, making it negative if necessary. In some cases there may be more than one possible answer, in which case you should explain the differences in meaning (if any) between the possible answers.

1 Under the new law, anyone buying a gun .... register with the police.

2 I don't feel like clearing up my room but I suppose I .... before my parents see it.

3 That was a delicious meal, but you .... gone to so much trouble – it must have taken you hours to prepare it.

4 You .... be willing to do any kind of job if you want to earn some money!

5 Henry will .... to return to his own country next year unless he can renew his work permit.

6 I'm afraid you will have to put those cigarettes back as I .... sell them to 12-year-olds.

7 It took me ages to fill in this application form but I .... done so as nobody read it.

8 Before Jules accepts this offer of work, he .... to know what the hours are.

9 I was going to buy a new dress for the party, but luckily my sister lent me hers so I ....

10 Now that the family next door have four children, they .... to buy a larger car as I don't see how they can all fit into their present one.

11 If you have been out of work for at least six months, you .... apply for financial help from the government.

12 When you get to their house, you .... to ring the bell as the door is always open.

13 You .... ever ride a bicycle on the motorway or you will be arrested.

14 You've been looking terribly pale for days now – don't you think you .... see a doctor?

15 Your passport photographs .... be either black and white or in colour, but they .... be signed on the back by someone who has known you for at least two years.

ENTER... ENTERTAIN...
ENTERTAINMENT

⊠ SPEAKING

Which film is which?

1 Match the shot from each film with its correct text and title, and then discuss which of the three films you would like to see with your partner.

a **Sharaku** b **Eat Drink Man Woman** c **The Story of Qui Ju**

1 The film is set in Taiwan. Elderly Mr Chu is the greatest living chef in Taipei, the capital of Taiwan. Unfortunately, Mr Chu has lost his sense of taste and he can no longer cope with his three grown-up daughters. One of them is 30 and fears being unmarried; another is an ambitious career woman and like her father is a perfectionist. The last and youngest daughter is a 20-year-old student and works in a fast-food restaurant.

2 This film is adapted from a novel set in rural China. It is a simple story about a young woman called Qui Ju, who is pregnant. Her husband has had an argument with the head of the village and has been injured in the fight. Qui Ju is determined that the chief must apologise for the injury to her husband. The film revolves around her efforts to get justice and ends with a bitter victory for her.

3 In 18th century Japan, Edo City was the centre of politics and economics. Art flourished, too, with many young artists working in the city. Juzaburo Tsutaya was famous for publishing *ukiyo-e* prints. One young artist working with him, Utamaro, knew that Tsutaya would be suppressed by the government. Then Utamaro betrayed Tsutaya to another publisher. In retaliation, Tsutaya made another, unknown, artist famous. But Utamaro was jealous of his talent ...

Make a list of all the other kinds of entertainment you can think of and underline your three favourite kinds of entertainment.

Now find as many other people in your class who share your preferences as you can.

2 Look at the pictures of various kinds of entertainment, sometimes referred to collectively as 'The Arts'. Write down the name of each one.

LISTENING

You will hear five people, each of them talking about one of the kinds of entertainment pictured above.
As you listen, write down the name of the entertainment which you think each person is referring to. (There will be 5 left over).

1 ....

2 ....

3 ....

4 ....

5 ....

GRAMMAR ▸ p.226 / **Third conditional**

1 Look at what the second speaker said:

If I hadn't joined the family business when I was 15, I would have gone to drama school.

The last speaker said:

I would've chosen the clarinet if I had learnt to play a musical instrument ...

In both these examples the speakers are talking about the past, about things which did **not** happen. This conditional pattern is used to speculate about things which might have happened in the past but didn't, and now it is too late for things to change.
Which two tenses do the two speakers use to talk about these situations which are now completely impossible?

2 Complete sentences 1–10 using the appropriate form of the verb in brackets.

1 If I'd known it was your birthday, I

.... (buy) you a present.

2 Jane would have been a dancer if she

.... (not grow) so tall.

3 If my parents .... (have) enough money, they would have built their own house.

4 The President .... (lose) the election if he hadn't agreed to reduce taxes.

5 Jo .... (drown) if her friend hadn't jumped into the pool and saved her.

6 If Pierre had .... (drive) more slowly, he .... (avoid) having an accident.

7 You .... (not make) so many mistakes if you

.... (listen) to your parents' advice.

8 If you .... (have) the opportunity, ... (become) a film star?

9 If the early explorers .... (realise) some of the dangers, they

.... (not leave) home.

10 The course of history .... (be) very different if people

.... (never fight) any wars.

⚡ SPEAKING What would you have done if you'd been there?

I'd have stayed to help.

I'd have run as fast as possible in the opposite direction!

If I'd been there, I think I'd have been too frightened to move.

Talk to people in your class about how you would have acted if you had seen or been in these situations. Ask each other what you would have done and why.

1 Look at this extract from the brochure *Arts Festival 97*.
What and where are the six events taking place?

Arts Festival 97

1 Camera Cult

This exhibition explores how photography reflects and shapes many aspects of social life. It ranges from the world of advertising and life in the city, to the more intimate world of the individual person revealed in personal photographs. There are three sections to the exhibition. **Cityscape:** explores past and present views of Bombay. **Intimate Lives:** takes a fresh look at the family album. **Media Gallery:** looks at the ways in which photography turns products into advertising images. Don't expect to see an exhibition of pictures on the gallery wall. This exhibition is electronic, and computer and video monitors will be available for you to find your way around, as well as expert guides who will talk you through the work if required.

2 Dance, dance, dance

For the first time the Festival reflects the growing popularity of modern dance with a selection of six productions. These new productions feature different professional dancers, all of whom are internationally famous. Each production has its own theme and lasts an hour. It is possible to see all six productions on two consecutive nights: simply entitled, Dances 1, 2 and 3 are staged on one night, with Dances 4, 5 and 6 the following night. Each performance is preceded by a short talk given by the choreographer, and members of the audience will have the opportunity to talk to the dancers as well as the designers at the end of the final performance on the last evening.

3 Hot Lights

It is not often one gets the chance to see such a wonderful collection of abstract paintings as feature in this year's Festival. These paintings are alive with colour – brilliant reds, yellows, blues and greens. The colours shout at you, demanding to be noticed! Some of the painters are exhibiting for the first time, others are artists well known for their powerful work. But you will find all the exhibits really exciting, like a blaze of colour at a carnival, full of light and movement. Many of the paintings are for sale although they cannot be removed until the end of the Festival.

4 Poetry 90

Poetry 90 was formed at the beginning of the decade to provide an opportunity for lovers of poetry and poets to come together to read and listen to their favourite works. Since Poetry 90 began, it has established an international reputation, bringing together people from South America, the US, Europe, North Africa and Australia. Most of the members are writers. Many have published collections, won competitions, received awards, given readings and workshops. As part of this year's Festival programme, Poetry 90 will present a series of poetry readings with the following themes: *Winter Ending; Twilight Zones; Rain over the Moon* and *Firefly Hearts.*

5 Open-air Sculpture

Each year the Festival organisers commission a different sculptor to produce a set of sculptures for the Festival Gardens. This year the young artist Mel Hardy has produced an exciting range of metal work. His copper designs include a fifteen-metre high clock which operates on solar energy. Visitors to the Festival will have fun exploring the grounds and discovering Hardy's work, sometimes in the centre of a lawn, sometimes hidden behind a bush or concealed in the branches of a tree. If you can't manage a visit during the Festival, the sculptures will remain in the Gardens for a further six months and will be open to the public at weekends.

6 Pick of the Potters

Last year's Festival exhibited pottery from the past. This year the exhibition is pottery from the present: modern, contemporary pottery full of imaginative ideas and designs, from a simple bowl to an elaborate statue. Many of the potters will be present at some stage during the Festival, giving workshops and demonstrations. There will also be an opportunity for visitors to try their hand at using a potter's wheel – under the watchful eye of a professional. But if you think pottery is all about pots, then you're in for a big surprise. The exhibits include plants, fish, jewellery – even a pottery plate of pottery fried eggs! As with the paintings, most of these exhibits are for sale at very reasonable prices.

VOCABULARY

2 Read through each text and find words or phrases which mean the same as:

Camera Cult

1 forms and defines (*vb.*)
2 personal and private (*adj.*)
3 knowledgeable (*adj.*)
4 explain (*phr. vb.*)

Dance, dance, dance

1 present (*vb.*)
2 one after the other (*adj.*)
3 is introduced by (*vb.*)
4 person who arranges dance sequences (*n.*)

Hot Lights

1 vivid (*adj.*)
2 dazzlingly bright (*n. phrase*)

Poetry 90

1 built up (*vb.*)
2 good name (*n.*)
3 creative group discussions (*n.*)

Open-air Sculpture

1 authorise a person to do something (*vb.*)
2 relating to the sun (*adj.*)
3 flat, cultivated area of grass (*n.*)

Pick of the Potters

1 present-day (2 *adjs.*)
2 plain (*adj.*)
3 complicated (*adj.*)
4 alert (*adj.*)
5 moderate (*adj.*)

3 Which event(s) would you recommend for someone who

1 enjoys outdoor exhibitions?
2 is interested in the past?
3 likes joining in activities?
4 wants to buy something?
5 would enjoy chatting to performers?
6 is prepared to interact with modern technology?

⟨I⟩ SPEAKING

1 In groups, talk about the events in *Arts Festival 97*.

Would you have gone to any of these events?

If I had been free, I would have gone to one of the Poetry 90 readings as I enjoy poetry.
I wouldn't have gone to Camera Cult as I'm not really interested in photography.

2 Now think of some form of entertainment which took place in your own town last year – maybe a fiesta, a fireworks display, a street procession or an event which you took part in.
Decide together which of these events you would have recommended to a foreign visitor and why.

3 Choose one of these events. Think of why you would (not) like to have been there.

You have about a minute to think what you are going to say to the others in your group.

1 You are going to write a short report about a trip. First, look at the points you need to think about when you write a report:

 ▶ how to introduce the topic

 ▶ selecting and organising the information

 ▶ linking the ideas

 ▶ how to end the report – include a personal comment at this stage if appropriate

2 Now read the report below which was written for a school newspaper by a student who went to Animation World.

Visit to Animation World

Each year our class makes a trip at the end of the summer term. We discuss where we want to go and then our teachers make the arrangements. This year we chose Animation World. We hired two coaches and met outside the school at 8a.m. Although the journey took two hours, we spent the time telling jokes and chatting to our friends.

Animation World opened last year in some old dock buildings, so all the attractions are brand new. It is designed like a museum but everything is based on cartoon characters from film and TV.

First of all we went to see the displays which are set out like film studios using the original scenery. You can see all your favourite figures from Disney films, like Mickey Mouse, Goofy and Donald Duck. The models are life-size, and the best thing is that you are allowed to touch them and have your photo taken!

In another part of the exhibition you can see the techniques the film makers use to turn the drawings into films. It was really interesting to see how they have to make hundreds of different drawings in order to get just two or three minutes of film.

At the end of the day we had a meal in one of the cafés and then went shopping. There are lots of different cafés and gift shops which are fun to wander around even if you don't want to buy anything. I thoroughly enjoyed the day; I also learnt how complicated it is to make cartoons, and I can recommend Animation World for your class trip.

3 Look at how *Visit to Animation World* has been organised.

The first paragraph gives the **purpose** for the trip followed by some very brief factual information.

The second paragraph mentions some **detailed information** about the place they went to.

The third paragraph tells the reader the **first thing** they did – with some examples.

The fourth paragraph goes on to give some **additional information** and mentions what else they did.

The last paragraph **concludes** the day, and the writer ends the report with a personal comment and recommendation.

4 Look at the pictures of the Flying Sculptures which you took whilst you were on holiday and which you had never seen before.

You have been asked to write a short report (about 200 words) for your student newspaper based on this event.

Choose two or three pictures and use *Visit to Animation World* as a basis for your report. Some phrases and vocabulary relating to the pictures have been included to help you.

the colours were really bright...

it looked just like a real...

it was made out of...

they were amazing...

the biggest balloon I've ever seen...

it floated...

it was shaped like...

1  Look at this sentence, from the student's report on Animation World, which uses a causative verb.

The models are life-size, and the best thing is that you are allowed to touch them and **have your photo taken!**

Now look at these three pairs of sentences and discuss the difference in meaning between each pair.

We're having our kitchen decorated.
We're decorating our kitchen.

I painted my portrait.
I had my portrait painted.

I checked my computer.
I had my computer checked.

2 When people get married, they need to have things done as well as doing things for themselves. Look at the examples and then complete the following sentences.

When we get married, we're having a film made of the wedding.

I'm getting my hair cut.

I'm having a new suit made.

I need to have my head examined!

1 They need to ....
....

2 He must ....
....

3 She has to ....
....

4 He has to ....
....

5 She needs to ....
....

3 Now write down three sentences of your own using *need*, *must* and *have to*.

 **SPEAKING** Write down three things you usually have done for you instead of doing them for yourself.
Find somebody else in the class who has written down three different things.

Now write down three things you would like to have done for you instead of having to do them for yourself.
Find someone who has written down three different things.

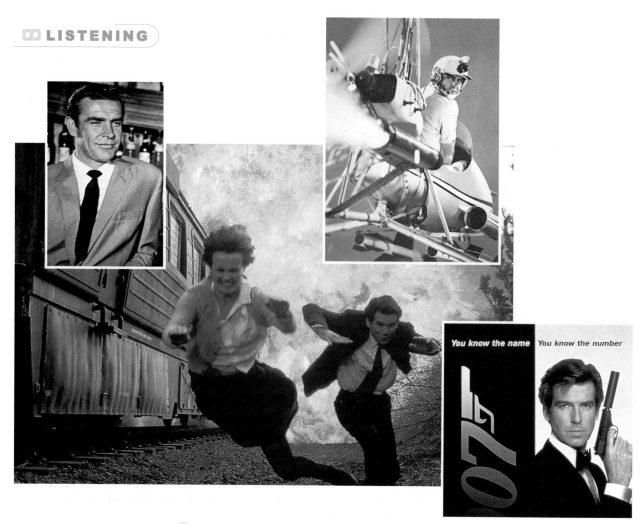

1 Have you seen any of the Bond movies? Which ones have you seen? Did
   you especially enjoy any one movie? If you haven't seen a Bond movie, do
   you have a particular reason for not wanting to?

   Perhaps you saw *Goldeneye* starring Pierce Brosnan? What did you think of
   it? Do you remember any scenes from the film? Was there anything you
   thought was particularly brilliant – like the special effects?

   For many years the actor Sean Connery played the part of James Bond in
   the films based on Ian Fleming's novels. The early Bond films, such as
   Octopussy, *Dr No* and *Diamonds are Forever*, have become cult movies.

2 Some students in a Media Studies class have been watching Bond films
   from the 1960s. You are going to hear them discussing their reactions to
   these films with their teacher.

   As you listen, choose the best answer to each question.

   1 The class has been working
      A as one group.
      B in pairs.
      C in two groups.

   2 Max says that the plot of each film
      A varies very slightly.
      B hardly ever changes.
      C is always identical.

3 Max says that the image of the woman painted gold is

   A quite magical.

   B extremely lifelike.

   C really impressive.

4 The gadgets used in each Bond film are

   A incredibly complicated.

   B new and unexpected.

   C surprisingly similar.

5 Cassie thinks the Bond films are

   A ridiculous.

   B amusing.

   C depressing.

6 Which word sums up Cassie's opinion of Bond's character?

   A dishonest

   B cruel

   C fantastic

7 According to Max the attraction of the Bond films depends on the fact that they are

   A wholly believable.

   B completely unreal.

   C morally convincing.

3 What do *you* think? Do you agree with Max or Cassie?

One of you should sum up Cassie's views and then write a sentence which expresses her main views.

One of you should sum up Max's views and then write a sentence which expresses his main views.

Check what your partner has written and see if you agree.

4 Do you agree with the person who said this?

`The whole appeal of the Bond we know and love is that he is not a responsible, decent adult. He's absolutely rotten and that's why we like him.´

1 ☒ Look at what the teacher says:
*Max, I'm beginning to get rather **im**patient.*

and what Carrie says:
*... the storyline is **im**possible anyway ...*

What do you notice about these two adjectives?
Can you think of any other words beginning
with *im-*?
Discuss with your partner any other ways in
which we can make adjectives negative.

2 Now listen again to the classroom discussion.
As you listen, write down the adjectives you
hear which begin with a negative prefix. There
are nine different ones altogether.

1 ....
2 ....
3 ....
4 ....
5 ....
6 ....
7 ....
8 ....
9 ....

3 How many different prefixes have you listed?
The list below contains other words which you
will have heard on the recording.
Discuss with your partner which prefix you
would use to make these words negative.

1 .... helpful   6 .... real
2 .... happily   7 .... predictable
3 .... responsible   8 .... conventional
4 .... important   9 .... logical
5 .... interesting

4 You will have heard the teacher say to Max:
*Good – that's more along the lines I was hoping for.
Very encouraging.*

Encouraging is an exception – can you make it
negative?

GRAMMAR Word building 5: nouns, adjectives, negative prefixes

☒ There are other words which you will have heard which you can also turn into
negative forms. Look at the example and then complete the table using your dictionary
if necessary.

noun	adjective	negative prefix
success	*successful*	un-
surprise	1	....
	2	....
attraction	....	....
expectation	....	....
development	1	....
	2	....

1 Ask each other the following questions.

Do you like entertaining people or being entertained? What can you do? Can you play a musical instrument? Do you sing? Can you juggle? Have you ever been on the stage? Would you perform in the street to earn money?

2 Look at these people who are buskers – they earn money by performing in public places. Discuss the following questions.

Would you give any or all of these buskers money if you saw them busking?
Is there somewhere in your town where people busk? Why do they choose that particular place?
Why do you think some people object to buskers? Do you agree with any of their objections?

GRAMMAR ▸ p.227   Using *it*

1 We use *it* in various ways; match the definitions 1–5 below with the examples A–E.

1 **it** in impersonal, rather formal structures
2 **it** when we talk about time, weather, distance
3 **it** when we want to refer to a person
4 **it** as a personal pronoun
5 **it** after certain verbs to describe reactions to things

A Have you seen *Goldfinger*? It's brilliant!
B Who's that? Is it Pierce Brosnan?
  No it isn't – it's Sean Connery.
C How far is it from here to the station?
D I hate it there.
E It is thought that there may be life on other planets.

2 Complete the following sentences using *it* + an appropriate structure.

1 It .... for Steve to remember people's names even when he knew them quite well.

2 .... five miles to the nearest video shop from here.

3 .... that scientists will have found a cure for cancer within the next twenty years.

4 .... children find it easier to learn to play a musical instrument than adults.

5 I really .... at my grandmother's place – it's so comfortable there.

6 Some people .... quite frightening to travel alone.

7 .... since I've seen you – where've you been?

8 .... that there are still some people who think that the earth is flat.

Key vocabulary

Apart from the vocabulary practised within this unit, you also need to know the following words in connection with the arts. Use your dictionary to look up any words you don't know and to help you with the incomplete words.

Places	& related words
arena	ais _ _
art gallery	balc _ _ _ _
arts complex	box
museum	circle
sta_ium	curt _ _ _ _
	f _ _ lights
	spot
	wings

People	& related words
ballerina	applause
choreog _ _ _ _ _ _ _	dub
compo _ _ _	encore
conduc _ _ _	interv _ _
playwr _ _ _ _	scri _ _
produ _ _ _	subtitles

My favourite
singer is ....
group is ....
actor is ....
album is ....

Vocabulary in context

Look at this picture and label the numbered parts.

Recycling: *would rather; it's time*

Complete the sentences below using either *would rather* or *it's time*.

1 I prefer the cinema to the theatre so .... go to a movie this evening.

2 .... I spent the money you gave me on a picture or a book?

3 .... you had your own art exhibition if you want to sell your work.

4 Despite the competitive atmosphere Michael .... go to music college than university.

5 After all the hours you've spent practising the cello don't you think .... you played something for us?

Learning record

When you have finished unit 8, try filling in this record of what you have learnt.

1 .... the film was on last week, I would have gone to see it.

2 I would've earned more money busking if
....

3 'We had a very intimate conversation.' What does *intimate* mean? ....

4 Can you think of another word for *contemporary*?

5 Your hair's really untidy – you need .... it cut.

6 I'm going to the dentist tomorrow .... two teeth ....

7 The opposite of *rational* is ....

8 The opposite of *encouraging* is ....

FCE Checklist

You should be able to complete this checklist without looking back now!

I have practised:

▶ speaking skills for Paper 5, Part ....
▶ listening skills for Parts .... and .... of Paper 4
▶ reading skills for Paper 1, Part ....
▶ writing skills for Paper ...., Part ....
▶ vocabulary skills for Part ...., Paper 3

EXAM ADVICE

15 Writing, Part 2

▶ In Part 2 of the Writing Paper you may have the choice of writing a **report** (or an account) of an event, a visit, etc.

▶ As with other similar questions in this part of the Writing Paper, you will be asked to identify with the situation.

▶ Underline or highlight the key points you need to include in your report. Is the report asking for any personal views?

▶ Make sure you understand who and what the report is being written for. Is it a report for a newspaper? Is it a report for your teacher? Is it a report for the police about something that has happened to you or that you have witnessed?

▶ Organise your ideas. Can you think of enough to write?

▶ Does your opening sentence make it clear what is going to follow? For example, if you are writing a report on a new restaurant:

Last night I visited the new restaurant which opened in the city centre a week ago. It is called ...

▶ Does the report require you to reach a conclusion?

▶ Are you asked to make a recommendation about anything, like the most interesting place to visit in your area, for example?

16 Listening, Part 2

Part 2 of the Listening Paper consists of either a single speaker or a conversation between 2 or 3 speakers and lasts for about 3 minutes. The listening task consists of writing short answers to 10 questions. These questions may be in the form of a note-taking exercise, completing sentences or filling in the answers to short questions.

▶ Use the preparation time to look carefully at the kind of information you are going to need in order to fill in the gaps. What kind of words can you expect to write? Will you have to listen for how old someone is, for the place where two people are going to meet, for the title of a course that someone is going to do, etc?

▶ By looking at the questions, can you guess what the piece is likely to be about?

▶ Does the instruction ask you for a word, a number, a few words or a short phrase? If you look at the length of the spaces where you have to write your answers on the answer sheet, you will see that you are not expected to write more than three or four words at the most.

▶ You don't have to write complete sentences.

▶ You will not lose marks for words that are incorrectly spelt, provided that the word is recognisable.

1 USE OF ENGLISH PART 5

For questions **1–10**, read the text below. Use the word given in capitals at the end of each line to form a word that fits in the space in the same line. There is an example at the beginning.

INTERNATIONAL SCHOOLS

International Schools offer one main ..... *attraction* ..... – continuity.   **ATTRACT**

Parents who lead lives where change is (**1**) ....   **EXPECT**

know that ordinary schools can be (**2**) .... when it comes   **RELY**

to their children's education. It is not (**3**) .... that if children   **SURPRISE**

move within the same system, they feel less (**4**) ....   **SECURE**

(**5**) .... international schools encourage the development   **SUCCESS**

of national as well as international identity, something which an

ordinary school may find (**6**) .... to achieve.   **POSSIBLE**

Many schools include children from dozens of countries, (**7**) ....   **TROUBLE**

by the fact that they may all speak different languages. It is not

that a child's mother tongue is (**8**) .... , but the school will focus   **RELEVANT**

on getting the children to work together in their different cultures.

It is interesting to note that few parents are ever (**9**) .... with   **SATISFY**

the education provided and report that their children are rarely

(**10**) .... while at school.   **HAPPY**

2 WRITING PART 2

You spent the evening at the cinema/the theatre/a concert. Write a report of what you attended, making it clear whether or not you would recommend the evening's entertainment to the people in your English class.

Write your **report** in **120–180** words in an appropriate style.

3 USE OF ENGLISH   PART 4

For questions **1–10**, read the text below and look carefully at each line. Some of the lines are correct, and some have a word which should not be there.
If a line is correct, put a tick (✓) beside it. If a line has a word which should **not** be there, write the word beside it. There is an example at the beginning.

SOMETHING TO KEEP THE KIDS QUIET THIS WEEKEND

1	✓	The Discovery Dome at Bodelwyddan Castle in Wales has something
2	....	for everyone. There are exhibitions, workshops and lots of more things
3	....	to see and do. The Dome provides hours of fun with different activities
4	....	where children can make weird-shaped bubbles, to construct boats and
5	....	fountains or build bridges over water. The workshop activities are
6	....	changed on a weekly basis so there's always something new to learn,
7	....	explore and enjoy. At the same time that as visiting the Dome it's also
8	....	possible to look well around the restored Castle. It has a fine collection
9	....	of pictures in the portrait gallery, a walled garden, an adventure in
10	....	playground and a children's play area.

4 Grammar: phrasal verbs and nouns

▶ Grammar reference p.216   Appendix 2 p.233

Use the words in the box to fill in the spaces in the passage.

through	down	on	out	for	into	with	up	off

People who are suffering from long-term pain are finding ¹ .... that exercise can be more effective than drugs. At Europe's largest Pain Relief Clinic in Liverpool in England, patients start ² .... the day with exercise and relaxation techniques followed by an hour on exercise bikes.

Many people who don't care ³ .... a lifetime of taking drugs are attracted to this new approach to treating pain. Professional athletes and dancers who are affected by physical injuries find that the pain can get them ⁴ .... to such an extent that they may be forced to give ⁵ .... their careers.

Swimming is another form of exercise strongly encouraged for chronic pain because it cuts ⁶ .... the physical stresses caused by gravity. Scientists are also looking ⁷ .... the possibility of funding research into hydrotherapy and why it is so popular in spa towns in Europe. Many people who have tried ⁸ .... treatment at these spas have reported experiencing less pain after exercising in water. A scientific break ⁹ .... which produced a cure for back pain, headaches and muscle injuries, would allow people to get ¹⁰ .... with their lives instead of spending months in bed.

5 Grammar: third conditional

▶ Grammar reference p.226

Rewrite the two sentences to make one complete sentence. Your new sentence must make it clear that it is now too late for what happened in the past to change.

Example

I didn't see you at the bus stop. I didn't give you a lift.

If I had seen you at the bus stop, I would have given you a lift.

1 I wasn't very musical. I didn't become a pop singer.

....

2 I didn't win the national lottery. I didn't buy a painting by Picasso.

....

3 I was late. I missed the start of the film.

....

4 I lost my job. I didn't buy a new music centre.

....

5 I didn't go to university. I didn't study theatre arts.

....

6 My camera was broken. I didn't take any photos of the jewellery exhibition.

....

7 I didn't earn any money. My parents were disappointed.

....

8 I arrived late at the pop festival. All the tickets had been sold.

....

9 I forgot my lines during the play. The audience laughed.

....

10 I had very little money when I was a student. I bought singles instead of albums.

....

---

6   READING   PART 1

You are going to read a magazine article about skyscrapers. Choose the most suitable heading from the list **A–H** for each part (**1–7**) of the article. There is one extra heading which you do not need to use.

A	Americans beaten by Malaysians.
B	High-rise buildings are basically unexciting.
C	Tall structures may not be safe.
D	What does the future offer?
E	Tall buildings are wasteful.
F	How the world's tallest structures line up.
G	Models for high-rise buildings originated here.
H	The powerful attraction of height.

HIGH AND MIGHTY

1

In the early years of the 20th century American skyscrapers were the symbol of modernity. The rest of the planet went green with envy and rushed desperately to copy this extraordinary American invention, the price of entry, so it seemed, into the modern world.

2

The Americans alone had the secret of building high. Above all, they packed their skyscrapers close enough together to create completely different ideas of what a city could be. However, the twin towers completed in Malaysia in 1996 have since become the world's tallest buildings and a symbol of economic and cultural achievement.

3

There is, of course, something rather childish about the urge to build high simply for the sake of being the world's highest. And yet the idea of extreme height shows no signs of relaxing its grip on the imagination of the world. The kind of people who present themselves as sensible and cautious businessmen rush headlong into attempts to build ever taller structures.

4

These are, moreover, structures that make no economic sense. Extreme height creates buildings that are hard to use efficiently. You cannot let them out until they are finished, so large sections remain empty, earning no income. And extreme height also means a much larger percentage of each floor is taken up with lifts and structure.

5

It is interesting to look at what tall buildings reveal about an architect's intentions. These buildings may be the best chance an architect ever gets to make his mark, but they are rarely the kind of mark an architect would like to make. For the most part, architects have found very little opportunity to create a meaningful design. It is just an object. There is not much of interest going on inside, just endless repeated floor plans. And there is a curious loss of scale. Once past the first 20 or so storeys, the architect finds little to interest him by way of design. The difference between a tall building and a very tall building is simply the difference between one large, boring box and another.

6

However, the twin towers in Malaysia are unlikely to remain the world's tallest for long. Even taller structures are on the drawing board for the 21st century in Russia, China and Australia. One Japanese architect has put forward a scheme for a building, not so much a skyscraper as a complete town which would accommodate as many as 52,000 people. But for the moment this looks likely to remain a dream.

7

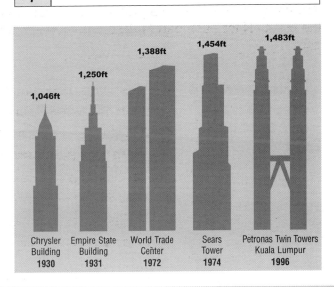

| Chrysler Building 1930 | Empire State Building 1931 | World Trade Center 1972 | Sears Tower 1974 | Petronas Twin Towers Kuala Lumpur 1996 |
| 1,046ft | 1,250ft | 1,388ft | 1,454ft | 1,483ft |

GLOBE-TROTTING

SPEAKING

Happy landings

Many airlines now show arrival videos to passengers on board the aircraft shortly before landing.

Look at the photographs.
Discuss which city you think these passengers are about to arrive at. There is a list of possible places to choose from at the foot of the page.

Imagine you could choose to land at one of these places in the next day or two.
Which one would you choose and why?
Which one would you not choose and why?

Singapore   London   Hong Kong   Rome   Los Angeles   Tokyo
Athens   Paris   Buenos Aires   Tangiers   Stockholm

1 In the following extract about Singapore some words have been missed out. Read the extract through carefully and decide on the missing words.

If you are not sure about the exact word which is missing, try to agree on the kind of word, for example, whether it is a noun, a verb or a preposition, etc.

When you have finished, check your answers with another pair of students.

Singapore

Just near the equator is a small tropical island so unusual that it is known by many names: 'Surprising Singapore', 'Garden City' and even 'Instant Asia'. It is small – just under 640 square kilometres, but following independence (1) .... 1965 Singapore has become (2) .... of south-east Asia's most modern (3) .... successful cities, where 2.8 million Chinese, Malays, Indians and Eurasians live and work side by side.

With temperatures averaging 24–32° C, Singapore's climate is pleasant all year round. There (4) .... a rainy season from November to February, but the showers help cool the air and rarely (5) .... long.

For more (6) .... 150 years Singapore River was the heart of the island's trade. However, today these old trading buildings have (7) .... restored as shops, restaurants, markets and bars, and the area has become (8) .... exciting leisure and entertainment centre.

2 How many of the missing words are link words?

Can you find any other link words in the passage?

ELEPHANT TREK

Dawn broke early <u>as</u> the sky gradually turned a pale grey and a thin mist rose above the forest. The group gathered in front of the largest hut and waited for the guide to appear. Although the sun was not yet up, the air was warm and everyone knew that in a few hours it would be hot and humid. In spite of that and the long trek ahead of them, they knew that this was the only way of seeing elephants at their watering hole. There was no guarantee of course that the elephants would be there, even though the villagers had told them that at this time of year the elephants always came back to the same watering hole. Nevertheless, everyone had been willing to get up at the crack of dawn and to walk the ten kilometres through the forest.

The guide came silently along the path and signalled to them to walk behind him. Nobody spoke. The undergrowth rustled and birds flapped in the trees above their heads. The ground under their feet was hard and dry, full of tangled tree roots and boulders so they had to keep their eyes on the track to prevent themselves from

falling. Once or twice a startled animal shot across their path; otherwise they only heard the forest and saw nothing. The guide stopped once in order for them to have a drink from their water bottles.

They must have been walking for about three hours because the sun had now risen and the forest was alive with sound. The sunlight filtered through the treetops; ahead of them they could see a clearing in the trees; the guide slowed down. Without turning round he motioned to them to wait while he went forward more cautiously. A large bull elephant was standing at the edge of the pool. Eventually he beckoned and people began to move, as quietly as they could and hardly daring to breathe. They knew that a sudden sound could disturb the herd and that elephants charged at terrifyingly fast speeds. However, one member of the group in his excitement dropped his camera.

'Quick, quick, run, run, the elephant is going to charge!' yelled the guide, and a look of terror spread across his face.

VOCABULARY

Match the words 1–9 from the passage with their correct meanings.

1 humid	large rocks
2 the crack of dawn	surprised and frightened
3 undergrowth	moved their wings up and down
4 rustled	indicated
5 flapped	made a whispering sound
6 tangled	damp
7 boulders	very early
8 startled	twisted
9 motioned	grass and bushes

2 Now read the passage again and this time underline the link words.
The first one has been done for you.

Link words are important: *not only* do they link the different parts of a sentence, *but* they *also* show how the ideas in that sentence are related.

Perhaps the simplest link word of all is *and*, which is used to connect ideas:

*... the sky turned a pale grey **and** a thin mist rose ...*
*... full of tangled tree roots **and** boulders ...*

There are other common link words which show how ideas can be contrasted or opposed:

***Although** the sun was not yet up, the air was warm ...*

***In spite of** that ...*

*... **even though** the villagers had told them ...*

***Nevertheless**, everyone had been willing ...*

***However**, one member of the group ...*

WRITING

Narrative

1 Look back at *Elephant Trek* and discuss these questions in groups.

▶ How does the story begin?
▶ What do we know about the kind of area where the tourists are?
▶ Why do you think the writer tells us more about the environment than about the people themselves?
▶ What are the phrases which help to create the atmosphere of the story?
▶ How does the writer convey a sense of panic?
▶ What do you think happened next?

2 Write another two or three paragraphs (about 150 words) to develop the story further.
Try to use some of the conjunctions which you have covered so far in this unit and the kind of language which will continue the atmosphere of the story.

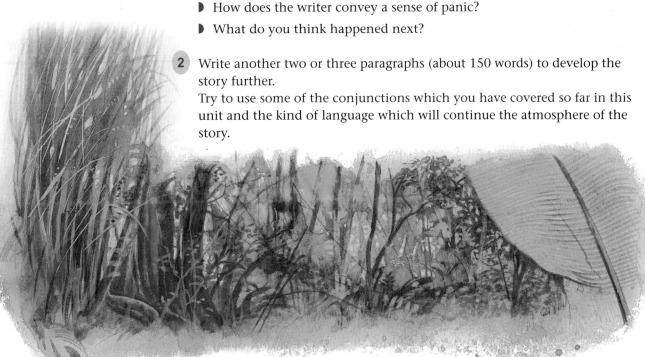

LISTENING

1 Talk about your ideal holiday in groups.
Then look at the questionnaire and decide if an active holiday would suit you.

Are YOU ready for a KATOOMBA adventure holiday?
WHICH OF THESE SPORTS WOULD YOU LIKE TO TRY AND WHY?

- rock climbing
- mountain biking
- trekking
- canoeing
- canyoning
- gliding

	Yes	No
Are you prepared to sleep rough?	☐	☐
Have you ever been camping?	☐	☐
Are you ambitious?	☐	☐

If you answered *yes* to the above questions, then Katoomba may be the place for you!
If you answered *no*, you may want to change your mind after listening to Hilary Easton!

2 You are going to hear part of a radio talk about a sport called abseiling which Hilary Easton did when she spent a day at Katoomba.
Before you listen, look at the notes below which are incomplete.
As you listen, complete the notes using a word or short phrase.

KATOOMBA — Blue Mountains

Mountaineering sports date from (1) ....

Distance from Sydney to Katoomba: (2) ....

Abseiling — much more than just (3) ....

A day at Katoomba begins with (4) ....

Everyone is taught about equipment, (5) ....

and fitting a harness

Height of practice slopes: (6) ....

Height of intermediate slopes: (7) ....

Face forward abseiling referred to as (8) ....

Hilary Easton especially enjoyed the (9) ....

Highest cliff Hilary abseiled down known as

(10) ....

160 **UNIT 9** *Globe-trotting*

1 If an adventure holiday still doesn't appeal to you, perhaps you'd prefer a trip to New York!

Look at the drawing of the Empire State Building in New York and the various things that people say about it.
What do their comments tell you about the words *so* and *such*?

> It's not surprising people want to visit it – it's such a unique building!

> It's such a high building that snow and rain can be seen falling up.

> When the building is lit up at night with such strong floodlights, it looks fantastic.

> The tower is so high that on a clear day you can see for 80 miles.

> I can understand why the Americans are so proud of the Empire State Building.

> There are so many windows they have to be cleaned on a non-stop basis.

> There are such a lot of landmarks to see from the top, as well as ships out at sea.

2 Now fill in the gaps in sentences 1–10.

1 It is .... hot in Singapore that most buildings are air-conditioned.

2 There was .... thick fog that we couldn't see anything from the top of the Empire State Building.

3 Elephants can charge .... fast that people have to be very careful if they go near them.

4 Typhoons can be .... strong that buildings in places like Hong Kong have to be specially constructed.

5 Explorers in the Antarctic must have been .... brave men!

6 The lottery winner gave away .... much money that in the end there was not enough left for a holiday.

7 Backpackers have the chance to meet .... a lot of different people.

8 There are .... few countries left which have not been developed for the tourist trade.

9 Some people don't take any notice of weather forecasts as they can be .... misleading.

10 Bali is .... a lush tropical island that holiday-makers are attracted all year round.

1 〔X〕 Could any of these pictures have been taken in your own country? Why/Why not?

Look at the world map which shows the five main kinds of climate: the tropics, the subtropics, the short winter zone, the long winter zone and the cold zone.

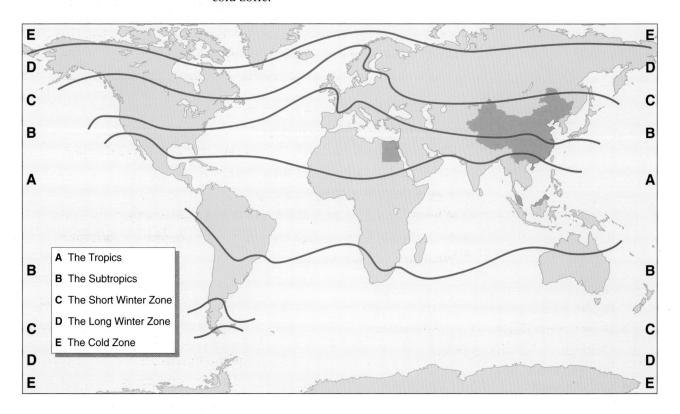

A The Tropics
B The Subtropics
C The Short Winter Zone
D The Long Winter Zone
E The Cold Zone

Discuss these questions.

Which category does your own country's climate fall into?
How would you describe the climate of the area you live in?
What do you like best and least about your climate?
Which other countries have similar climates to your own?

2 Read the text and fill in the missing names of the countries. (They are shaded on the world map to help you.)

Climate profiles

Everywhere on our planet has its own climate. No two places are identical in this respect, although there are plenty which are very similar. Broadly speaking, the five main types of climate are based on temperature and rainfall.

A .... falls into the subtropical category. It has long coastlines on the Mediterranean and the Red Sea, and a small part of the country, the Sinai desert, is in Asia. One of the hottest and sunniest countries in the world, most of the country is within the Sahara desert, with the exception of a coastal strip about fifty miles in breadth along the Mediterranean. The presence of the Nile makes the surrounding area very fertile and although the Nile has no tributaries, it fills up with heavy rain at its source in the tropical regions of East Africa.

B .... , the second largest country in the world, is affected by four main categories of climate – tropical, subtropical, short winter and long winter. In general, between May and September the country experiences monsoon rains but because it is such a vast country, there are considerable seasonal ranges of temperature.

C .... is an example of the tropical climate. There are high temperatures all year round, as well as regular rainfall which falls on as many as 200 days just about everywhere. Although the climate is hot and humid, the coastal areas of the country are freshened by sea breezes.

3 Now read the text again and answer the questions.
  1 Is it possible for places to have exactly the same climate?
  2 What two factors determine the description of a country's climate?
  3 Which part of country **A** is not in the desert?
  4 Why is the Nile unlikely to dry up?
  5 Why does country **B** fall into four different climatic areas?
  6 What helps reduce the high temperatures on country **C**'s coastline?
  7 What do **A** and **B** have in common?

VOCABULARY

4 Find words or phrases in the text which mean:
  1 apart from   4 starting point
  2 existence   5 enormous
  3 rich

5 What kind of weather do you think the poet was writing about in this poem? The missing title and the word in the first line are the same!

> ....
> The .... breathes
> Around the houses,
> Curling into corners
> Like a painter's brush
> With broad strokes
> Decorating the stones.
>
> **Lou D Miller**

1 People often choose a holiday destination for its weather. However, if you choose a skiing resort and when you arrive the snow has melted, it's not much use complaining to anyone. But glossy brochures can occasionally mislead people over buildings and facilities, so that on return from their holiday they may complain if they feel they have paid for something on the basis of the brochure description which, on experience, turned out to be very different.

A woman who recently went on a package holiday is complaining to the travel agent who arranged the holiday.

Listen to the first four lines of the dialogue and decide whether the woman's voice goes up or down at the end of her sentences.

> You did say the hotel overlooked the harbour, *didn't you?*
> But you haven't stayed there yourself, *have you?*

When the woman is unsure of the reply, her voice goes up on the question tag (*didn't you?*).
When she is certain of the reply, or expects agreement, her voice goes down on the question tag (*have you?*).

2 Now listen to the whole of their conversation which is printed below, and as you listen mark each question tag to show whether it rises (⌣ʼ) or falls (⌐ˎ).

Customer = **C**   Travel Agent = **TA**

C You did say the hotel overlooked the harbour, didn't you?

TA That's right.

C But you haven't stayed there yourself, have you?

TA No – but some of my colleagues have.

C And did they tell you it overlooked the harbour?

TA Well, not exactly. I don't think I asked them actually.

C And I believe you said the food was excellent, didn't you?

TA I can't remember what I said.

C Well, I think you said the food was excellent and that the chef had an international reputation, didn't you?

TA Well, I may have exaggerated slightly.

C Slightly? You won't be surprised if I tell you that you exaggerated a great deal, will you? In fact you exaggerated so much that I intend asking for a complete refund.

TA I'm afraid that's out of the question.

C But on your booking form it says that I am entitled to my money back unless I'm completely satisfied, doesn't it?

TA Well …

C And I *am* far from satisfied, aren't I? I haven't come all this way to your office to tell you that I had a wonderful holiday, have I?

TA Well …

C I would not be standing here complaining if everything had been perfect, would I?

TA Would you like to speak to the manager?

C You're the manager, aren't you?

TA I don't think I will be for much longer!

3 Now you will hear the same woman asking more questions, but this time the question tags are missing. After each question you must add the question tag and then practise the intonation pattern.

1 I spoke to you personally when I booked the holiday, ... ?

2 You did tell me this was one of your best package holidays, ... ?

3 Don't forget to speak to your colleagues about this hotel, ... ?

4 I'm not likely to book another holiday with your company, ... ?

5 You told me this hotel was very popular, ... ?

6 You do realise that if you don't refund my money, I shall take you to court, ... ?

7 This is the first time I have ever complained about your travel company, ... ?

8 You wouldn't want me to write to my local newspaper, ... ?

9 You don't expect me to believe that the chef has an international reputation, ... ?

10 You can't blame me if I book my next holiday with another company, ... ?

WRITING

Formal letter 4

1 🎧 One way of avoiding this woman's experience is to arrange a self-catering holiday where you can cook for yourself. This may sound like hard work but in a small group it becomes part of the fun of the holiday. In any case, if you happen to see a good restaurant, you have the freedom to stop and have a meal if you want.

Look at the advertisement below which you have seen in a magazine. Although you and your partner don't have your own bicycles, you would like to arrange a self-catering cycling holiday some time during the summer months when the weather is good.
Discuss the further information you would need before you could book. Some ideas to help you are already included.

Are helmets included?

RENT A BIKE

Luggage-how do we carry it?

Daily or weekly rental?

Rent one of our new bikes and have fun touring. We can arrange for you to collect and return your bike from your nearest rail station at no extra cost. We can advise you on your route and where to stay overnight. Inexpensive eating places also recommended. Book now to avoid disappointment!

How much?

2 When you have decided what else you need to know, write a letter to the holiday firm asking for further details. Write your letter in 120–180 words. Look back at page 46 if you need to remind yourself about how to set out a formal letter.

1 ☒ The phrases below occurred on page 161 when you were studying how to use *so* and *such*.

Look at the words in bold type which describe the quantity of something. Decide what kind of noun – singular or plural, countable or uncountable – each one should be used with.

1 There are so **many** windows they have to be cleaned on a non-stop basis.

2 There are such **a lot of** landmarks to see from the top …

3 It is so hot in Singapore that **most** buildings are air-conditioned.

4 The lottery winner gave away so **much** money that in the end …

5 There are so **few** countries left which have not been developed …

---

2 Read the text below and decide which answer A, B, C or D best fits each space.

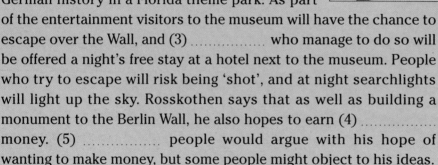

THE WALL MOVES OVER THE OCEAN

The Berlin Wall has been rebuilt, and before you raise your eyebrows, this new Berlin Wall has been built in the US. In fact, (1) …………… stone making up a 100m section of the real Berlin Wall was transported to Fort Lauderdale as part of a $30 million museum project. West Berliner Jürgen Rosskothen and his business team have recreated (2) …………… the aspects of recent German history in a Florida theme park. As part of the entertainment visitors to the museum will have the chance to escape over the Wall, and (3) …………… who manage to do so will be offered a night's free stay at a hotel next to the museum. People who try to escape will risk being 'shot', and at night searchlights will light up the sky. Rosskothen says that as well as building a monument to the Berlin Wall, he also hopes to earn (4) …………… money. (5) …………… people would argue with his hope of wanting to make money, but some people might object to his ideas.

1 A other   B either   C every   D several

2 A most   B all   C few   D many

3 A both   B any   C another   D each

4 A many   B much   C all   D some

5 A little   B another   C few   D all

UNIT MONITOR

Key vocabulary

Apart from the vocabulary practised within this unit, you also need to know the following words in connection with travel and the weather.

Use your dictionary to look up any words you don't know.

Then use the words to label the numbered parts of the pictures.

underground (station)	flood	motel
customs & immigration	snow	voyage
passport control	lane	cruise (ship)
baggage claim	charter flight	excursion
check-in desk	on board	ticket machine

camp-site	motorway	ferry
hard shoulder	storm	hail
thunder	coach	dock
motorway toll	lightning	port
heatwave	escalator	tube

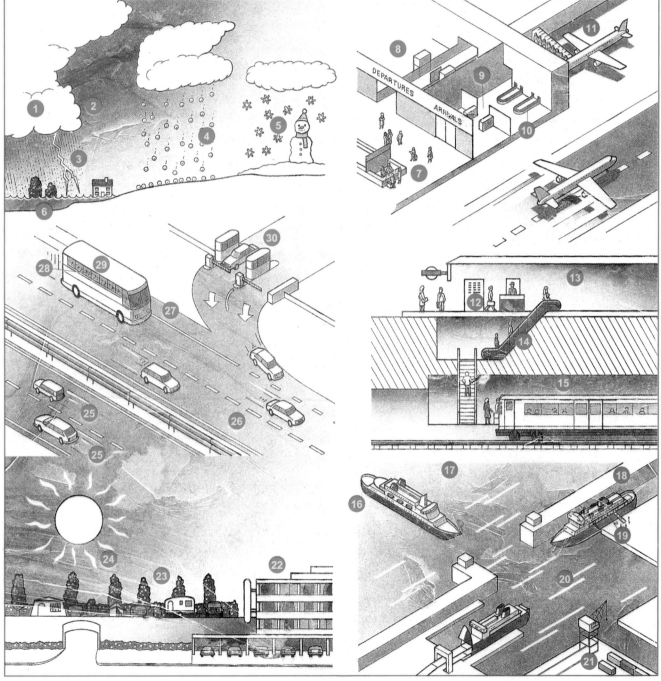

1 *thunder*   **17** *voyage*   **28** *excursion*

Complete sentences 1–10 using the appropriate words from the list on page 167.

1 In an emergency you can pull onto the .... of a motorway but you can't use it for any other purpose.

2 The rising tide threatened to .... the coastal road.

3 An unexpected .... brought crowds of people to the seaside as everyone tried to find ways of keeping cool.

4 The .... from Bombay to Liverpool took three weeks as the ship called in at a number of (5) .... on the way to load and unload cargo.

6 The best way to get around the city is to use the .... , as the tubes are not delayed by traffic jams!

7 Although the package holiday includes all meals and accommodation, you will have to pay extra for any .... organised by the hotel.

8 After passing through passport control, follow the signs to the .... area to collect your luggage.

9 A .... is usually cheaper than a scheduled one although they may not depart and arrive at such convenient times.

10 A .... often appeals to elderly people as it is very relaxing being able to eat, sleep and be entertained on board ship for the entire holiday.

Recycling: negative prefixes

Complete the sentences by adding the correct prefix to each adjective.

1 If you are .....satisfied with your hotel accommodation, you should complain to the manager.

2 This list of holiday resorts is .....complete – according to the brochure there should be more choice.

3 Some people feel .....capable of organising their own travel and accommodation arrangements and prefer to take a package holiday.

4 It is .....legal for tourists to take plants into Australia from abroad.

5 It is considered .....polite if you ignore the customs and traditions of a foreign country.

6 Some people are very .....willing to try strange or different food.

7 Very hot and humid temperatures can be .....pleasant.

8 People who seem .....friendly may simply be nervous about dealing with strangers.

9 If you are an .....sociable kind of person, you should not go on a group holiday.

10 It is .....correct to assume that everyone will speak your language.

Learning record

When you have finished Unit 9, try filling in this record of what you have learnt.

1 Join the two parts of the sentences below using an appropriate link word.

A I hope to spend a year travelling around India .... my parents are not very keen on the idea.

B The climbers carried on walking .... the fact that it was getting very foggy.

c I need a holiday .... I have worked very hard all year.

2 *so* or *such*?

A It's .... a lovely day; why don't we go for a walk?

B There are .... many countries in the world I can't imagine anyone has ever visited them all.

3 Finish the sentences with the correct question tag.

A You've never been camping, ... ?

B You will come on holiday with me, ... ?

4 Correct the sentences; each of them contains one mistake.

A Not much tourists visit the seaside in winter.

....
....

B Only a few rain fell this summer so water supplies are limited.

....
....

You should be able to complete this checklist without looking back now!

I have practised:
> speaking skills for .... , Part .....
> writing skills for .... , Parts ..... and .....
> listening skills for .... , Part .....
> reading skills for ....
> grammar skills for ....

EXAM ADVICE

17 Writing, Part 2

In Part 2 of the Writing paper you may have the choice of writing a story or a narrative. You may be given a title, or the question may take the form of a sentence which you have to use either as the beginning or the end of a story.

> This kind of writing needs careful planning in order to make sure your story has a beginning, a middle and an end and keeps within the required length of 120–180 words.

> Keep your storyline fairly simple.

> Try to include as much descriptive vocabulary as you can.

> Don't introduce too many characters.

> Make sure you know the rules for using direct speech as this kind of writing gives you the opportunity to use direct speech if you want.

> Make sure that you use the correct tense(s); it is likely that you will need to use the past tenses for story writing.

> In order to link the ideas in your story together, you will need to use link words and time expressions. (Grammar reference page 227)

> If you are going to end your story with the sentence which has been supplied in the question, be clear how you are going to include it **before** you start writing. Make sure you plan how to work the sentence convincingly into your story!

18 Listening, Part 3

Part 3 of the Listening paper consists of 5 short extracts, either monologues or short dialogues, and a multiple matching task. There are 5 questions and a list of 6 possible answers to choose from.

> You hear the complete recording of all 5 extracts twice.

> Use the preparation time to read through the list of answers so that you have an idea of what you will be specifically listening for in order to match the extract with the appropriate answer.

> The answers are lettered A–F, and one answer will not be needed.

> Don't use an answer more than once.

> As you listen for the first time, try to select the correct answer, and as you listen for a second time, check your understanding by focusing on the information in the listening text which corresponds with the information in the answer.

1 Reading

Below is a short story, but the paragraphs are in the wrong order. Read through the story and put the paragraphs in the correct order so that the story makes sense. Then underline the words and phrases that helped you to do this.

Disappearance

A   Then, hurrying back to the house to consult with his mother, he heard a faint voice: 'Help! Help me!' It was Jim's voice beyond all question. It seemed to come from the air.

B   It was an event of the first, even of shattering importance, to the whole country. With the warming up of the spring days, though still audible, the cry seemed fainter and fainter, more and more distant, till finally in the great heats of the Texan summer it died away completely and was never heard of again.

C   With his mother and a younger brother he ran a farm in a rather isolated part of the state. One evening in winter, after a snowfall that had lasted all day, the wind shifted, the clouds vanished, and a full moon blazed down on the carpet of fresh snow. In that clear, dry air it was almost bright enough to read; and the mercury in the thermometer shot down to below zero.

D   Total disappearances – where a human being just vanishes from the face of the earth without explanation – have always interested me. And here is perhaps the strangest that ever came my way. For it seems to involve a different kind of space to the ordinary space we are familiar with. It was told to me by a farmer from Texas, a fellow I met in 1891 or 2 when I had a dairy farm in Ontario.

E   However, no answer came. It frightened him, for no conceivable reason came to him. For the first time in his life, he told me, he was aware of goose-flesh.

F   His mother, when she rushed out, heard it too. But though they both stood there shouting and shouting, and Jim's voice, now fainter, now louder, now close, now far away, answered, they could never decide exactly the direction it came from. Indeed it seemed to come from all directions, though always from the empty air about them, and never from below.

G   Furthermore, the neighbours heard it too next day when the older brother had ridden out to fetch them. All came from several miles away, so isolated was the farm. No explanation was forthcoming. Jim never came back. He was never seen again. As winter passed, the voice grew fainter, but hardly a day went by without the cry for help being heard.

H   But the lad did not come back, and his brother, who told me the story, went out himself to see what was the matter. No question of danger arose. None was possible. There on the otherwise untrodden snow were Jim's footmarks, clear as daylight, the only tracks visible. And there, about halfway to the well, lay the two buckets on the ground. Following the tracks, he reached the buckets. The tracks stopped dead beside them. No track of any kind was visible along the farther 20 metres to the well. It was mysterious to say the least. No sign of flurry or disturbance. He shouted his brother's name.

I   It was while preparing supper that the mother, needing water, asked Jim, the younger of the two brothers, to fetch some from the well. This was a daily commonplace job. The well, their only house supply, never ran dry. And Jim, putting on his fur mitts and cap, went out with a couple of buckets as usual. The distance to the well was about 100 metres.

The correct order is: ....

Now answer the following questions based on the story. Choose the answer (A, B, C or D) which you think fits best according to the text.

1 The writer was interested in Jim's disappearance because it

    A was so strange and mysterious.

    B took place on a winter's evening.

    C was told to him by his older brother.

    D had a feeling unlike anything else.

2 On the evening of Jim's disappearance, the weather was

    A cloudy.

    B freezing.

    C windy.

    D snowing.

3 Jim's footprints in the snow

    A were not really clear.

    B reached as far as the well.

    C went beyond the buckets.

    D were the only marks.

4 Jim's voice could be heard from

    A a variety of places.

    B under the ground.

    C one main direction.

    D the air beneath them.

5 What does the writer think happened to Jim?

    A He died during the spring.

    B The summer heat killed him.

    C He simply doesn't know.

    D He probably ran away.

6 In two or three sentences write what you think happened to Jim in *Disappearance*.

2 WRITING PART 2

You have been asked to write for a magazine about this statement: *Young people don't know how to spend their money sensibly; most of them waste it on sweets and magazines.*

Write an **article** on this topic in **120–180** words in an appropriate style.

3 USE OF ENGLISH   PART 1

For questions **1–15**, read the text below and decide which word **A, B, C** or **D** best fits each space.

___

SWEET TEMPTATION

Every day British Airways offers to its passengers worldwide an amazing total of some 49,350 chocolates. (**1**) .... average, 95% instantly disappear off the trays. Hardly (**2**) .... , it seems, can (**3**) .... the temptation of a delicious-looking chocolate. Actually there are no (**4**) .... figures on how many are eaten immediately they are seen, or how many get (**5**) .... into a pocket or a handbag to be enjoyed (**6**) .... .

A great (**7**) .... of serious effort has to go into (**8**) .... sure that tens of thousands of chocolates a day get airborne in perfect (**9**) ..... . In a year, some 26 million passengers fly (**10**) .... the airline and almost as many chocolates are consumed.

Fine chocolates require careful handling. They are well known to be very choosy about the (**11**) .... of their surroundings, dislike being shaken about and the more (**12**) .... flavours like rose creams, for example, cannot be placed too close to (**13**) .... flavours.

Chocolates need to look smart, and wrappings and boxes have to be stylish and travel well. Research has (**14**) .... that many people actually like to take home the little boxes which have two or three chocolates (**15**) .... for their children.

1	**A**	On	**B**	In	**C**	By	**D**	At
2	**A**	nobody	**B**	someone	**C**	anyone	**D**	everyone
3	**A**	respect	**B**	resist	**C**	remove	**D**	relieve
4	**A**	careful	**B**	ready	**C**	exact	**D**	right
5	**A**	slipped	**B**	pulled	**C**	slapped	**D**	preserved
6	**A**	further	**B**	again	**C**	later	**D**	more
7	**A**	amount	**B**	deal	**C**	share	**D**	quantity
8	**A**	having	**B**	proving	**C**	deciding	**D**	making
9	**A**	position	**B**	state	**C**	condition	**D**	arrangement
10	**A**	with	**A**	by	**C**	in	**D**	to
11	**A**	cold	**B**	temperature	**C**	degree	**D**	environment
12	**A**	delicate	**B**	fine	**C**	fragile	**D**	colourful
13	**A**	tougher	**B**	stronger	**C**	bigger	**D**	darker
14	**A**	said	**B**	made	**C**	done	**D**	shown
15	**A**	beside	**B**	into	**C**	inside	**D**	over

4 Grammar: phrasal verbs

▶ Grammar reference p.216   Appendix 2 p.233

Complete the following sentences with the correct form of one of the phrasal verbs in the box.

get away with	go in for	turn back	feel up to	show off
drop in	rub out	keep up with	count on	break off

1 It's too late to .... now as we're almost there and they'll have dinner ready for us.

2 If you've made a mistake, ... it .... and start again.

3 Jo didn't .... the climb so he stayed at the camp-site and prepared the evening meal.

4 I don't think Ruth is really interested in the places she visits; she just likes .... to everyone about where she's been.

5 I think I'll .... that competition – the prize is a two-week cruise around the Caribbean!

6 I do hope you can come to the party as I'm .... you to entertain the younger children.

7 Can you slow down a little – you've got such long legs I can't .... you.

8 He was complaining about the company and had to .... as his boss walked into the office.

9 If you're free this evening, why don't you .... for a coffee?

10 Whilst the jeweller's back was turned, the thief managed to .... one of the watches she had pretended to admire.

5 Grammar: link words

▶ Grammar reference p.227

Join the two sentences together using the word(s) in brackets and making all the necessary changes. In all cases there is more than one possibility.

1 The weather was not particularly good. Alice enjoyed the excursion to the castle. (**despite**)

....

2 Pavel took a taxi to the airport. He wanted to make sure he caught his flight. (**in order to**)

....

3 The price of package holidays has risen. There has been an increase in airport taxes. (**owing to**)

....

4 The hotel had its own swimming pool. It also had a small gym. (**as well as**)

....

5 The rail company will offer passengers a refund. There were unexpected delays. (**as a result of**)

....

6 Travel brochures drop through my letterbox. I feel it is time for a holiday. (**whenever**)

....

7 I like fairly active holdays. My husband prefers lying on a beach all day. (**whereas**)

....

8 Yuko hung a notice outside her bedroom door. She did not want to be disturbed. (**as**)

....

9 The car was a bargain. We decided to buy it. (**such ... that**)

....

10 Axel had been to the same hotel for the past 20 years. He still went there every year. (**even though**)

....

THE GOOD LIFE?

SPEAKING

The way we live

1 Look at the photograph and discuss the following questions.

Where do you think it was taken?
Could it be in your country? Why or why not?
Do you think the little girl climbed into the crate by herself?
Could she be a refugee? Why or why not? Is it possible to be a refugee in one's own country?
If you saw a child who looked warm and comfortably asleep in circumstances like this, how would you react? Would you do anything?
If you saw a child whom you knew sleeping in the street, would you do anything?

Living conditions, which vary from country to country, affect our health and happiness. Does it matter where you grow up?
Are children whose parents have a lot of money likely to be happier than children whose parents are not well off?
What do you think is essential for a child to enjoy a comfortable upbringing?

2 The list below includes things that some people consider essential in order to give a child a happy and comfortable upbringing.
Choose the eight which you consider the most important, with reasons for your choice.
You can add to the list if you think there is something missing.

> toys   sweets   computer   bicycle   own bedroom   attention
> own television   music lessons   brother and/or sister   pet
> plenty of pocket money   private education   holidays abroad
> family outings   affection   eating out

READING

The way we behave

1 In your experience, are children who have a comfortable lifestyle more likely to be well-adjusted adults?
Is it possible to spoil children with too much affection or only with material things?

Read the newspaper article about scientific investigations into violent behaviour and then answer questions 1–4 by choosing the best answer A, B, C or D.

Hamsters help scientific studies

HAMSTERS, WHICH ARE normally kept as pets by millions of children, are helping scientists to understand whether violent teenagers are created by a violent childhood.

Hamsters have in their brains the same chemical signals that regulate behaviour in human beings. Studies which are being carried out by scientists show that when the brain chemistry in young hamsters is affected by fear, the hamsters become extraordinarily anti-social and violent to their fellow animals. The studies focus on the chemicals in the brain which regulate and help to control aggression.

These findings add weight to the belief of many who think that aggression in adults can be blamed on youngsters being neglected or badly treated, as opposed to those who think that some people are born violent.

Social scientists think they can help young people who become aggressive when they face unemployment, drugs or violence, but the earlier they can intervene during childhood the better. This suggests that genetic behaviour can be changed or modified by upbringing. Another obvious example, heart disease, which is known to be genetic, is also made worse by poor diet and environment.

The relationship between genes and environment, particularly diet, in affecting people whose behaviour reveals criminal tendencies is also being studied. This research is building on a study that shows some connection between glucose or sugar consumption and violent behaviour.

Some studies which have been carried out in a US prison show that when the prisoners' diet was improved, the incidence of violence and anti-social behaviour fell by about 40%. It seems that good nutrition can make a difference to behaviour: other studies show that diets with limited amounts of sugary and refined foods also reduce suicide rates.

Some people are now worried that a murderer whom a judge has sentenced to life imprisonment may be able to walk free if it can be proved that a bad diet was to blame.

1 In what way are hamsters and human beings identical?
  A They both attack others when frightened.
  B Chemical messages operate in the same way.
  C They are both violent when they are younger.
  D Chemicals govern the same brain structure.

2 The scientific investigations into the behaviour of hamsters support the theory that violent
  A adults are violent from birth.
  B behaviour is due to lack of money.
  C behaviour is due to poor upbringing.
  D children are unemployable.

3 Some scientific studies suggest that
  A prisoners eat too much sugary food.
  B improved diets can reduce aggression.
  C suicidal people eat too much glucose.
  D violent people often commit suicide.

4 What might a criminal be able to plead in future?
  A 'I ate the wrong food.'
  B 'My parents were unkind.'
  C 'I can't help myself.'
  D 'My diet lacked sugar.'

VOCABULARY

2 Now find words or phrases in the article which mean:

Paragraph 2
 1 influenced
 2 concentrate on

Paragraph 3
 3 support
 4 not properly looked after
 5 contrary to

Paragraph 4
 6 become involved
 7 inherited

Paragraph 5
 8 likely to turn to crime

Paragraph 6
 9 rate
 10 processed so that the nutritional value is removed

1 ⚏ Look at these examples of relative clauses. Match the statements A–E with the ways the relative pronouns in 1–5 have been used.

1 If you saw a child *who looked warm and comfortably asleep* …

2 If you saw a child *whom you knew* sleeping in the street …

3 Are children *whose parents have a lot of money* …

4 The list below includes things *that some people consider* …

5 Living conditions, *which vary from country to country*, affect our health …

A the possessive pronoun refers to people

B the pronoun refers to things and is the object

C the pronoun refers to a person and is the subject

D the pronoun refers to things and is the subject

E the pronoun refers to a person and is the object

In which of the examples can you omit the relative pronoun, especially in spoken English, without it making any difference to the meaning of the sentence?
Are these examples of identifying or non-identifying relative clauses?

2 Now read the newspaper article on hamsters again, this time underlining the relative pronouns; there are twelve altogether. Then decide which relative clauses are identifying and which are non-identifying.

Remember that in identifying clauses the information is essential to the meaning, and in non-identifying clauses the information can be removed without affecting the meaning of the sentence.

3 Identifying relative clauses

In the following exercise, numbers 1–5, rewrite the two sentences as one by joining them with a relative pronoun, and make any other necessary changes.

Example
The thief was caught by the police. He had already broken into six other homes.
The thief who was caught by the police had already broken into six other homes.

1 The boys stole the car. They used it for joyriding.

2 The prisons are overcrowded. They are going to be demolished.

3 Some lawyers earn very high salaries. They are famous.

4 That is the girl. Her friend has been accused of shoplifting.

5 The person committed the crime. He was mentally unstable.

Non-identifying relative clauses

Now do the same with numbers 6–10. As well as making any necessary changes, remember to add the comma(s) which separate the relative clause from the main clause.

Example
The teenager was 17 years old. He was charged with attacking the old-age pensioner.
The teenager, who was charged with attacking the old-age pensioner, was 17 years old.
OR
The teenager, who was 17 years old, was charged with attacking the old-age pensioner.

6 The bank theft was carried out by a team of professional thieves. It had been carefully planned.

7 The members of the jury were getting bored. They had been sitting in court for eight hours.

8 International terrorism is seen as a growing threat to world peace. It concerns many governments.

9 The actress was sent to prison for a number of years. She was arrested for carrying drugs.

10 The witness's evidence was very important. He was proved to be lying.
(Begin with *The witness …*)

1 ⧖ In Unit 7 you discussed how old you had to be before you could do certain things.

Do you remember how old you have to be in your own country before you can …

get married?　vote in an election?　get a job?
have a driving licence?　join the army?　leave school?

Do you agree with these age limits?
Do you think you should be older or younger in any of these cases?

2 You are going to hear part of a radio programme called *Rites of Passage*, which describes the ways in which different cultures celebrate a child's entry into adulthood.
After you have listened for the first time, answer the following question:

What do young men from the Masai tribe, the Antipodes and nineteenth century Europe have in common?

3 Before you listen again, read the notes below which are incomplete.
Listen and complete the notes by writing a word, a number or a short phrase – no more than four words – in each box.

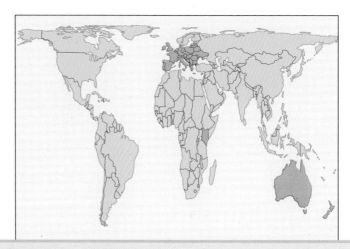

Rites of Passage

In the UK young people used to learn a trade at the age of (1) ....

Today in the UK you can become a soldier at the age of (2) ....

In some cultures children become adults as early as (3) ....

For how long are boys from the Masai tribe taken away? (4) ....

Who advises African girls before they are considered adults? (5) ....

In the Wonghibon tribe a boy became a man by (6) ....

At the end of the Wonghibon ceremony the boy lost (7) ....

What could happen to people who disobey tribal rules over watching the ceremony? (8) ....

What does the speaker call the journey around European cities? (9) ....

What drives youngsters from Australia and New Zealand to visit Europe? (10) ....

1 In some countries it is considered illogical that you can fight for your country by entering military service before you are allowed to drive a car or get married.

Some people used to think of compulsory military service as a rite of passage, something that distinguished a child from an adult.

Today many countries which have retained compulsory military service offer alternative schemes in which young people can participate, like social service programmes.

In the articles below two young Frenchmen describe their experiences within the French system. Quickly read through each article to discover whether they share similar or dissimilar views.

Olivier Unlike many of my friends, I actually looked forward to doing my ten months' military service. Adventure was guaranteed, and after two years at a business school in Paris it was just what I needed. I was based in south-east  France, near Geneva, with a regiment called the 'Chasseurs Alpins'. Deep in the Alps, these soldiers are among the most active in the French army and famed for their mountain exploits.

Before going, I barely knew how to ski and knew absolutely nothing about survival in the mountains. By the end of the year, however, I could ski, mountain climb and hike for days on end, even with a heavy backpack and a gun, and thought nothing of sleeping in bivouacs* at over 3,000 metres. The training was tough but rewarding, and one of the best aspects is that I learnt all these new skills for free. I was made a lance-corporal*, which meant I was given a platoon* to command and was responsible for its success.

In a way, it would be a shame if military service were scrapped. My ten months taught me so much, and both physically and mentally I've become more robust*. I consider myself a good citizen of France, and am grateful for the opportunities my military service provided. Its disappearance would mean that students in a few years' time would not have my opportunties.

*
bivouacs – temporary open camp
lance-corporal – lowest rank officer
platoon – small army unit
robust – strong

David I did not want to go into the army, so I became a *coopérant du service national*, which should have meant spending sixteen months as an aid worker. Fortunately my degree in material physics meant I was able to become a maths  teacher in a school in the Côte d'Ivoire, an old French colony. The idea of such a different culture frightened me, especially as I had not been outside Europe before, and it took me a whole year to feel at home in Bondoukou, a small town near the border with Ghana. People were wary of a white Frenchman, as well they might be given France's history, but in the end I made some good friends among the locals. In my second year, I was even in charge of the school volleyball team and taught private maths lessons as well.

There is no doubt that I had a very hard time towards the beginning of my stay there. Arriving in a completely strange country and being given a class of 60 children between 11 and 18 to teach is always going to be difficult. However, the whole experience has transformed me and made me much stronger mentally. I would never have believed how much I could enjoy my time there, especially after university.

Military service would probably not be missed by most young people, and I think the present system does not suit a modern France. However, instead of being scrapped, military service should be shortened to a few months and switched to a more peaceful and useful role like the one I hope I performed.

2 Group A: Read through the text about Olivier and pick out the positive reasons that Olivier puts forward in favour of doing military service.
Group B: Read through the text about David and pick out the positive reasons that David puts forward in favour of doing military service.

Now compare your reasons and see how many reasons the two men have in common. In what ways do their reactions differ?

If you had to do a similar period of service in your own country, whose experience would you prefer and why?

What do you think today's British students mean by the 'gap year'?
What do you think teenagers are talking about when they ask each other, 'Are you doing a gap year?'

WRITING
Article

Imagine you have been asked to write a short article on rites of passage for some UK teenagers who are interested in your country and its culture.

Discuss in your group the rites of passage in your own country and culture. You should be able to draw on your own experience and that of your family and friends. Try to think of as many celebrations as possible, from religious occasions like baptism or *bar/bat mitzvah*, to birthdays, name days, examination successes like graduation from high school or university, to engagement parties, and so on.

Jot down the ways in which a celebration is organised, who is invited, how important it is to you and other people.

Using some of the ideas which you have discussed, write 120–180 words on the ways in which your own culture celebrates one significant, personal occasion. (Try to include some relative clauses.)

1 Does it matter where you live? Why or why not?
Have you always lived in the same house or apartment?
What do you like best/least about the building where you live? Why?
Which room in your house or apartment is the most important to you?
Would the other people who live in the building agree with you?

2 Read the six texts below. Do you agree or disagree with the comments?
Find out what the other people in your class think. How far do their
comments match what these people had to say?
Does any one particular extract attract more or less agreement or
disagreement?

1 I care about kitchens. Not kitchens with all the latest electrical equipment, but kitchens to live in. I long ago realised that a good kitchen makes more difference to the life of a household than any other room in the house.

3 For human beings shelter is based on the family – and for a very good reason. Human children take a very long time to grow up, and while they're developing they must be looked after.

5 It's an enviable life, in some ways, having no ties, cooking in the open air, moving about the country as fancy takes you. I think gypsies are better off than most of us.

2 Even while they're still living in the parents' home, teenagers are already planning the homes they'll make themselves.

4 Worse than even the worst house is no house at all, for a house represents our status in the community.

6 It's better to rent than buy property, because when you rent you can move on whenever you want without the problem of trying to sell the place.

1 Look at the pictures of the various buildings where people live.
Which of these buildings do you like best? Why?
Which one would you definitely not want to live in? Why not?

2 You are going to hear four different people talking about the buildings they live in.
As you listen for the first time, match the place they describe with the correct building A–H.

Speaker 1 .... Speaker 3 ....
Speaker 2 .... Speaker 4 ....

3 As you listen for the second time, note down some of the **key words** which helped you decide.

VOCABULARY

4 These are some of the words which you heard the speakers use; pick them out on the photographs.

Speaker 1: *block   landscaped gardens   top floor*
Speaker 2: *town centre   apartment   above the shop*
Speaker 3: *semi-detached   ground floor   balcony
           french windows   roof garden*
Speaker 4: *wooden   bungalow   chalet   lake*

5 Look at the photographs which were not mentioned and decide which words from the list below belong to each photograph.

detached ......   lamppost ......
waste ground ......   brick ......
stone ......   partly demolished ......
cobbled street ......   towers ......
shutters ......   blind ......
tarmac ......   window boxes ......

WRITING

Description

1 You saw an advertisement for an organisation called 'Holiday Swap', which enables people to exchange homes with each other for holiday purposes. You wrote off for some further information and here are some examples of what 'Holiday Swap' sent you. Look at them and answer the questions below. How would you describe the tone of these two descriptions?

If you're looking for a fabulous place for a holiday, then I can recommend my villa, which is situated on a hilltop miles from anywhere, surrounded by olive groves and pine trees. There's a great view across the bay from all the rooms in the house.

It's a typical white-washed house made of stone, with marble floors and a flat roof which is great for sunbathing. On the ground floor is a large, well-equipped kitchen with an oven, a gas hob and a fridge. There is a patio outside the kitchen where you can eat your meals. Also on the same floor there is a shower room, a laundry and a dining room if you should ever want to take your meals inside.

On the first floor there is a lounge with big french windows leading onto a terrace. There are three double bedrooms and a bathroom and all the windows have shutters which keep the house cool.

Our apartment is in one of the best locations in the city, close to the old town square and the main shopping streets. There is an underground car park and each apartment has two parking spaces. The apartment is on the sixth floor of a modern block but as all the windows are double-glazed, there is no problem with traffic noise.

The apartment consists of a large kitchen with all modern appliances like microwave, dishwasher, freezer, breakfast bar and espresso coffee machine. The comfortable lounge (with TV and music system) has french windows leading onto a small balcony which overlooks the street.

There are two single bedrooms, each with an en-suite shower room. In the basement of the block there are communal laundry facilities and a sauna room for the use of all the residents.

If you want a holiday with all the advantages of city life – boutiques, department stores, cinemas, theatres, concert halls, restaurants, musems, discos and lots more – then swap your home for our apartment!

Which of these two places would you swap your home for? Why?
What are the kinds of things people need to know if they are going to stay in your home?

2 Using some of the vocabulary which you have learnt so far in this unit, write the description of your home which the organisation will send to people who might be interested in swapping homes with you. Make your description as attractive as possible. You can use the letters on page 183 to help you. Write 120–180 words.

GRAMMAR ▶ p.230 Phrasal nouns and compound nouns

1 Look at what people said when they were talking about where they live.

*There have been quite a few **break-ins** ...*

*... – one room, kitchen and **bathroom** – but it suits me fine ...*

*... as I work in the **take-away** ...*

*... we live opposite a **car park** ...*

In Unit 2 you learnt about phrasal verbs, which combine a verb and preposition(s).

Phrasal nouns are formed in the same way, although not all phrasal verbs can be turned into phrasal nouns.

Which of the nouns in bold type above are phrasal nouns?

Sometimes it is quite easy to guess the meaning of a phrasal noun from the context.

Example

Chinese take-away – you take the food away

break-in – a person enters a place using force (a burglary)

2 Match the phrasal nouns 1–10 with their meanings.

1	turnover	a nervous collapse
2	let-down	a road leading from another road
3	breakup	a physical exercise session
4	workout	a wrecked vehicle
5	breakdown (1)	a disappointment
6	take-off	mechanical failure
7	write-off	an escape – usually fast
8	turn-off	the amount of trade made by a business
9	getaway	the end of a relationship
10	breakdown (2)	leaving the ground

3 It is also very common to form nouns by putting two words together, and these nouns (e.g. *bathroom, ground floor*) are called **compound nouns**.

Look back at the lists of words on page 183 which you matched with the photographs. Can you find any more examples of compound nouns?

Match the words in the left-hand column with a word in the right-hand column to make a compound noun and decide which words could be written as one word. Some words can be matched more than once.

night	collector
door	side
half	dress
land	day
sea	shade
birth	lady
air	master
lamp	line
head	step
ticket	time

1 Look back at Unit 7 and the Grammar reference on page 225 if you need to remind yourself how to form comparative adjectives.

In the first few lines of this article, pick out two examples of comparative adjectives.

Now read the rest of the article and pick out two examples of comparisons which are made using a different grammatical structure.

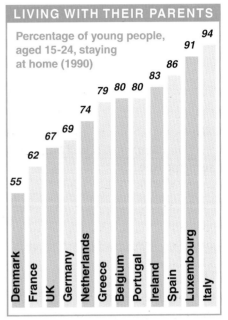

LIVING WITH THEIR PARENTS

Percentage of young people, aged 15-24, staying at home (1990)

Denmark 55, France 62, UK 67, Germany 69, Netherlands 74, Greece 79, Belgium 80, Portugal 80, Ireland 83, Spain 86, Luxembourg 91, Italy 94

Leaving home, that rite of passage into adult life, is becoming harder and harder for young people across Europe.

In Mediterranean countries, where family traditions are stronger, young people tend not to leave home until they marry. Figures published in 1990 show that the more difficult economic conditions become, the less chance there is of young people leaving home.

Not all young people, however, have the option of staying at home. A significant proportion find themselves forced to be independent. In northern Europe, where families are not used to supporting their children late into life, it can cause domestic tensions if grown-up children have to live at home. The more money parents earn, the longer they are usually willing to support their children. But if parents are unemployed, then they are unlikely to be able to financially support their children.

These sentences both make comparisons using one structure followed by a similar structure:

*... **the more** difficult economic conditions become, **the less** chance there is of young people leaving home.*

***The more** money parents earn, **the longer** they are usually willing to support their children.*

2 Now complete the sentences below using suitable comparative structures.

1 The .... parents treat their children, the .... likely it is that those children may develop into anti-social adults.

2 The sooner a young person gets a job, the .... they can become financially independent.

3 The more money you earn, the .... you become.

4 The more violent the crime, the .... the prison sentence.

5 The less some parents see of their children the .... , as they always quarrel.

6 The more parents and their children argue, ... children will want to move away from home.

7 The greater the rise in unemployment, the .... society can expect young people to be discontented.

8 The .... the police arrest the vandals, the better.

9 The more numerous the reports of crime in the newspapers, the .... people become about their own safety.

10 The more crime on the street increases, the .... likely it is that people will go out alone at night.

3 Look at the graph on page 185. According to the figures:

> Young Danish people are **not as/so keen** on living with their parents as young Italians (are).

It is possible to express a comparison more exactly:

> ... nearly **twice as many** young Italians live with their parents compared with young people in Denmark.

Sometimes the meaning may be modified by another word in front of the first **as/so**:

> Girls are not **nearly** so violent as boys.
> The crime rate in some rural areas in the UK is **almost** as high as that in some cities.
> The figures for stolen cars are **just** as high this year as they were last year.

4 Look at the pictures and write down the comparisons which each picture describes. Use as many different ways of comparing as possible based on the examples above.

For picture 4 you could say, for example:

> *That skyscraper is three times as high as that apartment block.*
> *That apartment block is not nearly as high as that skyscraper.*

Key vocabulary

Apart from the vocabulary practised within this unit, you also need to know the following words in connection with crime and the law.

Use your dictionary to look up any words you don't know and to help you with the incomplete words.

Crime

assass _ _ _ _ _ _ _
blackm _ _ _
for _ _ _ _ _
fra _ _ _
hooli _ _ _ _
kidna _ _ _ _ _ _
shoplif _ _ _ _ _
smugg _ _ _ _ _
vanda l _ _ _ _

Law and order

barris _ _ _ _
capit _ _ punishment
corpo _ _ _ _ punishment
death pen _ _ _ _ _
defend _ _ _ _
gao _ (British English)
ja _ _ _ (American English)
guil _ _
just _ _ _ _
offe _ _ _ _
prosec _ _ _ _ _ _
solic _ _ _ _ _
tri _ _
verd _ _ _ _

Vocabulary in context

Complete sentences 1–10 using the appropriate words from the list above.

1 Some countries impose very stiff penalties for drug ....

2 .... was abolished in UK schools many years ago, and no teacher is allowed to use any form of physical punishment.

3 Some banknote .... are so good that they are very difficult to detect.

4 At the end of his .... the accused was found not ....

5 .... people and demanding money for their release is a serious ....

6 The .... of JF Kennedy took place in Dallas in 1963.

7 It took the jury over four days to reach their .... of not guilty.

8 It is not unusual for store detectives to find that people who are arrested for .... have plenty of money on them.

9 People who feel that they have been wrongly imprisoned will continue to fight for .... by appealing against their sentence.

10 The death penalty – or .... – has been abolished in many countries.

Recycling: link words

Read the article and fill in the gaps using a suitable link word or phrase from the box. Use each link once only.

if despite in order to while however
because although and when unless

I went to university abroad after leaving school, but looking back I now wish that I had taken a year off.
(1) .... my parents supported me throughout my four-year course, there were times (2) .... I felt very short of money.
(3) .... I had worked for a year before starting my course, I would have been able to live at home (4) .... save some money at the same time.
There were certain people at university who took a job in the evenings (5) .... earn some money. (6) .... being financially better off, (7) .... , their academic work tended to suffer (8) .... they were so tired a lot of the time. (9) .... your parents are really well off, I think you have to accept that (10) .... you are a student, life has to be lived very economically.

Learning record

When you have finished Unit 10, try filling in this record of what you have learnt.

1 Add any necessary punctuation to the following sentences.

   A The hooligans whom the police caught last night were all under twelve years old.

   B Mali where Yann used to work is one of the poorest countries in the world.

   C I know the policeman who was awarded a medal for bravery.

2 Complete the following sentences with a suitable phrasal noun.

   A The .... on the motorway caused a huge traffic jam.

   B From the estate agent's description I had expected the house to be very attractive, so it was a real .... when I saw how old and shabby it was.

   C The .... was so bumpy that quite a few passengers felt sick.

3 Fill in the following gaps with a suitable comparative structure.

   A The .... Sam works, the .... his chances of passing the exam.

   B There are not .... women judges .... men.

   C The .... serious the offence, the more likely you are not to go to prison.

   D There is almost .... credit card fraud .... cheque book forgery.

FCE Checklist

You should be able to complete this checklist without looking back now!

I have practised:

 ❯ speaking skills for Paper ...., Parts ......
 ❯ reading skills for Paper ...., Part ......
 ❯ use of English skills for Paper ......
 ❯ listening skills for Paper ...., Part ......
 ❯ writing skills for Paper ...., Part ......

EXAM ADVICE

19 Listening, Part 4

The last part of the Listening paper, Part 4, consists of either a monologue or a conversation involving 2 or 3 speakers and lasts about 3 minutes. It will always have 7 questions, but the question type will vary: it may be three-option multiple choice, True/False or Yes/No questions, or questions requiring you to identify which speaker said what by writing the speaker's initial in a box. The questions will always be objective, and you will not have to write any words or short answers.

 ❯ Each part of the Listening paper focuses on a different kind of listening skill.

 ❯ In this part you can expect the questions to focus on your ability to understand both the gist and the main ideas contained in the whole piece, as well as the attitudes, feelings and opinions expressed by the speaker(s).

 ❯ There will be fewer questions in this part which test your understanding of detail and specific information.

 ❯ The questions will follow the order in which you hear the information.

20 Speaking

Paper 5, the Speaking paper, is taken by pairs of candidates and lasts about 15 minutes. It is divided into 4 parts and 2 examiners are present; one examiner acts as the interlocutor and the other examiner, who does not take part in the conversation, carries out the assessment.

 ❯ Whether or not you know your partner in the interview makes no difference to your assessment.

 ❯ In Part 1 of the test you will be asked to talk about yourself, your interests and your personal and family background.

 ❯ In Part 2 you and your partner will each be given 2 photographs in turn. Look carefully at your photos and listen to what the examiner asks you to talk about in relation to the photographs. If you are not sure what you have been asked to do, then ask for the instruction to be repeated. You do not lose marks by asking for something to be repeated, but if you sit in silence for too long the assessor will not be able to judge whether you actually have the language skills to talk about the photographs. Don't expect to just describe what you can see in the photos; you will also be asked to express opinions about the situations, and the similarities and/or contrasts between the photographs.

- In Part 3 the interlocutor will give you some new material to look at. It may be another photograph, a drawing, an advertisement, a leaflet, etc. You and your partner are expected to work together on whatever task you are given; the interlocutor will listen but not join in. You need to show that you can take turns in discussing things with your partner, that you can agree or disagree if necessary, that you can express opinions and exchange information together. You might be asked to plan something, to solve a particular problem or to prioritise, that is to place things – like holiday destinations, for example – in order of importance from your own point of view.

- Don't try to include the interlocutor in what you are saying.

- Be supportive towards your partner.

- Try to use appropriate language which shows that you understand that you are working together, for example:

What do you think?
I'm not sure I agree with you.
Shall we take this point/picture first?
So what's our conclusion?
Yes, that's what I think too.
So what shall we decide?

- Don't dominate the conversation.

- Don't feel too shy to say what you really think.

- You have about 3 minutes for this part so don't rush into making conclusions too early in the conversation.

- In Part 4 of the Speaking test the interlocutor will join in the discusssion and extend and develop the theme or the topic which you have been talking about in the third part. The skills which you have to use in dealing with Part 4 are very similar to those you used in Part 3, but this time it is a three-way discusssion. Listen to what the others have to say and try to reply appropriately and naturally. You may be asked to expand on something which you previously mentioned or to consider another viewpoint.

- At the end of the test the examiners will say thank you and say goodbye. Don't expect or ask for any comment on how you have performed.

1 READING PART 2

You are going to read an article about living underground. For questions **1–7**, choose the answer (**A, B, C** or **D**) which you think fits best according to the text.

For five years, Simon Ormerod and his wife Maureen have lived a secret life up a forest track in a remote corner of south-west England. Why secret? They live underground.

From the inside, their home looks like any other bungalow, with its pot plants, carpets and neat furniture. From the outside it looks like nothing on earth. It is under a field. The Ormerods constructed it without seeking planning permisssion, and, for fear of being found out by the local authorities and forced to demolish it, they kept the secret even from friends – until a sharp-eyed planning official noticed that building supplies were being delivered to the site.

To their surprise and delight, however, far from being criticised they were regarded by local officials as eccentric innovators, slightly odd but harmless people attempting to create something original. The Ormerods now hope that they will be able to keep their home and not be forced to dig it out.

Their remote property is hidden in an area of woodland and meadows near the coast. They have no mains electricity or water, using a water wheel and diesel generator for power and a pump to get water from a spring. They moved to the site nine years ago, and after living in a caravan for a while they eventually began building the two-bedroom underground home. Once they had moved in they never invited friends home and their self-sufficiency meant there was virtually no need for visitors. Even the postman was asked to leave letters in a box at the end of the lane. A farmer harvesting his crops close by did not realise the property existed.

Simon Ormerod is now estimated to be worth quite a lot of money. 'I didn't build it to beat the planners,' he said. 'I did it because I had a piece of land which I was attached to, and I think it's right to build this sort of energy-saving home. We wanted a home here in the woods, and we didn't want to interfere with anyone nor be interfered with. I wanted to live here and be buried here.'

The house has most of its roof and three sides covered by earth; the chimney pot sticks out in a field. Only a solar heating area of roof and the glass front open to let in light. Their weekly heating bill is less than £1. Building in the open countryside is usually forbidden because of the effect on the environment, but this property has no electricity supply, no obvious road to it and no water supply. It fits beautifully into its surroundings.

1   Why did the Ormerods keep their house such a secret?

   A   It was in a private forest.
   B   They didn't want others living near.
   C   It was built under the earth.
   D   They were building it illegally.

2   How was their house eventually discovered?

   A   Their friends told the planning officials.
   B   A planning official was very observant.
   C   A building supplier told their friends.
   D   The local authorities saw their supplies.

3 What has pleased the Ormerods?

    A official lack of concern about the house
    B official permission to build the house
    C official interest in the future of the house
    D official praise for the idea behind the house

4 When the Ormerods originally found the site, they

    A had a temporary home.
    B hid in the nearby woods.
    C built a small caravan.
    D dug a well for water.

5 How did the Ormerods manage to avoid being noticed?

    A They never left the forest site.
    B They needed little outside help.
    C They had no proper letter-box.
    D They never had any visitors.

6 Which statement best describes Simon Ormerod's philosophy?

    A I have a right to this land.
    B I am trying to save money.
    C Let me live my own way.
    D Let me alone to die here.

7 Why do you think the Ormerods' house is likely to remain?

    A It doesn't affect the environment.
    B It doesn't cost a lot of money to run.
    C It is well designed and economical.
    D It is a new and original building idea.

2 Grammar: relative clauses

▶ Grammar reference p.229

Fill in the gaps in the following sentences using a suitable word from the box. In some cases there may be more than one possible answer. Put brackets ( ) around relative pronouns which are not necessary.

who	which	that	whom	whose

1 The house, ... owner has emigrated, has still not been sold.

2 My father, ... everyone greatly admired, was a very modest man.

3 Do you know .... is coming to stay next week?

4 I'm afraid I've lost that book .... you lent me.

5 I saw your mother in town; she was with someone .... I didn't recognise.

6 We decided to go on holiday to a place .... we hadn't been to before.

7 The old lady .... lives next door has been a very good neighbour over the years.

8 Have you any idea .... painting has won the competition?

9 It was the first road accident .... she had ever had.

10 People .... live in flats have to be prepared to get on with their neighbours.

3 USE OF ENGLISH   PART 5

For questions **1–10**, read the text below. Use the word given in capitals at the end of each line to form a word that fits in the space in the same line.

WHERE DO COMPUTERS GO WHEN THEY DIE?

Every year around one million (**1**) .... computers are thrown	**PERSON**
away. There are now a number of (**2**) .... to help those trying to	**ORGANISE**
get rid of their old computers. Some recyclers will remove (**3**)	**VALUE**
metals and strip machines of (**4**) .... parts, although the bulk of the	**USE**
machine still remains. Another (**5**) .... is to give them to charities	**SOLVE**
who will gladly make use of them.	
Companies simply wipe clean the hard disk to avoid the (**6**)	**POSSIBLE**
of secret (**7**) .... falling into the wrong hands. But this leaves the	**INFORM**
recipients with an (**8**) .... machine unless some new	**WANT**
software is introduced.	
There is even one US firm which (**9**) .... in recycling the little	**SPECIAL**
polystyrene 'peanuts' used for (**10**) .... in the computer packaging!	**PROTECT**

4 Grammar: phrasal verbs and nouns; compound nouns

▶ Grammar reference p.230   Appendix 2 p.233

Use a word from list 1 combined with a word from list 2 to complete the sentences below, making any necessary changes. Some words will need to be used more than once.

1		2	
heart	hold	shine	box
break	let	light	away
take	window	off	down
day	pass	out	attack
write	pick	up	in
sun	lamp	post	
carry			

1 I'm not surprised the president had a .... : he's overweight. He never has time to exercise and he drinks far too much. He was lucky to survive.

2 Thieves .... through the skylight, managed to avoid setting off the alarm system and got away with a number of valuable pictures.

3 The car was so badly damaged that the insurance company agreed to .... it ....

4 When I don't have time to cook a meal, I pop out to the Indian .... in town.

5 We had paid for very expensive tickets, so when the concert was cancelled at the last minute it was a real ....

6 If you would like a lift, I'll .... you .... at nine o'clock outside your house.

7 A faint ray of .... broke though the clouds.

8 Jon is brilliant at imitating other people – have you seen him .... his boss?

9 The lorry hit the .... with such force that it was brought crashing onto the pavement.

10 The dance hall was so hot and stuffy that a couple of people .... and had to be carried outside for some fresh air.

11 Although the robbery happened in broad .... , nobody appears to have seen anything.

12 As radiators boiled over in the heatwave, a number of vehicles .... on the motorway.

13 One of the things I like most about chalets in Switzerland is the way people fill their .... in summer with wonderful displays of bright red flowers like geraniums.

14 Scientists have been .... research into a cure for the common cold for years.

15 The was a traffic .... which caused a 5 mile long queue as thousands of motorists tried to reach the coast.

---

5   USE OF ENGLISH   PART 2

For questions **1–15**, read the text below and think of the word which best fits each space. Use only **one** word in each space.

CAN'T WORK, DON'T MAKE ME

'Why don't you work, Fiona?' has **(1)** .... the cry of countless despairing friends over the years. It's a very silly **(2)** .... , really. If I knew the answer, I'd be able to do **(3)** .... about it.

For most **(4)** .... my childhood and adolescence I **(5)** .... protected from my natural tendencies **(6)** .... the education system. Also my friends worked, and it was socially unacceptable **(7)** .... to. At university, **(8)** .... , I decided to reveal my intentions.

Reactions to my total **(9)** .... of activity were mixed. The university environment is a very relaxed one, **(10)** .... gives you time to work out your own feelings. But my parents, who were rather traditional, were **(11)** .... impressed. They were not pleased to discover **(12)** .... daughter's attitude to work.

So **(13)** .... don't I work? Well, I don't like it. I hate mental effort. I prefer to lie on my bed dreaming of **(14)** .... a great journalist. I am one stage further on from the woman **(15)** .... liked work and could sit and look at it for hours. I know I loathe it!

---

6   WRITING   PART 2

Your teacher wants to know what you think about Fiona's attitude to work in the text *Can't work, don't make me*. Do you approve or disapprove?

Write a short **article** for your school magazine in **120–180** words based on your reactions and your own personal attitude to work.

GREAT ESCAPES

SPEAKING

Story time

1 Try to guess the answers to the following questions.

What is this mythical monster called?

a yabbie
a jerula
a bunyip

Where is it believed to live?

Nigeria
Australia
Mongolia

If you guessed correctly, was it luck or did you have a reason for choosing those particular answers?

2 Can you remember the names of any favourite stories about monsters that you enjoyed reading when you were younger? Write them down and be ready to discuss them later.

LISTENING

1 You are going to hear a story about the monster in the picture above. First look at the pictures of the lyrebird, the centipede and the mountains known as the 'Three Sisters', all of which feature in the story. Some of the vocabulary which you will also hear is listed below; make sure you understand these words and then listen to the story.

chirp – a high-pitched noise made by birds and insects
ledge – a narrow horizontal surface like a shelf
perch – to sit or stand on something above the ground
lurch – to stagger or walk as if drunk
devour – to eat up greedily

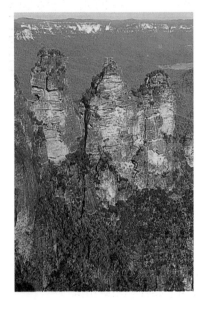

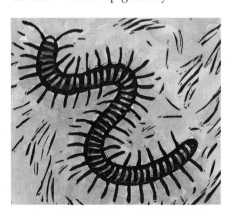

2 Now listen to the story again, and put the ten pictures below in the right order so that they form a story strip of *The Three Sisters*.

3 The story about the three sisters is part of traditional Aboriginal folklore. Look at the names of the stories which you wrote down that people remembered from their childhood, and discuss the following questions in groups.

Are there any similarities between these stories and *The Three Sisters*?
Are monsters always bad?
Does part or all of the enjoyment of these stories depend on magic or fantasy?
Did you actually *enjoy* being frightened?

Jot down some of the things which make these stories and legends so enjoyable for young children, and keep your list for later in the unit.

1 Look at these sentences from the story which you have just listened to:

A *They were a happy family, leading a quiet and contented life.*

B *Only one creature, feared by all, threatened their happiness ...*

C *Tyawan knew where the Bunyip lived and as he had to pass the hole when going into the valley to collect food, ...*

D *One day, having said goodbye to his daughters, he descended the cliff steps.*

E *... and the angry Bunyip emerged from a deep, satisfying sleep.*

Pick out an example of the following participles:
▶ present ▶ past ▶ perfect

Now answer these questions.

1 In which example could the participle be replaced with a phrase to show that the action in both the main and the subordinate clauses happened simultaneously?

2 In which example does the participle act like an adjective?

3 In which example does the participle make clear the sequence of events: that one action happened before another?

4 In which example(s) could you replace the participle with a relative clause beginning with *who*?

2 　CD　You are going to hear the story of *The Three Sisters* again. This time note down the various participles as you listen. Your teacher will pause the tape occasionally; don't try to write down complete sentences, just the participles. Check the participles with your partner.

3 Rewrite sentences 1–5 using an appropriate participle or participle clause.

Example
I worked with Aborigines for many years so I learnt a great deal about their culture.
***Having worked** with Aborigines for many years, I learnt a great deal about their culture.*

1 I lived in the desert, which was very exhausting at times.
.... was very exhausting at times.

2 I didn't speak any of the Aboriginal languages so I had to learn a few words.
Not .... ,
I had to learn a few words.

3 As they believe that all animals have spirits, each Aboriginal tribe takes on the spirit of a particular animal.
.... ,
each Aboriginal tribe takes on the spirit of a particular animal.

4 Aborigines who had lost their land decided to fight back against the British.
Aborigines, ...
decided to fight back against the British.

5 One Aboriginal leader who was wounded was taken to hospital but managed to escape.
....
....

Now rewrite sentences 6–10 and reverse the pattern.
Example
Known as Pemulwuy, he organised local resistance groups until he died in 1802.
He was known as Pemulwuy and he organised local resistance groups until he died in 1802.

6 Diseases carried by Europeans were responsible for killing thousands of Aborigines.
Diseases which ....
were responsible for killing thousands of Aborigines.

7 Not having any resistance to new diseases made it impossible for people to recover from smallpox.
As people did ....
.... , it was impossible for them to recover from smallpox.

8 Being given the status of Australian citizens in 1966 was the result of a long legal struggle.
When they .... ,
it was the result of a long legal struggle.

9 The battle for land rights, famously won by Eddie Mabo in 1992, has become increasingly successful.
The battle for land rights, ...
.... ,
has become increasingly successful.

10 The Aborigine population, still feeling discriminated against even today, continues to fight for its rights.
....

1 How do you escape? Have you got a particular hobby that takes you into another world?

Do you know anyone with a really unusual hobby?

For some people reading provides a form of escapism. Do you think computer games and high-tech toys have replaced books for children, or will stories and books always have a place in children's imagination?

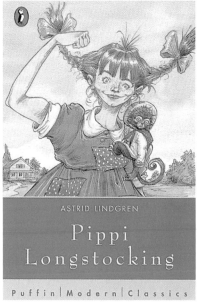

2 The Swedish writer Astrid Lindgren used to tell her daughter Karin bedtime stories. Those stories have since been published and translated into sixty languages.

Quickly read the magazine article overleaf once to find the answers to the following questions.

1 How long ago were the Pippi Longstocking stories written?

2 What had happened to give Astrid Lindgren the opportunity to write the stories?

3 Is there any connection between Astrid Lindgren's childhood and Pippi's?

3 Now read the article again. There are six gaps in the article where sentences have been removed. Choose from the sentences A–G the one which fits each gap. There is one extra sentence which you do not need to use.

Few children's authors can claim to have been on first name terms with prime ministers, to have changed their country's tax system or to have put a law on the statute book. **1** [____]

In 1995 the Swedish novelist Astrid Lindgren celebrated the fiftieth birthday of her most famous creation, the freckle-faced tomboy, Pippi Longstocking.

In Sweden it is reckoned that every literate person has read at least one of her books. Various literary critics have suggested that the Pippi Longstocking stories were written to explore aspects of Swedish society. **2** [____]

'It was 1941 and my daughter Karin was ill with pneumonia. Each night I sat by her bedside telling her stories. One night I asked her what she wanted to hear and she said: "Tell me about Pippi Longstocking." She just made up the name there and then, and as it sounded strange I started telling strange stories.'

Three years later Astrid Lindgren, in bed herself with a sprained ankle, began writing down all the stories. She gave them to her daughter as a tenth birthday present and thought she would try her luck with a publisher. **3** [____]

Later they won first prize in a literary competition, and from that moment Lindgren found herself a national heroine. Her 70 books are published in 60 languages, making her one of the world's ten most widely translated authors. There is a video game based on Pippi's escapades, and an Astrid Lindgren theme park in her native town of Vimmerby. **4** [____]

Despite being voted Sweden's most popular woman five years in a row, she has remained a deeply private person. She was born in southern Sweden, the second of four children, and the theme of carefree childhood in the country that runs through all her books was modelled closely on her own experiences.

'No childhood could have been happier or freer. **5** [____] My father's dearest possession was a certificate he got for moving more stones than other farmers. The land was so rocky it couldn't be ploughed or planted until thousands of tons of boulders had been removed. Yet we had a pleasant, natural landscape, clean water to swim in and clean air to breathe.' **6** [____]

Pippi, with her unruly, liberated lifestyle which allows her to keep her horse on the verandah and to party all night with her pet monkey, is an obvious ideal for children. However, some adults have objected to the influence which such behaviour has, and one Swedish newspaper once described nine-year-old Pippi as a dangerous role model. Such criticism never worries Astrid Lindgren: 'I never write for adults. I don't even write for children. I write for the child I once was who is inside me still.'

A We had nothing.

B In Germany alone 94 state schools are named after her.

C If you don't respect animals, you won't feel respect for children or adults.

D Fewer still live to see postage stamps issued in their honour.

E Astrid Lindgren, however, disagrees and says that the stories developed by chance.

F It is a world that has completely vanished.

G They were rejected.

VOCABULARY

4 Find words or phrases which mean:

1 a series of documents recording legal decisions made by parliament
2 a small brown mark on the skin
3 a girl who acts and dresses in a boyish way
4 someone able to read and write
5 invented
6 twisted
7 adventures full of mischief
8 without worry or responsibility
9 something owned by someone
10 disobedient
11 free from restrictions
12 example of expected behaviour

WRITING

Story

Imagine you are going to enter a short story competition which is being organised by an English language magazine which will publish the winning entry.

The story should be in 120–180 words and has to begin or end with the sentence: *It was the last time they ever saw him.*

Before you begin writing, work out a simple plot, or storyline.

Don't start writing until you are quite clear who the *him* in your story is. Is it going to be an adult, a child, an animal … ?

Think about some of the new vocabulary you have learnt which you could now try and include.

Look at the suggestions for link words, relative clauses and participles on pages 227, 229 and 230 in the Grammar reference.

Look up the rules for using the past tenses on pages 218 and 220 as these are the tenses you are most likely to use for writing a story.

If you want to include direct speech, remember to use speech marks (inverted commas) either side of what a person actually says. For example, look back at page 158 at the end of the story *Elephant Trek*.

Don't forget your story must begin or end with the sentence: *It was the last time they ever saw him.*

1 ☒ Pippi Longstocking is described as a *freckle-faced* tomboy.

Freckle-faced is a compound adjective and means that Pippi's face was *covered with freckles*.

Similarly, **nine-year-old** Pippi uses a compound adjective as another way of saying *Pippi, who is nine years old, ...*

Match the words on the left with appropriate past participles on the right to form compound adjectives used to describe people; you will need to use certain adjectives more than once.

	shaven
	dressed
good	educated
hard	behaved
hot	aged
middle	built
broad	shouldered
short	working
well	tempered
clean	hearted
kind	sighted
left	looking
bad	handed
	spoken

2 Divide your list into those words which we use to describe a person's appearance and those which we use to describe a person's character.
Pick three words that apply to you, and three words that apply to your partner.
Exchange your lists – did you each pick the same words?
Use some of the compound adjectives you have learnt to describe these people.

3 Now look at the sentences below and rewrite each one using a compound adjective.

Example
This carton contains one litre of milk.
*This is a **one-litre** carton of milk.*

1 The journey from London to Paris takes three hours by train.
It is a .... train journey from London to Paris.

2 We have recently bought a house with five storeys.
We have recently bought a
.... house.

3 The flight lasts two hours.
It is a .... flight.

4 Gino, who is twelve years old, has gained a place at university.
.... Gino has gained a place at university.

5 The interval will last 30 minutes.
There will be a .... interval.

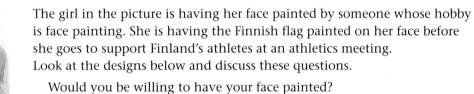

Did you find anyone whose hobby was face painting when you were discussing unusual hobbies earlier in this unit?

The girl in the picture is having her face painted by someone whose hobby is face painting. She is having the Finnish flag painted on her face before she goes to support Finland's athletes at an athletics meeting.
Look at the designs below and discuss these questions.

    Would you be willing to have your face painted?
    Is it a way of escaping from your identity or drawing attention to your identity?
    If you were going to watch your country in a football match, would you be prepared to have a flag painted on your face?
    Which designs do you prefer?
    Would you rather have or see one or two designs on each cheek?
    Is there anything you would like to have painted on your face that doesn't appear here?

1   □ Does it matter what you look like?
Are clothes important? If you want to look smart, what do you wear?
What are your favourite clothes?
Would you like to wear (or have worn) a school uniform?
What advantages and disadvantages do uniforms have?
Do you think girls spend more time on their appearance than boys?

2   Traditionally, beauty salons have catered for women, but the extract below
is from an article about the reasons behind the increasing popularity of
male beauty salons in the UK.
Discuss your opinions of male beauty salons.

Now read the article and answer the questions below.

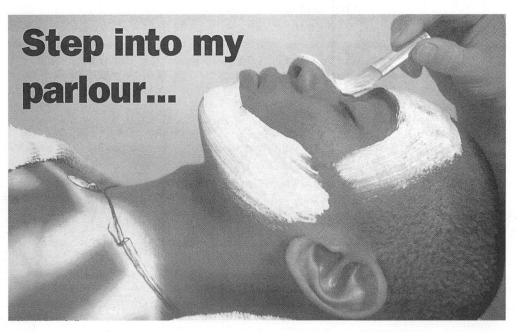

Step into my parlour...

Adrienne Ashcroft is one of a growing number of beauticians who cater for men. 'I have found that men, in general, are becoming more interested in their appearance,' she says. 'The current interest is a natural extension of the health craze.'

According to the editor of a magazine on men's health, films have also had an influence on male appearance, with Hollywood being the main influence. 'There is an increase in the number of men who are paying attention to their appearance, and the number of readers writing in to the magazine for advice. Often they are pressured into change by their girlfriends, and the big cosmetics companies are now targeting men.'

A survey carried out by one market research organisation shows that sales of male cosmetics in the UK have risen by 37% over the past five years. One cosmetics company which launched a range for men says its sales have doubled during this period.

A shop assistant who works on the cosmetics counter of a well-known store says, 'Men's attitudes have changed – they are no longer coming in with wives or girlfriends but by themselves.'

There are five different sources of information which the writer quotes in this extract. What are they?
Pick out the phrases which show that the sources of information agree with each other about the reasons for the growth of the male beauty business.

VOCABULARY

3 Match the words from the text with their meanings:

1 current   **2** craze   **3** pressured   **4** targeting   **5** launched

aiming at   present, topical   produced   short-lived fashion   compelled

▶ SPEAKING

1 Discuss the following questions in groups.

Now that you have read the article, have your opinions of male beauty salons changed in any way?

Do you agree with any of the reasons which the different people give for men's increasing interest in their appearance?

What kind of image do you want to create? A conventional one?

Do you want to fit in with a crowd or do you want to stand out in a crowd?

Do crazy fashions fill you with excitement or bore you?

Are clothes another form of escape from ourselves?

Do clothes help us pretend to be someone different? Or do they state who we are?

Did you like dressing up when you were a child?

Would an invitation to a fancy dress party terrify you or excite you?

2 Do these photos have anything in common?

Do you think the various people are wearing clothes which are suitable for the occasion?

Do you think any of them looks really smart?

Do you think anyone looks scruffy?

⊙ LISTENING

1 You are going to hear an interview with an American fashion designer called Maudie Levertov.

Before you listen, read the statements below. When you have heard the recording once, decide whether the statements are true or false and be ready to explain your answers.

1 Maudie must be middle aged.

2 The interviewer's attitude suggests that he thinks fashion designers are rather shallow people.

3 Maudie is probably rather well built.

2 Listen again and answer questions 1–5 by choosing the best answer A, B or C.

1 In Europe Maudie has already
  A opened two shops.
  B set up offices.
  C bought a market.

2 At the beginning of her career, Maudie
  A had to borrow money.
  B rented a showroom.
  C worked from home.

3 What does Maudie say about her new business move?
  A She's copying other designers.
  B She's not competing with anyone.
  C She's probably over-expanded.

4 Maudie's shops currently sell
  A clothes, shoes and beauty products.
  B clothes, perfume and cosmetics.
  C clothes, shoes and perfume.

5 What does Maudie aim for in designing clothes for women?
  A to make a woman feel like a supermodel
  B to enable a woman to look her best
  C to allow a woman to escape from reality

GRAMMAR ▶ p.231 *make / let / allow*

1 ⬚ What did Maudie mean when she said:

1 'I want to **make** *my customers feel* a million dollars.'

There are two ways *make* is used when we want to convey the idea of being compelled to do something, although in the context of what Maudie says customers obviously have a choice as to whether or not they buy her clothes.

Once having bought them, however, Maudie intends they should feel *like a million dollars*. A customer might say:

'Maudie's clothes **make** *me feel* wonderful!'

In this context, *feeling wonderful* is the natural result or consequence of wearing Maudie's designs, and obviously there is no sense of compulsion.

Compare this with sentence 2, which suggests that children have no choice and are more or less forced to do what adults want.

2 Most small children *are* **made to** *wear* clothes chosen by adults.

Now compare sentences 3 and 4. Do they mean the same?

3 My mother **let** *me wear* what I wanted when I was younger.

4 I was **allowed to** *wear* what I wanted to (by my mother) when I was younger.

2 Write about the situations described in the statements 1–4 using *make*, *let* and *allow* to express the ideas. Each situation can be expressed in more than one way.

Example
Uniform was compulsory at my secondary school.
We were **made to** *wear uniform at my secondary school.*
My secondary school **made** *us wear uniform.*
My secondary school did not **let** *us wear casual clothes.*
We were **not allowed to** *wear casual clothes at my secondary school.*

1 Beth wanted to be a fashion designer, but her parents wouldn't agree.

2 I did not want to go to university, but my teachers insisted I should apply.

3 I wanted to go on holiday alone, but my parents said I had to go with a friend.

4 Alan wanted to go skydiving, but his parents told him it was too dangerous.

Key vocabulary

Apart from the key vocabulary practised within this unit, you also need to know the following words in connection with clothes and the body. Use your dictionary to look up any words you don't know. Rearrange the words below under the two headings.

Clothing	Parts of the body

sweater anorak chin eyebrow blouse pants pyjamas hip forehead toe bra elbow jeans scarf jaw tongue tights socks tracksuit raincoat belt throat wrist heel knickers stomach palm bikini overcoat gloves chest ankle nostril slippers suit waist cardigan bottom swimsuit trunks neck mac(kintosh) shorts jumper T-shirt nail eyelash thumb dressing gown

Recycling: relative clauses

Read the text which is adapted from *Pippi Longstocking* by Astrid Lindgren and fill in the gaps using the words in the box. Add any punctuation you think necessary.

| who | which | that | whom | whose |

When Pippi decided to set up her own home, she took two things with her, a little monkey (1) .... name was Mr Nelson and a big suitcase (2) .... was full of gold pieces. When she arrived at her cottage, the thing (3) .... made people stare was, of course, the monkey. There were two other children (4) .... were spending a week with their grandmother in the cottage next door when Pippi arrived. They watched her walk up the path. Her hair (5) .... was the same colour as a carrot was tied in two plaits. Her nose was the shape of a very small potato and was dotted with freckles, and she had a very large mouth. She wore a blue dress with red patches and long stockings – one brown and one black. She had a pair of black shoes (6) .... were twice as long as her feet. Her father (7) .... Pippi hadn't seen for years had bought them for her in South America. But it was the monkey (8) .... really attracted the children's attention. It was little and long-tailed, and dressed in blue trousers, yellow jacket and a white straw hat.

Learning record

When you have finished Unit 11, try filling in this record of what you have learnt.
Fill in the gaps in the following sentences so that the second sentence means the same as the first.

1 Not being very old, Rebecca still likes dolls.
As Rebecca .... , she still likes dolls.

2 When Matthew had finished reading *Pippi Longstocking*, he bought *Lotta's Bike*.
.... *Pippi Longstocking*, Matthew bought *Lotta's Bike*.

3 The flight is delayed for two hours.
There is a .... on the flight.

4 A baby who was kidnapped yesterday was only four weeks old.
A .... baby was kidnapped yesterday.

Complete these sentences with a suitable compound adjective.

5 Tony looks very different now that he's .... , although I think I prefer him with a beard.

6 Sarah is a very .... woman: she has a string of qualifications as well as a doctorate in astrophysics.

Complete these sentences using the correct form of *make, let* or *allow*.

7 My father can't .... me go to university if I don't want to.

8 The students .... to play loud music in the common room but not in their study bedrooms.

9 The prisoner was .... stand in the heat for so long he almost fainted.

10 Would you .... me to make a suggestion?

FCE Checklist

No looking back! I have practised:
▶ .... for Paper 1, Part ....
▶ .... for Paper 2, Part ....
▶ .... for Paper 3, Part ....
▶ .... for Paper 4, Part ....
▶ .... for Paper 5, Parts ....

21 Writing, Part 2 (set texts)

Question 5 on Part 2 of the Writing paper is always based on the set texts.

There is a choice of texts, and each text stays on the syllabus for two years. For example, in 1997 the books were *Great Expectations* by Charles Dickens, *Brave New World* by Aldous Huxley, *Crime Never Pays* in the Oxford Bookworm Collections, *Rebecca* by Daphne du Maurier and *Pygmalion* by GB Shaw. Some of these texts would have been on the 1996 syllabus so you should always check the current regulations* to see what changes have been made to the list for the session in which you want to take the FCE. The regulations will also tell you which edition to read, as some of the long novels will be published in an abridged or shortened version and you are not expected to read the original.

▶ Unless you have read and prepared a set text, don't be tempted to pick this question!

▶ The kinds of question based on the background books will vary.

▶ Underline the key words in the question and organise your ideas as with any other piece of writing.

▶ Are you being asked to write an article, perhaps recommending the book for your college magazine?

▶ Are you being asked to write about your favourite character(s) in the book?

▶ You may be asked to write about whether the events in a book could happen in your own country.

▶ You may be asked to discuss the title of a book, or the picture on the front cover of a book.

▶ You are **not** expected to use the language of literary appreciation, but you should be able to write about the plot (the storyline), the characters and the significant ideas in your chosen book, if relevant to the question.

▶ Be prepared to write about your own personal reactions to what you have read and what you have enjoyed or not enjoyed in your reading.

* The regulations are available from:
University of Cambridge Local Examinations Syndicate
1 Hills Road
CAMBRIDGE
CB1 2EU
UK

22 Using computerised answer sheets

For Paper 2 your answers must be written (in ink) in the printed spaces on your question paper, and you do not need to write anything on your mark sheet for Paper 5. However, on pages 237–239 in this course book you will find sample answer sheets for Papers 1, 3 and 4.

It is a good idea to familiarise yourself with how to fill in these mark sheets and to use them for practice purposes when you do the FCE Practice Exam.

▶ Use a soft pencil to fill in the boxes

which are called lozenges.

▶ If you make a mistake, rub it out with a clean rubber; don't use white-out fluid.

▶ In Paper 1, the Reading paper, if you decide to copy your answers from your question paper onto your answer sheet (instead of answering directly onto your answer sheet), make sure that you copy across very carefully and that your answers don't get out of order.

▶ In Paper 3, Use of English, you should use ink for answering Parts 2, 3, 4 and 5; use pencil for Part 1 as you have to fill in lozenges for the first 15 questions.

▶ Write clearly, especially in Paper 2, and don't write outside the spaces which are allowed for your answers in Papers 3 and 4.

▶ If your handwriting is very big or occasionally difficult to read, you must be prepared to modify it in your own interests.

▶ Don't leave gaps but make a sensible guess instead – you could always be right!

▶ In Paper 4, Listening, you are allowed 5 minutes at the end to transfer your answers, so don't try to fill in the answer sheet while you are listening to the recordings. In Parts 2 and 4 you should record your answers in ink if possible; Parts 1 and 3 can be answered using pencil to fill in the lozenges.

1   USE OF ENGLISH   **PART 3**

For questions **1–10**, complete the second sentence so that it has a similar meaning to the first sentence. Use the word given and other words to complete each sentence. You must use between two and five words. **Do not change the word given.**

Example
The piano is not small enough to get through the door.
too

The piano _is too large to_ get through the door.

___

1   I find my boss very difficult to work with.
   difficulty

   I have .... my boss.

2   Ayako pays £60 for a music lesson of 45 minutes.
   minute

   A .... Ayako £60.

3   Students are forbidden to smoke in their study bedrooms.
   allowed

   Students .... in their study bedrooms.

4   They carried on playing volleyball even though it was raining.
   despite

   They carried on playing volleyball .... was raining.

5   'Don't put that hot saucepan on the table,' Helen said to her son.
   warned

   Helen .... put the hot saucepan on the table.

6   Can you connect me with the ticket office, please?
   through

   Can you .... to the ticket office, please?

7   I wish you would tidy up your desk.
   time

   It's .... your desk.

8   The flooded road meant we couldn't get through.
   prevented

   The flooded .... through.

9   Could I invite a few friends to a party?
   mind

   Would .... a few friends to a party?

10 The exam was not as difficult as I had expected.
   than

   The exam .... I had expected.

2 Grammar: *do* or *make*?

This exercise helps you revise when to use *do* and when to use *make*, two verbs which are often confused.

Decide whether the words and expressions below are used with either *do* or *make* and put them under the appropriate heading.

a suggestion   a complaint   a decision   a test   an exam   homework
an excuse   a journey   money   an arrangement   a mistake   one's bed
business   an offer   a profit   exercise   certain   a choice   love
a favour   harm   a trip   an inquiry   damage   work   one's best
a discovery   housework   an effort   sure

do	make

Now fill in the missing verbs in their correct form in the sentences below and add four sentences of your own, two using expressions with *do*, and two using *make*.

1 Rick doesn't bother to check his work and often .... careless mistakes.

2 Before you leave the house, ... sure all the lights are switched off.

3 We've .... business with this firm for years and never had any problem with unpaid bills before now.

4 The police .... inquiries into last night's bank robbery.

5 When it comes to taking the FCE, ... your best!

6 He .... a decision to emigrate weeks ago and he has no intention of changing his mind.

7 ....

8 ....

9 ....

10 ....

3 Writing

Look back at the notes which you made at the beginning of this unit about what makes certain stories and legends so enjoyable.

Your teacher is putting together a collection of stories which can be recommended for young children.

Write a brief outline of a story which you enjoyed; in more detail say what you enjoyed about it and why you recommend it.

Use the title of the story as a heading and write about 150 words.

---

4 USE OF ENGLISH   PART 4

For questions **1–15**, read the text below and look carefully at each line. Some of the lines are correct, and some have a word which should not be there.
If a line is correct, put a tick (✓) beside it. If a line has a word which should **not** be there, write the word beside it.

SUMMER JOB

1 .... When I answered an advertisement for a summer job, I had no idea

2 .... what I was letting myself in for. The advertisement did not to say very

3 .... much, except that a busy parents were looking for someone to take

4 .... care of their two young children during the school holidays. The pay

5 .... was generous; I rang the number and the job was becoming mine. I

6 .... arrived the next day and to my surprise found the front door of a large

7 .... house wide open. I called out and, while I was wondering so what to do,

8 .... heard some laughter from the top of the stairs. As I just looked up I saw

9 .... two small figures being about to empty a bucket of water. I moved back

10 .... too late to avoid being soaked from the head to foot, with cries of delight

11 .... coming from above. I asked where their parents were, only to be told

12 .... that they had already left for their work and would not be home until

13 .... late. 'You're the fourth person who's come in two weeks. No one stays

14 .... for very long,' they announced. Hardly rather surprising, I thought to

15 .... myself. 'I think I'll stay long enough for to dry my clothes and then I'll
   be off,' I replied grimly.

5 Grammar: participles and participle clauses

▶ Grammar reference p.230

Complete sentences 1–5 using the words in the box to make either a present or past participle acting as an adjective.

| irritate | guard | exhaust | stain | steal |

Example

worry
*This is a very **worrying** situation, which must be discussed.*

frighten
*The **frightened** child took one look at the mouse and screamed.*

1 I'm afraid I fell fast asleep during a very .... journey which took more than 24 hours.

2 This badly-........................ carpet needs a good clean.

3 This must be the .... Ming vase which the police have been looking for.

4 She's an .... child, always arguing over one thing or another.

5 The king's arrival was such a closely-........................... secret that nobody knew anything about it until the last minute.

Complete sentences 6–10 using either a present or perfect participle.

Example
***Arriving late** at the theatre, I had to wait for the interval before I could take my seat.*
***Not having received** an invitation, Henry didn't attend the reception.*

6 .... you like Cantonese food, I've booked a table at our local Chinese restaurant.

7 .... at least one Indian sunset, I was disappointed that the sky remained permanently overcast throughout our holiday.

8 .... all my savings on a house, I had no money left for a new car.

9 .... a loud bang in the street, they ran out expecting to see an accident.

10 .... out of the train window, I watched the landscape flash by.

You are going to read a newspaper article about an 'intelligent house'. Seven sentences have been removed from the article. Choose from the sentences **A–G** the one which fits each gap (**1–6**). There is one extra sentence which you do not need to use.

HELLO HOUSE – I'LL BE HOME IN 45 MINUTES

Home is about to become less of a castle and more of a user-friendly palace. An 'intelligent house' is already under construction in Britain. **1** _____ When you turn off the motorway, the car phone can be used to order it to turn on the heating, start the oven, switch on the lights and open the garage doors.

For the past century, inventors and film-makers have dreamed of the completely automated house. **2** _____ Technology that could successfully achieve the task has been around since the 1960s, but despite occasional bursts of excitement, home automation has been restricted to a few enthusiasts. **3** _____

The cost of such systems has so far discouraged ordinary buyers. **4** _____ However, two things are now happening that could make home automation a reality for everyone. The cost of microchips is rapidly falling, and once computer power is everywhere, linking them up could become extremely cheap. **5** _____ Many people are now prepared to pay for electronic networks around their homes for computer terminals, phones and televisions. Such systems could later be used for home automation.

6 _____ Using the computer terminal in the home, all the domestic appliances in every room could be wired up. For example, your fridge would be able to tell your phone to ring your car and remind you to pick up some milk on the way home.

A The facilities such a system would open up are amazing.

B The second thing is people's desire to communicate.

C Not many people are willing to pay more than £100 for an electric curtain-drawing mechanism.

D It would do eveything from making the early morning tea to switching off the light last thing at night.

E This is a house that will understand and obey telephoned instructions.

F The computer can respond to a knock on the door.

G These enthusiasts drive their families mad by installing systems that frequently break down.

UNIT 1

Reported speech 1

When we want to tell or report to another person what someone has said, we have to make certain changes.
There are two ways of reporting:

▶ repeating the actual words which the person originally spoke, using inverted commas around their actual words:
  Peter said, 'I want to go to university in Spain.'

▶ reporting what they have said indirectly:
  Peter said (that) he wanted to go to university in Spain.

Note When we use **that** + clause we often leave out *that* – especially in spoken English.

The main rule to remember in reporting indirectly what people have said is the verb change which usually moves the tense into a tense further back in time.

Direct speech		Reported speech
Present simple *'I go to university in Spain,'* *Peter said.*	→ →	Past simple *Peter said (that) he went to* *university in Spain.*
Present continuous *'I am taking my final exams* *soon,' Mariann said.*	→ →	Past continuous *Mariann said (that) she was* *taking her final exams soon.*
Present perfect *'I have never been to* *university,' Rory said.*	→ →	Past perfect *Rory said (that) he had never* *been to university.*
Past simple *'I went to university in my* *home town,' Carla said.*	→ →	Past perfect *Carla said (that) she had been* *to university in her home town.*
Past continuous *'I was joking,' Lars said.*	→ →	Past perfect continuous *Lars said (that) he had been* *joking.*
Simple future (*will*) *'I'll buy a new dictionary,'* *Monika said.*	→ →	*would* *Monika said (that) she would* *buy a new dictionary.*
can('t) *'I can't leave school until* *later,' Jacques said.*	→ →	*could(n't)* *Jacques said (that) he couldn't* *leave school until later.*
may *'I may go to art college,'* *she said.*	→ →	*might* *She said (that) she might go to* *art college.*
must *'You must get a job,' her* *mother said.*	→ →	*had to* *Her mother told her (that) she* *had to get a job.*

Note The past perfect tense does not change in reported speech. Similarly the modal verbs *could, should, would, might* and *ought to* do not change.

Time, place and other changes

Other changes that generally need to be made include:

Direct speech		Reported speech
now	→ →	then
here	→ →	there
next	→ →	the following
last	→ →	the previous/before
yesterday	→ →	the previous day/the day before
tomorrow	→ →	the day after/the next day/the following day
today	→ →	the same day/that day
come	→ →	go
I, you, etc.	→ →	*she, him,* etc. (changes depending on the situation and who is speaking to whom)

Example

'I went shopping yesterday,' Nesta said. 'Tomorrow I'm going shopping again, but I think it will just be window shopping this time.'

Nesta said (that) she had been shopping the day before and she was going shopping again the following day, but she thought it would just be window shopping that time.

If we report something using a reporting verb in the present tense, then **no changes** are made **to either the original verb or the time and place references**, although the pronoun still changes:

  *It **says** here that the prime minister **is thinking** of resigning.*
  *Your daughter **says** she **needs** a lift from the station.*

We tend to use reporting verbs in the present tense when we want to report something which we happen to be reading at the time, from a magazine or a letter, or give someone a message.

Even if we report something using a verb in the past tense, if the consequences affect present time and we want to emphasise this aspect, the original present tense can be used:

  'I still love her,' Jake said.
  *Jake **said** he still **loves** her.*

Note Reported speech is far more commonly used than direct speech except when we want to tell jokes or stories.

Reported questions

As well as all the changes described above, when we report questions the question changes into a statement (so there is no question mark) and the word order changes to that of a statement.

If it is a question without a question word, when we report it we use the word **whether** as the person's answer could be either *yes* or *no*:

'Are you good at languages,' Maria asked Peter.
*Maria asked Peter **whether** he was good at languages.*

It would also be possible to use **if**, and most people, especially in spoken English, would not bother to distinguish between using *if* and *whether*:

*Maria asked Peter **if** he was good at languages.*

If the question begins with a question word (**what**, **how**, **when**, etc.), then that question word is repeated at the beginning of the reported speech clause:

What do you want?
*He asked me **what** I wanted.*

Gerunds 1: after certain verbs

After certain verbs we have to use the **gerund** (the *-ing* form) if we want to use another verb:

*I would **recommend studying** abroad to anyone.*

The verbs listed below must always be followed by a gerund if we want to use a verb.

It is worth learning this list – *it is worth* (meaning *it is a good idea*) also takes a gerund!

admit	deny	mention	recommend
appreciate	finish	mind	resist
avoid	imagine	miss	risk
consider	involve	postpone	suggest
delay	keep	practise	

The gerund is also used after some very common verbs which express our reactions to things, especially things we like or dislike:

- verbs which convey a positive reaction: *enjoy, adore*
- verbs which convey a negative reaction: *dislike, can't stand, can't bear, loathe, detest*
- verb which conveys a neutral reaction: *don't mind*

A gerund is a verbal noun and may act as the subject or the object of a sentence:

***Studying** abroad was a great experience for Mariann.*
*Mariann enjoyed **studying** abroad.*

Articles

1 The **definite** article **the** is used with most nouns when we:
- refer to something specific
  *Are you going to **the** cinema this evening?*
- refer back to something that has already been mentioned or something the listener already knows about
  – *Have you seen my jacket?*
  – ***The** black one?*
  – *Yes.*
  – *It's hanging up.*
- refer to the fact that there is only one of its kind in a particular context
  ***The** new prime minister gave his first speech in **the** Houses of Parliament.*

Other uses
- in superlative constructions
  *This is **the** best book I've read for ages.*
- with the names of certain countries and groups of islands, as well as individual islands
  ***the** United States of America, **the** Canaries, **the** Isle of Wight*
- with the names of rivers, oceans, seas, mountain ranges
  ***the** Rhine, **the** Atlantic, **the** Red Sea, **the** Andes, **the** Himalayas*
- with adjectives when they are used as plural nouns:
  ***The** Americans were the first to land on the moon.*
  ***The** injured were taken to hospital by helicopter.*

2 The **indefinite** article **a/an** is used:
- when we refer to something generally
  *I've always wanted to buy **a** new car. (doesn't refer to a particular car)*
- with singular countable nouns
  *Can you lend me **a** pencil, please?*
- when we mention something for the first time
  ***A** large majority of people are against building the new motorway.*
- with numbers and fractions
  ***A** thousand pounds is a lot of money.*
  *I'd be happy with **a** quarter of that!*
- when we talk about people's jobs or occupations
  *My father's **a** lawyer.*
  *Is he? My mother's **a** judge!*

3 **Zero/No article** is used:

- with plural countable nouns
  I love apples.
  Shops open at 8 a.m. and close at 6 p.m.
- with uncountable nouns
  I gave up eating butter years ago.
- with the names of towns, cities, most countries, lakes, mountains, shops
  I spent my holiday in Salzburg.
  Do you like living in Chile?
  I would love to live beside Lake Constance.
  Mount Fuji is the highest mountain in Japan.
  Have you ever been to KaDeWe in Berlin?
- with certain institutions which have a specific name
  I spent two years at London University.
  Have you ever been to Westminster Abbey?
  No, but I've been to Westminster Cathedral.
- with common phrases connected with place or movement.
  *I live **at home** with my parents.*
  *Sam wasn't **at work** today.*
  *I prefer travelling **by train** at night.*
  *He was buried **at sea** as he had always wanted.*
  *Are you going **on foot** or **by car**?*
  *She spent most of her life **in prison**.*

Present tenses

The **present simple** is used:

- for a situation which is true for a period of time
  *I **go** to university in Spain.*
- for scientific truths
  *The sun **rises** in the east and **sets** in the west.*
- for regular, habitual actions
  *We **see** our friends every week.*
- for verbs **not normally used in the continuous** form; the most common are
  appear, believe, belong, hear, imagine, know, love, mean, seem, smell, taste
- in spoken English, when telling a joke, or in written English when we want to make something seem more immediate
  *What **is** yellow and **goes** up and down?* (a banana in a lift!)
  *So there I **am** at the top of the stairs when the door **opens** and in **comes** …*

The **present continuous** tense is used:

- for an action that is happening at the same time as you are speaking
  *Wait a minute – the doorbell**'s ringing**.*
- for an action which carries on over a period of time
  *People **are spending** more money on eating out.*
- with *always* for emphasis – often to show surprise or irritation
  *It**'s** always **raining** when I want to go out.*

The **present perfect** simple tense is used when we:

- refer to something that happened in the recent past but is still connected to the present
  *I**'ve missed** the beginning of the TV programme, but it **hasn't finished** yet so I'll watch the rest of it.*
- talk about something in the past which has no specific reference point
  *I've never **seen** such a boring play!*
  ***Have** you **met** my father?*
- refer to something which happened in the past but has a result relevant to the present
  *You look very pale – **have** you **been** ill?*

The **present perfect continuous** tense is used:

- when we want to emphasise something which happened in the past but still continues into the present
  *I**'ve been learning** the piano for ten years and I still can't play very well!*
- for actions which seem to have finished but the effect is still visible
  *Your eyes are very red – **have** you **been crying**?*
  *The floor's covered in water – what **have** you **been doing**? I**'ve been bathing** the dog!*

UNIT 2

Phrasal verbs

A **phrasal verb** is a verb combined with a particle (a preposition, an adverb or sometimes both) in which the meaning is very often **not literal**.

Not all verbs followed by a preposition, for example, are necessarily phrasal verbs. Compare the following two examples:

  a *I **went out** to the cinema last night.*
  b *The fire **went out** as soon as it began to rain.*

In a) the ordinary verb is followed by a preposition to explain where the speaker went.

In b) the combination of *went + out* has a completely different meaning: *to be extinguished.*

Phrasal verbs are very important and you will *come across* them (phrasal verb meaning *to encounter*!) a great deal, especially in informal, spoken English. You may occasionally be able to guess their meaning from the context in which they are used, but you should be prepared to learn the meanings of most important phrasal verbs as well as how to use them.

You do not need to worry about whether the particles are prepositions or adverbs. It is more important to know whether the verb and its particle(s) can be separated or not. There are three types of phrasal verb, and in order to use these verbs accurately you need to know where to put the particles – the prepositions and/or the adverbs. Word order is therefore very important.

In Appendix 2 on page 233 there is a list of phrasal verbs with examples to help you with your preparation for the FCE. This list also tells you which phrasal verbs may have more than one meaning.

1 Intransitive phrasal verbs

An **intransitive** verb is one which does not take an object. The verb is **always** followed by its particle(s), so word order never changes:

  *What time do you **get up** every morning?*
  *She **passes out** at the sight of blood.* (meaning *faint*)

2 Separable phrasal verbs (verb + adverb + object)

If the object is a noun, it can be placed before or after the adverb:

  *He **gave** the book **back**.*
  *He **gave back** the book.*

  *She **took** her coat **off**.*
  *She **took off** her coat.*

If the object is a pronoun, for example *it*, then the object must come before the adverb:

  *He **gave it** back.*
  *She **took it** off.*

Similarly, *He **turned down** my offer.*
  *He **turned** my offer **down**.*   (meaning *refuse*)
But *He **turned me down**.*

3 Inseparable phrasal verbs
(verb + preposition + object OR
verb + adverb + preposition + object)

Whether the object is a noun or a pronoun, it must come after the particles:

  *Could you **look after** the baby for a couple of hours, please?* (meaning *be responsible for*)
  *Could you **look after her** for a couple of hours, please?*

  *We must **cut down on** our telephone bill.* (meaning *reduce*)
  *We must **cut down on it**.*

Zero and first conditionals

The zero conditional

***if* + present tense + present or imperative** (the verb base without *to*)

The zero condtional is frequently used when we:

▶ want to talk about general truths, especially scientific observations
  *Some doctors believe that **if you feel** unhappy, **you sleep** badly.*

▶ want to give orders or instructions
  ***If you see** William, **give** him my best wishes.*
  ***Buy** me some crisps **if you're going** to the shop, please.*

The first conditional

***if* + present tense + future**

The first conditional is used when we want to talk about something which is possible and likely to happen; we often use it when we are giving advice, warning or persuading, or making a promise:

  ***If you don't leave** that dog alone, **it will bite** you.*
  ***If you tell** me when you're coming, **I'll meet** you for a drink.*
  ***You'll never regret** it **if you work** hard at school.*

It is also possible to use other modal verbs in place of *will*:

  ***If you wait** outside Buckingham Palace, **you may see** the Queen.*

As well as using *if* to join conditional patterns, there are other common conjunctions, especially **unless** (meaning *if not*) and **provided that/as long as** (meaning *if and only if*).

Punctuation When the *if-* clause comes first, it is followed by a comma; when the main clause comes first, there is no comma.

Adjectival order

In English the adjective(s) are placed before the noun. The order in which we put the adjectives may occasionally vary, but for FCE you should learn the following order:

personal opinion + age/size/weight + shape + colour + country of origin + material (+ noun)

> *Amy has bought a lovely, large, circular, red and gold, Indian, cotton cover for her bed.*

Try writing your own sentence to help you remember this basic order. Have you bought anything new recently?

Adverbs

Formation

Most adverbs of manner end in *-ly*, which is added to the adjective:

> *beautiful – **beautifully**, quick – **quickly**,*
> *lucky – **luckily***

Note the spelling change if the adjective ends in *y*: *-ily*. There are some common exceptions when the adverb is the same as the adjective:

> **early   far   fast   hard   late   next   straight**

Note The adjective *good* = *well* when used as an adverb. If the adjective already ends with *-ly*, for example *friendly*, *lovely*, *silly*, *ugly*, it cannot be turned into an adverb. In this case we use a phrase:

> *His behaviour is **very silly**.*
> *He behaves **in a very silly way**.*

> *She gave me a **lovely** smile.*
> *She smiled at me **in a lovely way**.*

Position

The position of an adverb in a sentence varies: it can come at the beginning, in the middle or at the end.

▸ Adverbs of manner which tell us *how* something is done most often come at the end of the sentence as the adverb is essential to the meaning of the verb, although other positions in the sentence are also possible:

> *How did she drive home?*
> *She drove home **slowly**.*
> *She **slowly** drove home.*
> *She drove **slowly** home.*
> ***Slowly** she drove home.*

> *How did they move the injured man?*
> *They moved him **carefully**.*
> *They **carefully** moved the injured man.*
> ***Carefully** they moved the injured man.*

▸ Adverbs which tell us *where* something takes place or the position that something is placed usually come at the end of the sentence:

> ***Where** shall I put your pen?*
> *Put it **over there**, please.*

> ***Where's** John going?*
> *He's going **downstairs**.*

▸ Adverbs of frequency which tell us *when* or *how often* something happens most often come at the end of the sentence, although other positions are also possible if we want to add particular emphasis:

> ***When** did you see your cousin?*
> *I saw him **yesterday**.*

> *Are you seeing your cousin **today**?*
> *No, **today** he's off to New York.*

> ***When** did your flight arrive?*
> *It **finally** arrived six hours late.*

▸ Adverbs of frequency which do **not** tell us precisely *when* usually come before the verb, except when the verb *to be* is used in which case they come after the verb:

> *They **never go** abroad on holiday.*
> *They **are always** pleased to see their friends.*

▸ Adverbs of frequency which are used in sentences which have more than one part to the verb come after the first part of the verb:

> *They **have often been** abroad on holiday.*
> ***Will** I **ever see** you again?*

▸ Adverbs which tell us the **degree** or the **extent** of something usually come in the middle of a sentence and before the adjective or the verb which they modify or intensify:

> *How old is he?*
> *I don't know exactly, but he's **very old**.*

> *Have you done your homework?*
> *I haven't **quite** finished.*

> *Are you sure Tessa is coming today?*
> *I'm **fairly** sure.*

Note An adverb cannot go between a verb and an object.

UNIT 3

Second conditional

if + simple past + would/could/might + verb base

The second conditional is used when we want to talk about something which is unlikely to happen, although that does not stop us from speculating or hypothesising about it:

*If I **had** the chance, **I would like** to learn Arabic.*
*She **might feel** less nervous living alone **if she lived** in an apartment block instead of a large, detached house.* (in other words, she does live alone in a large detached house)
*If he **saved** more money, **he could retire**.*
*If I **was/were*** younger, **I might take up** roller-skating.*

*When the verb *to be* is used in the *if-* clause, the traditionally correct form of the verb is *were*. However, most English speakers would consider *were* to be rather formal, especially in spoken English, and are more likely to use *was*.

The modal verbs *might* or *could* can be used in place of *would* in the main clause if we want to speculate with less certainty.

Punctuation When the *if-* clause comes first, it is followed by a comma; when the main clause comes first, there is no comma.

Modal verbs 1: expressing possibility and certainty

When we are not sure of something, we can express our ideas as **possibilities**. If we are talking about the present, we use:

$\left.\begin{array}{l} may \\ might \\ could \end{array}\right\}$ + verb base

*The sky is very dark – it **might rain** later.* (you are not sure)

If we are talking about the past, we use:

$\left.\begin{array}{l} may \\ might \\ could \end{array}\right\}$ + have + past participle

*I haven't seen her for so long she **could have changed**.* (it's possible)

Note Continuous forms can also be used:

*She may **be waiting** outside now.*
*They might have **been trying** to phone us, but our line's been engaged.*

When expressing a **negative** possibility, it is not customary to use *may* in contracted form although *mightn't* is acceptable.

*That **may not** have been my brother you saw yesterday.*
*Don't worry about seeing the doctor over the pain in your back – it **mightn't** be serious.*

When we know that something is almost definite because there are certain facts that lead to this conclusion, we can express our ideas as **certainties**. If we are talking about the present, we use:

$\left.\begin{array}{l} must \\ can't \end{array}\right.$ + verb base

*She **must like** Italy as she goes there on holiday every year.* (you are almost certain she likes Italy)

*The rail ticket **can't be** expensive as it's only a short journey.* (you are almost certain it isn't expensive)

If we are talking about the past, we use:

$\left.\begin{array}{l} must \\ can't \end{array}\right.$ + have + past participle

*I'm sure Mick doesn't play golf so you **can't have seen** him on the golf course.* (you are almost certain it wasn't Mick)

*You **must have enjoyed** that concert – I heard it was brilliant!* (you are almost certain of your facts)

Note Continuous forms can also be used:

*You must have **been sitting** there for hours waiting for the bus to arrive.*

Past tenses 1

The regular **past simple** tense in English is formed by adding *-(e)d* to the verb base:

walk → *walked*   **hope → *hoped***

However, many verbs are irregular and the past forms of these do not necessarily follow any pattern:

eat	ate	make	made
fly	flew	put	put
go	went	shrink	shrank
light	lit	throw	threw

In Appendix 1 on page 232 there is a list of irregular verbs which you need to learn in preparation for the FCE examination.

The **past simple** tense is used to describe completed actions or events which took place at a fixed point in the past, or to refer to circumstances which happened in the past:

*When I **was** six, I **lived** with my grandparents for two years.*
*The second world war **ended** in 1945.*
*He **worked** in China from 1988 to 1994.*

The **past continuous** tense is formed by using *was/were* + *-ing*:

> The phone **was ringing**.
> They **were smiling**.

The past continuous tense is used to describe actions or events in the past which were not necessarily completed but were in progress at a point in the past:

> I **was studying** for my exams during my summer holidays in 1995.
> The sun **was shining** as we set out for the mountains.

Sometimes the past continous tense can be 'interrupted' so that while one action is taking place, another action – using the past simple tense – cuts across it or interrupts it:

> I **was talking** to my mother when the doorbell **rang**.

The same tense is also used to describe two (or more) actions which were happening simultaneously in the past:

> While we **were waiting** at one bus stop, our friends **were waiting** for us at another.

Gerunds 2: gerund or infinitive

Some verbs can be followed by *either* the **gerund** *or* the **infinitive** *without making any difference* to the meaning of the sentence:

> **begin   start   continue**

> I **began learning** French when I was six.
> I **began to learn** French when I was six.

With other verbs there is a very slight difference in meaning:

> **like   love   prefer   hate**

Usually the *-ing* form of verbs connected with feeling (or perception), has a generalised meaning:

> I love **going** to festivals in the summer.

When we use these verbs followed by the infinitive, then we often mean that we have an alternative choice or preference in mind:

> I like **to go** to music festivals in the summer.

Some verbs, however, *do change their meaning* depending on whether they are followed by the gerund or the infinitive:

> **remember   forget   stop   regret   go on   try   mean**

remember

> Ali remembered **to phone** his father.
> Ali remembered **phoning** his father.

The use of the infinitive refers to a specific action which Ali had to do, but the use of the gerund means that Ali recollected something he had done in the past.

forget

> I forgot **to buy** some postcards when I was in Pisa.
> I will never forget **meeting** an Ashanti chief in Ghana.

When *forget* is followed by a gerund, it refers back to an event or action. Used with the infinitive, however, it refers to an event or action which has (or has not) been done.

stop

> She stopped **to speak** to her mother.
> She stopped **speaking** to her mother.

The use of the gerund tells us that she is no longer speaking to her mother. The infinitive tells us that she interrupted whatever she was doing in order to speak to her mother.

regret

> I regret **to say** that I have to cancel my holiday.
> I regret **wasting** so much money on that present.

When followed by a gerund, regret refers to an event or situation in the past which you feel sorry about; when followed by the infinitive, however, it means that you feel apologetic about what you are about to say.

go on

*After studying languages, she went on **to become** an interpreter.*

*He went on **moaning** for ages about how unhappy he felt.*

Followed by a gerund *go on* means that an action carries on or continues; followed by the infinitive it means that after one thing finishes, another thing starts.

try

*He jumped into the water and tried **to save** the dog.*
*I tried **learning** Mandarin but it was too difficult.*

When *try* is followed by the gerund it has the idea of attempting something, rather like an experiment; followed by the infinitive it refers to a specific attempt to do something rather difficult.

mean

*He meant **to clean up** the mess in the kitchen but he forgot.*
*Going to university means **studying** for a number of years.*

When followed by the gerund, *mean* has the sense of *involve*. With the infinitive it can only be used in the perfect and past tenses and conveys what a person intended to do but probably didn't do.

The verbs **need** and **want** can be followed by either the **gerund** or the **infinitive**, but the use of the **gerund** makes the meaning **passive**:

*My house **needs/wants painting**. I **need to ring** the decorator as I want to ask him how much it will cost.*

Reported speech 2

The most common reporting verbs are **say** and **tell**:

'You should get a job,' her mother said.
*Her mother **said** (that) she should get a job.*

However, if the reporting verb contains an additional element such as advising, as in the example above, a reporting verb that conveys that element can be used:

*Her mother **advised her to get** a job.*

This structure – **verb + object + infinitive** – is used with certain verbs, including **tell**:

*Her mother **told her to get** a job.*

The most common verbs that use this pattern are:

**advise ask beg force order persuade request
tell warn**

Other useful verbs for reporting speech are used with a **that** clause: **admit complain promise suggest**

'I'll take you to the basketball match on Sunday, Nicky,' his father said.
*Nicky's father **promised that he would take** him to the basketball match on Sunday.*

Promise can also be used with the **infinitive** but **without an object**. The same pattern can be used with **threaten**.

*Nicky's father **promised to take** him to the basketball match on Sunday.*

Expressing wishes and regrets; complaints

The verb **wish + past tense** is used to talk about something which we would like to be different.

Another way of expressing the same idea, but more strongly, is to use **if only**.

When referring to the **present or the future**, both **wish** and **if only** are followed by a past tense:

*I wish I **felt** better – then we could go out.*
*If only I **felt** better – then we could go out.*
(meaning I don't feel better; we can't go out)
*I wish I **was/were*** really rich.*
*If only I **was/were*** really rich.*
(meaning I am not really rich)

***Were** is generally considered to be more formal than **was** (see Unit 3, Second conditional, page 48)

Wish + would (not) is used when we don't like something and/or want to complain about it:

*I wish you **wouldn't** make such a noise. (meaning You are too noisy and I am complaining about it)*

When we want to express a wish about something that happened in the **past**, then we use a **past perfect tense**. For example, imagine you went on holiday with some friends but the holiday was not a success:

*I wish I **hadn't wasted** so much money on that holiday.*
*If only I **hadn't wasted** so much money on that holiday.*

Past tenses 2

The **past perfect simple tense** is formed using **had + past participle** and the **past perfect continuous** using **had been + -ing**.

The past perfect simple is used to refer to an action, event or circumstance in the past which happened **prior to** another action, event or circumstance in the past:

*When he finally got to the airport, the plane **had already left**.*

If we use a **conjunction to indicate the sequence** in which two events happened, then the past simple tense can be used to refer to both events and the **past perfect is not necessary**:

*After he **put/had put** the cat out, he went to bed.*

The past perfect continuous refers to an action, event or circumstance which carries on or is incomplete prior to another action, event or circumstance in the past:

*I **had been sitting** on the grass for quite a while before I realised how damp it was.*

UNIT 5

Linking conditional sentences

There are four ways apart from using *if* to link the two parts of a conditional sentence; the four additional linking words which you need to know at this level are:

1 *unless (if ... not)*
   Unless we do something urgently, the panda will become extinct. (meaning *if we don't act now, the panda will not survive*)

2 *provided (that)*
   Provided (that) people care about the world they live in, there is a good chance that rare species of animals will survive.

3 *as long as*
   As long as people care about the world they live in, there is a good chance that rare species of animals will survive.

2 and 3 are very similar in meaning and suggest that circumstances or conditions depend on other circumstances or conditions.
In 2 the rare species of animals will survive if people care enough about their world.
In 3 *as long as* suggests that rare animals will survive for the length of time people continue to care about their world.

4 *suppose*
   Suppose we all behaved just as we liked, the world would be a very selfish place. (meaning *imagine what would happen if we behaved just as we liked ...*)

Verbs followed by the infinitive

Just as certain verbs must be followed by a gerund, so other verbs are followed by the infinitive.
   *I've **decided to move** to a house in the country.*
   *Kay is **learning to drive**.*

The most common verbs which take the infinitive are:

afford	expect	offer
agree	fail	pretend
appear	happen	promise
arrange	hope	refuse
ask	learn	seem
choose	manage	threaten
decide	mean	

   want (active use only, e.g. *I want to see you*)
   need (active use only, e.g. *I need to see you*)

too/enough (+ for) + infinitive; so + that

If we want to show that something is excessive or more than is desirable, we use *too* + **adjective or adverb**:
   *As for life on other planets, Mercury is **too** hot on one side and **too** cold on the other.*

This pattern is often used with *for* + **infinitive** to show a consequential relationship:
   *Mercury is **too** hot **for** us **to live** there.*

The same idea can be expressed using *so + that*:
   *The heat is **so** great **that** we couldn't live there.*

We can also use **enough** in a similar way to mean that something is adequate or sufficient to meet one's needs:
   *The tent is big **enough for** us **to use** when we go camping again this year.*
   *Mercury is **not** temperate **enough for** anyone **to live** there.*

Not enough can therefore be used to express the same idea as *too* with an adjective that means the opposite:
   *It's **too small**.*
   *It's **not big enough**.*

Future tenses 1

The **future** can be expressed in many different ways. The choice of which tense to use depends on the speaker's intention and the degree of emphasis in what is said.

The **simple future tense** – *will/shall* + **verb base** – is used for:
▸ predictions
   *Tomorrow it **will be** cold and cloudy throughout the country.*
▸ promises
   *After getting into so much trouble, I'll never **tell** another lie.*
▸ threats
   *Don't tell my secret to anyone or I'll never **speak** to you again.*
▸ offers
   *I'll **take** you to the concert.*
▸ suggestions
   ***Shall** we **eat** out this evening?*
▸ making a sudden or spontaneous decision
   *What a lovely day! I'll **make** a picnic to take to the beach.*
▸ expressing opinions
   *I expect you **will be** hungry after all that exercise.*

Note It is unusual to use *shall* other than when making suggestions and then it is generally only used with the first person singular and plural.

The **present continuous tense** (+ **time reference**) is used for talking about arrangements in the future which have already been made:

I'm meeting my brother this evening.

The **present simple tense** is used for talking about future fixed events, programmes and timetables:

Lunch is at 1 o'clock on Saturdays.
The train leaves at 16.45.

The *going to* form is used for expressing plans and intentions and events that are likely to happen:

I'm going to take a holiday in August.
I'm going to ask for a pay rise.
There's going to be a storm – it's so dark.

UNIT 6

Using the passive

When we use the **passive form**, the subject of the sentence is the thing or the person affected by the action.

Most verbs which take an object (**transitive verbs**) can be used in the passive:

Shakespeare wrote many plays.
Many plays were written by Shakespeare.

Verbs which do not take an object (**intransitive**) cannot be used in the passive:

The moon rose high in the sky.

The passive is formed using the verb *to be* in an appropriate tense + **the past participle** of the main verb.

Tense	Subject	Verb *to be*	Past participle
Present simple	*Newspapers*	**are**	**printed** *daily.*
Present continuous	*A new airport*	**is being**	**built**.
Past simple	*The company*	**was**	**established** *in 1943.*
Past continuous	*A hole*	**was being**	**dug** *for a new water tank.*
Present perfect	*Applicants who*	**have been**	**offered** *a job will hear soon.*
Past perfect	*People at risk*	**had been**	**given** *vaccinations.*
Future simple	*You*	**will be**	**told** *when you can go in.*
Future perfect	*Your fax*	**will have been**	**received** *by now.*
Modals (present)	*Your feet*	**should be**	**looked** *after.*
	Your heart	**must be**	**checked**.
Modals (past)	*This letter*	**shouldn't have been**	**opened**.
	This parcel	**can't have been**	**weighed**.

Note The present perfect continous, the future continuous and the future perfect continuous passives are rarely used.

Verb + direct object + infinitive without *to*

Some verbs take a **direct object** before the **infinitive without** *to*:

> *make   let*
> *His father **made him finish** his meal before leaving the table.*
> *Can you **let me know** what time your train gets in?*

The most common verbs using this pattern, sometimes referred to as verbs of perception, are:

> *feel   hear   notice   see   smell   watch*

They are used without *to* when the action is completely experienced:

> *I **felt the cobwebs brush** my face as I opened the attic door.*
> *I **heard him shout** as he slipped on the ice.*
> *I **saw him give** the stranger a small package.*

The same verbs of perception can be followed by the **gerund** when the action is only partly experienced:

> *I **heard his key turning** in the lock.*

Note *Help* can be used with or without *to* with no change of meaning.

Gerunds 3: after prepositions

The **gerund** is used after all **prepositions**:

> *Marcia was awarded a prize **for coming** top in the exams, and **on hearing** the news she burst into tears.*

As well as knowing that verbs following prepositions take the gerund, it is important to know which prepositions follow certain adjectives and verbs.

Adjective + preposition + *-ing*

> *When I was at school I was **afraid of making** mistakes.*

afraid capable frightened terrified	+ of
bad clever good skilled	+ at
bored fed up	+ with
interested	+ in
keen	+ on
sorry responsible	+ for

Verb + preposition + *-ing*

> *She **succeeded in learning** Spanish while working for a year in Argentina.*

depend insist rely	+ on
be accustomed look forward object	+ to
apologise arrest someone	+ for
succeed	+ in
congratulate someone	+ on
warn someone	+ about
prevent someone	+ from

Future tenses 2

The **future continuous tense** – *will + be + -ing* – is used for:

- plans taking place in the future
  > *What **will you be doing** in August?*
  > *I'll **be playing** in two concerts then I'll **be taking a holiday**.*
- developments or changes that we expect will happen at some point in the future
  > *In a hundred years' time perhaps **we will be taking** holidays on the moon.*

The **future perfect simple** and **future perfect continuous** tenses are used for anticipating a specfic point in the future when a situation or circumstance taking place over a period of time will be completed:

> *By 1998 **I'll have been** at university for 5 years.*

> *How long have you been learning English?*
> *By the end of this month **I'll have been learning** English for 3 years.*

223

would rather; it's time

We use **would rather/it's time** + **past** tense to convey wishes referring to the present or future:

> *I'd rather you didn't tell anyone my secret.* (meaning *I'd prefer it if you didn't …*)
> *It's time you told me your secret!* (conveying slight impatience as well as a feeling that you have waited long enough for something)

If we want to convey greater impatience as well as a feeling that time is important, we use the more emphatic **it's about time** or **it's high time**:

> *It's about time you grew up!*
> *It's high time she learnt how to behave.*

Modal verbs 2: expressing obligation and necessity; permission and prohibition

Obligation and necessity

Must + **verb base** expresses strong obligation and is used:

▶ when we need to convey legal conditions as well as an individual speaker's authority
> *You **must** apply for a visa if you want to visit China.*

▶ when we want to exert pressure, even if the situation is quite informal
> *You **must** get your hair cut; you look a real mess!*

▶ for personal obligation
> *I **must** study harder and go out less.*

In its **negative** form it is used to:

▶ express what is forbidden by law
> *You **mustn't** drive without a licence or you'll be arrested.*

▶ convey strong advice
> *You **mustn't** go into the recording studio when the red light is on or the producer will be furious.*

Note The past tense of *must* is *had to:*
> *He **had to** wear a uniform when he was in the army.*

Have to + **verb base** is used in impersonal contexts to:

▶ convey indirect authority from a third person, rather than an individual
> *We **have to** check in at the airport at least two hours before the flight.*

▶ express a rule or law in an emphatic way
> *You will **have to** wear a uniform when you start school in the UK next year.*

In its negative form with the auxiliary verb *do*, it is used to express the absence of obligation or necessity:

> *You **don't have to** wear school unifrom if you want to go to school in Germany.*

Have got to + **verb base** is more informal than *have to* and is often used in spoken English when the speaker may feel rather irritated and wants to place emphasis on what is being said:

> *You **have got to** learn to look after your belongings more carefully – I almost stepped on that brand new watch which you'd left on the bathroom floor!*

In its **negative** form it also carries an emphatic tone, suggesting that the speaker's intention is the opposite of what is being said:

> *You **haven't got to** take the FCE but it will be very useful in your future career if you do.*

Should + **verb base** and **ought to** + **verb base** are used when the idea of obligation is not as strong as an order but is closer to giving advice, or making a suggestion or recommendation. There is no difference in meaning between the two verbs:

> *You **should** wear a thick coat when you go out as it's bitterly cold.*
> *You **ought to** wear a thick coat when you go out as it's bitterly cold.*

In their **negative** forms they are also used to express advice, suggestions and recommendations in a more emphatic way:

> *You **shouldn't** leave without saying goodbye to your tutor.*
> *You **oughtn't to** leave the lights on when you go out.*

Need (to) is not strictly a modal verb, but it is included here as it is used to express the idea of something being necessary, although not (legally) obligatory:

> *If you want to be invited to Nina's party next week, you will **need to** apologise for being so rude to her last night.*

In its **negative** form it is used, like *don't have to*, to express the absence of necessity or obligation. It can be used without *to* or with the auxiliary verb *do*:

> *You **needn't** read the whole book, just the opening chapters.*
> *You **do not need to** read the whole book, just the opening chapters.*

Needn't have + **past participle** is used when we want to refer to something that happened in the past which turned out to be unnecessary:

> *I paid a booking fee when I reserved the tickets by phone. However, when we arrived, the theatre was half empty, so in fact I **needn't have** booked the tickets in advance.*

Did not need to + **verb base** is used to refer to something in the past which was not done because it was unnecessary:

> *I **didn't need to** ring my cousin to tell him the news as I would see him that evening anyway.*

Permission and prohibition

The most common way of asking for and refusing permission is to use *can/can't:*

> *Can I borrow your camera?*
> *No, you can't.*

May is also used, although this is rather formal as it is less direct than *can* and is therefore considered to be more polite. The negative is similarly very formal and sounds very emphatic:

> *May I borrow the car tomorrow?*
> *No, you may not. (not mayn't)*

Comparatives and superlatives

Adjectives and adverbs

Adjectives

When we want to compare things, we use the following patterns with *than*.
Adjectives of one or two syllables usually add *-er* and *-est*; look carefully at the spelling rules in bold type:

Adjective	Comparative	Superlative
cheap	cheap**er**	cheap**est**
wise	wis**er**	wis**est**
big	big**ger**	big**gest**
happy	happ**ier**	happ**iest**

> *A second-hand VW is cheaper than a Fiat 500, but a 2CV is cheapest of all.*

Adjectives of three or more syllables use *more/less* and *most/least:*

> *A Fiat 500 is more expensive than a 2CV, but a Rover 100 is the most expensive car.*

Although most long adjectives use *more, most* etc., some adjectives with two syllables can be used in their comparative and superlative forms with either the suffix endings *-er, -est* or in conjunction with the comparative/superlative adverbs *more, most* etc.:

> *The road was at its **narrowest** where the mountains ran down to the edge of the lake.*
> *The **most narrow** part of the road was where the mountains ran down to the edge of the lake.*

Certain adjectives of two syllables, however, only use *more, most* etc., e.g. *careful, boring.*

IRREGULAR ADJECTIVES

Adjective	Comparative	Superlative
bad	worse	worst
far	farther/further	farthest/furthest
good	better	best
old	older	oldest
old	elder*	eldest*

* used to talk about the order in which children are born:
> *Charles is the elder (of two), but he is older than me (not elder than me).*

It is also possible to form comparisons using:
as + **adjective/adverb** + **as** + **noun/pronoun** etc.
> *Insurance for a 2CV is **as expensive as** insurance for a Fiat.*

In a **negative** structure it is possible to use **not so/as** + **adjective** + **as**:
> *A 2CV is **not so expensive as** a Fiat.*

In informal structures especially, **pronouns** can be used in the position of the object after **as**:
> *Hilary doesn't play the piano **as well as me**.*

In more formal language, however, the structure is more likely to be:
> *Hilary doesn't play the piano **as well as I do**.*

We can use a variety of words to **modify** these expressions. Some of the most common (or commonest!) include:
> ***nearly   a lot   much   a little   (quite) a bit***

> *A 2CV is **nearly** as fast as a Fiat.*
> *A Rover is **a lot** faster than a 2CV.*
> *A Jaguar is **much** faster than most cars.*
> *A Fiat 500 is **a bit** faster than a 2CV, but **not much** (faster).*
> *A Porsche is **a little** faster than a Rover.*

Adverbs

Adverb	Comparative	Superlative
carefully	more carefully	most carefully
wisely	more wisely	most wisely
quickly	more quickly	most quickly

IRREGULAR ADVERBS

badly	worse	worst
little	less	the least
much	more	the most

IDENTICAL ADVERBS AND ADJECTIVES

fast	faster	fastest
hard	harder	hardest
long	longer	longest
straight	straighter	straightest

used to, be used to, get used to

Used to + **verb base** refers to a **past habit** or **discontinued state**:

> I **used to drive** a bubble car but now I drive a Citroën ZX.
> I **used to love** ice-cream when I was a child, but now I hate the stuff.

Used to + **gerund** refers to something that is a **regular occurrence** where it may have taken some time to adjust to the circumstances:

> I'm **used to driving** fast cars.
> I've worked at home for 3 years now so I'm **used to being** on my own all day.

Get used to + **gerund** refers to the action of **adjusting to new circumstances**:

> It took me a long time to **get used to driving** on the right when I moved to France. (but I am used to it now)
> I've **got used to being** on my own and now I think I'd find it quite difficult to share a place with anyone else.

UNIT 8

Third conditional

if+ **past perfect** + *would/could/might* + **past participle**

The third conditional is used when we want to talk about something in the past which didn't happen, although that doesn't stop us from speculating or hypothesising about it:

> **If I had had** the opportunity, **I would have become** an actress.
> **You wouldn't have got** wet if you **had taken** an umbrella.

The modal verbs *might* or *could* can be used in place of *would* if we want to speculate with less certainty.

Punctuation When the *if*- clause comes first, it is followed by a comma; when the main clause comes first, there is no comma.

have/get something done

Have/get + **object** + **past participle** are known as **causative verbs** – they cause something to be done; there is no difference in the passive meaning of the past participle, but *get* is slightly more informal than *have*.
This structure is used when we want to refer to things which are **done for us** or **to us** by other people:

> He had to **have** the computer **repaired** before he could finish the project.

Have/get can also be used in a **non-causative** way when we want to say that something happened to a person but they were not responsible for the action:

> Jill **had** her car **broken into** after leaving it in the street overnight.
> Dick took so many biscuits off the plate that he **got** his hand **smacked**.

Negative prefixes

The most common **negative prefix** is *un-*; although there are no fixed rules for which prefix to use when, other negative prefixes include:

> *dis- il- im- in- ir-*

Words beginning with *l* often take *il-*: **illogical**
Words beginning with *m* or *p* often
take *im-*: **impossible**
Words beginning with *r* often take *ir-*: **irrelevant**

Using *it*

We use *it* as a personal pronoun when we want to refer to something which is neither male nor female – like the title of a film or an object, a place, or an abstract idea or concept. We also use *it* when we either don't know the sex of what we are referring to or it isn't necessary or important to even mention it:

*I must show you my new camera – **it** takes excellent pictures.*
Did you go to Hollywood when you were in the States?
  *Yes – **it** was an amazing place but I wouldn't want to live there.*
***It** is not a good idea to make cinema prices too expensive otherwise people won't want to go.*
*Look at the baby – isn't **it** sweet!*
*You can pick up the kitten – **it** likes being stroked.*

When we want to refer to a person or identify someone, we use *it* – even though we know whether the person is male or female.

*Who's that waving to you – is **it** your brother?*

It is used impersonally to make any comment about time, weather, distance, temperature or just an existing situation. In these examples *it* does not refer back to any noun or noun group:

***It**'s very hot in this theatre.*
***It**'s lovely to see you again!*
***It**'s eight o'clock – time to go.*
***It**'s about two kilometres to the concert hall.*
***It**'s really not fair to keep everyone standing in a queue for so long.*

After certain verbs, those which describe how we feel or react to places or situations (*enjoy, dislike, hate, like, love, prefer*), *it* is used as an object:

*They hate **it** here – I would prefer **it** if they didn't come.*

In certain **impersonal expressions** when we want to avoid mentioning who is responsible for an opinion, we use *it* with a passive verb form. This structure is very useful in written English in reporting ideas, for example:

***It** is generally believed that happy people are healthy people.*
***It** has been said that we can expect to live longer in the 21st century.*

Other common verbs used with *it* in impersonal structures:
accept   agree   consider   decide
feel (in the sense of *consider*)   hope   know   realise
report   suggest   understand

Link words

Link words are used to join ideas in sentences in a variety of ways.

To express contrast:

▶ *but, while, whereas*
*I plan on going to Tenerife, **but** my daughter is going to Madeira.*

These link words usually occur between two clauses.

▶ *although, (even) though*
***Although** it was very cold, Bill went for a walk without a coat.*
***Even though** it was very cold, Bill went for a walk without a coat.*

These link words can come before or after the main clause:
*Bill went for a walk without a coat **although** it was very cold.*

▶ *however*
*I am very busy. **However**, I hope to be able to take a short holiday.*

However can be placed at the beginning, in the middle or at the end of a sentence; if it is used in the middle of a sentence, it has a comma before and after:
*I am very busy. I hope, **however,** to be able to take a short holiday.*

▶ *despite the fact that, despite + -ing, in spite of the fact that, in spite of + -ing*
***Despite the fact that** she was very tired, she managed to complete the climb.*
***In spite of being** very tired, she managed to complete the climb.*

▶ *on the one hand ... on the other hand*
***On the one hand**, I dislike flying; **on the other hand**, it's the fastest way of travelling long distances.*

On the other hand can be used alone to begin a new sentence:
*Scientists are worried about the effects of global warming. **On the other hand**, it is possible that their predictions may be wrong.*

To express purpose:

▶ *in order (not) to, so as (not) to*
*He opened the door very quietly **in order not to** wake anyone up.*

▶ *in order that, so that*
*I am saving all the money I can **so that** I'll be able to go on a round-the-world trip.*

To express reason:

▶ *as, since, because*
  *They are entitled to cheap travel **since** they are over 65.*

▶ *owing to the fact that*
  ***Owing to the fact that** there was a rail strike, more people went to work by car.*

These link words can come before or after the main clause.

▶ *due to the fact that*
  *The breakdown in the programme was **due to the fact that** there was a major power failure at the TV centre.*

To express result:

▶ *so*
  *She was hungry **so** she had something to eat.*

▶ *so + adjective (**that**), such + noun (**that**)*
  *The film was **so** good (**that**) I saw it twice.*
  *It was **such** a good film (**that**) I saw it twice.*

▶ *consequently, as a result, therefore*
  *Cathy was feeling under a lot of pressure. **Consequently**, she cancelled her trip abroad.*
  *She was very good at her job as and **as a result** was offered promotion to managing director.*
  *He has decided to retire next year and **therefore** is selling his house.*

To express time:

▶ *when, as, while*
  *I'll see you **when** I get back from holiday.*
  ***While** she was waiting for the bus, it began to rain.*

▶ *whenever*
  ***Whenever** I see Carol, she's always wearing something new.*

For emphasis or extra information:

▶ *furthermore, besides*
  *I've been to the US a number of times. **Besides**, I'd like to go somewhere new for a change.*

These link words usually occur at the beginning of a sentence.

▶ *as well as + -ing/a phrase/an individual word:*
  ***As well as being** beautiful, she is also extremely clever.*
  *He married her because she was clever **as well as** beautiful.*

▶ *moreover*
  He had spent a great deal of money on furnishing the new apartment. ***Moreover***, everything he had bought was made to order.

Moreover can be used at the beginning, in the middle or at the end of a sentence; if it is used in the middle of a sentence, it has a comma before and after.

So and *such*

So and *such* are used when we are expressing result and we want to emphasise an adjective or adverb:

▶ *so + adjective/adverb (**that**)* (see Link words)
  *I think Marta is **so** kind.*
  *He does his homework **so** quickly (**that**) he makes lots of mistakes.*

▶ *such + adjective + plural countable noun (**that**)*
  *She tells **such** wonderful stories (**that**) I could listen to her for hours.*

▶ *such + adjective + uncountable noun (**that**)*
  *He makes **such** good furniture (**that**) it lasts for years.*

▶ *such a + adjective + singular countable noun (**that**)*
  *He's **such** a bad-tempered man (**that**) I'm not surprised he's so unpopular.*

Question tags

Question tags are used with a **rising intonation** in spoken English if we are asking a question and **we are not sure** of the answer:

*Dave's not really resigning, **is he?***

(The speaker doesn't know whether the answer will be *Yes, he is* or *No, he isn't*.)

Question tags are used with a **falling intonation** if we are **seeking confirmation or agreement**:

*Cézanne was a superb artist, **wasn't he?***

(The speaker expects the answer to be *Yes, he was*.)

Question tags usually come at the end of a sentence; they are usually contracted, although they may not be in very formal English:

*You're his brother, **aren't you?***
*He did say the court case had finished, **did he not?***

Generally speaking, questions tags are used after statements and not questions.

If the statement is positive, then the question tag is negative; if the statement is negative, the tag is positive:

*It's a lovely day today, **isn't it?***
*It's **not** raining, **is it?***

After a **full verb** in a statement, the question tag is formed using the auxiliary verb *do*. It must be in the same tense as the full verb:

*The train leaves soon, **doesn't it?***
*He played that piece really well, **didn't he?***

If the statement contains an **auxiliary verb**, e.g. *have*, or a **modal auxiliary verb**, e.g. *can*, or **non-auxiliary verb** *be*, this is then repeated in the question tag:

> *You **haven't** seen my pen, **have you**?** *
> *You **can** meet me tonight, **can't you**?*
> *I'm next in the queue, **aren't I**? (not amn't I)*

*When we want to ask for information or help politely, it is common to put the statement in the negative and add a question tag.

After **imperatives** it is customary to use *will you/won't you/would you/can you/could you*:

> *Pass me the salt, **will you**? (or **won't you/would you/can you/could you**)*

When the imperative is in the **negative**, then only *will you* is possible: ***Don't touch** that wet paint, **will you**?*

When the statement contains words like *everybody, no one, nobody* and *somebody*, the question tag uses *they*:

> ***Nobody** called while I was out, **did they**?*
> ***Somebody** told you the truth, **didn't they**?*

Using determiners to express quantity

There are some basic rules for using **determiners**; the following list shows those words which can **only** be used with:

▶ **singular countable nouns**
  another each either every neither
  Every package holiday has free insurance.

▶ **plural countable nouns**
  both few many other several
  Several tourists felt unwell during the trip.

▶ **uncountable nouns**
  less little much
  *The countries in the northern hemisphere have **less** sun than those on the equator.*

Note *Much* and *many* are generally used in **negative** statements and questions, and *a lot of* is generally used when the statement is in the **affirmative**:

> *How **much** foreign money **have you got** left?*
> *I **haven't many** notes but I've got **a lot of** coins.*

Take care when using **(a) little** and **(a) few**; look at the difference in meaning in these examples:

> *A **little** rain fell during the summer months.* (meaning *some rain, but not much*)
> ***Little** rain fell during the summer months.* (meaning *almost no rain*)
> *There were **a few** of my friends at the party last night.* (meaning *some friends, but not many*)
> *There were **few** of my friends at the party last night.* (meaning *hardly any friends*)

The determiners which can be used with **both singular** and **plural countable** and **uncountable** nouns are:

▶ *all any no enough more most some*
  *Is that **all** the **butter** that's left?*
  *Have you bought **enough books** or not?*

UNIT 10

Relative clauses: identifying (defining) and non-identifying (non-defining)

A **relative clause** uses a **relative pronoun**: *who, whom, which, whose, that*, or **no relative pronoun** at all – which is often the case in spoken English.

Deciding which pronoun to use depends on whether:

▶ the pronoun refers to a person or a thing
▶ it is the subject, object or possessive of the relative clause
▶ the relative clause is identifying (defining) or non-identifying (non-defining).

There are two kinds of relative clause

1 **Identifying clauses**
  The information in the identifying relative clause is **essential** to the meaning of the sentence as it identifies and explains what is being referred to. The sentence would not make sense without the relative clause:
  *The person **who** broke that vase should offer to replace it.*
  *The language area **which** is really difficult for me is grammar.*

The relative clause usually comes straight after the noun it refers to and is not separated by commas (in written English) nor any break or pause in spoken English.

2 **Non-identifying clauses**
  In the non-identifying relative clause the information is **not essential** in order to understand what the sentence means as it conveys additional information about the noun it refers to:
  *Living conditions, **which** vary from country to country, affect our health.*

Non-identifying clauses tend to be more formal, and less common in informal speech. This type of relative clause also usually comes straight after the noun it refers to, but it is generally marked by commas in written English and by breaks or pauses in rhythm and intonation in spoken English.

The relative pronouns are usually used as follows:

▶ *who* and *which* are usually used to refer to people and are more common in written English
▶ *that* is usually used to refer to things and is more common in spoken English. It can never be used in non-identifying clauses
▶ *who, which* and *that* can be omitted from identifying relative clauses when they refer to the object of the verb in the clause:
  *If you saw a child **(whom)** you knew sleeping in the street ...*

However, it is not possible to omit the relative pronoun when the verbs are in the passive:

> Studies **which are being carried out** by scientists show ...

Remember that in identifying clauses the information is essential to the meaning, and in non-identifying clauses the information can be removed without affecting the meaning of the sentence.

Compound nouns and phrasal nouns

Compound nouns and **phrasal nouns** may be written as one word, two separate words or with a hyphen (-) between the two words, e.g. *take-away*.

However, the use of the hyphen in these nouns is not very clear; so you should use a dictionary to check whether a word has a hyphen or not. If you can't look it up, then leave out the hyphen and write the word as one word if it is a fairly short word, e.g. *bathroom, weekend, football* and as two words if it is longer, e.g. *bus driver, heart attack*.

Making comparisons

Apart from using the comparative and superlative, it is also possible to make comparisons using this double structure:
the + comparative + *the* + comparative:

> **The more** people earn, **the meaner** they become.
> **The more tired** I am, **the better** I sleep.
> **The less** I see of Mick, **the better**.
> **The less** I eat, **the more** weight I'll lose.

Common expressions for comparing quantities are:
twice/three times etc. + *as* + adjective:

> I am **twice as fond** of coffee **as** I am of tea.
> There are **three times as** many girls **as** boys in my class.

It is also possible to use words in front of the first *as* or *so** in the *as/so ... as* pattern, which modify the meaning:

> Boys are not **nearly so** giggly **as** girls.
> Jan is not **quite as** tall **as** her brother.
> The figures for smoking among teenage girls are **almost as** high **as** those among teenage boys.
> The figures for divorce in the UK are **just as** high this year **as** they were three years ago.

*So can only be used in the negative.

UNIT 11

Participles and participle clauses

There are three types of participle:

▶ **present participles**, formed from the **verb base + -*ing*:**
> *She was a model student, **working** hard to get her degree.* (*working* replaces the relative clause *who worked*)

> *He called in to see his mother when **going** to collect the children from school.* (*going* could be expressed by *as he went* to show that the action in both the main and subordinate clauses happened simultaneously)

> *I have just read the most **entertaining** book.* (*entertaining* acts like an adjective before the noun *book*)

▶ **past participles**, formed from the **verb + -*(e)d*** or its irregular form and often passive in meaning:
> *A short poem, **written** by a young child, won first prize.* (*written* replaces the relative clause *which was written*)

▶ **perfect participles**, *formed using **having** + past participle*
> *Last week, **having caught** the train to work, I realised I had left my briefcase at home.* (the use of the perfect participle makes the sequence of events clear: *I caught the train **before** I realised I had left my briefcase at home*)

> *Sally was the most **admired** teacher in the college.* (*admired* acts like an adjective before *teacher*)

Negative participles are formed using **not**:
> ***Not** having paid his phone bill, Ted had his line disconnected by the telephone company.*

Note The subject of the participle and the other verb in the sentence must always be the same.

Compound adjectives

A **compound adjective** is made up of an **adjective + participle** and is frequently used to describe people:
> *He is a **well-built, hot-tempered** young man.*

Compound adjectives made up of a **number (adjective) + noun** are frequently used to describe the size, the age, the weight or the length of things:
> *a **two-litre** bottle of water*
> *a **five-year** old girl*
> *a **three-kilo** bag of potatoes*
> *a **twenty-mile** journey*

Compound adjectives are usually hyphenated if they occur before a noun – *a **well-known** writer* – but not hyphenated if they occur after the noun – *a writer who is **well known**.*

make / let / allow

Make often means cause something to happen:

> He **made** me laugh even though I didn't think he was really
> funny.
>
> He **made** me look a fool.
>
> (*make* + object + infinitive without *to*)
>
> She **made** me angry; she **made** me sad.
>
> (*make* + object + adjective)

Make is also used when we want to convey the idea of
wanting to compel or force, and give little or no choice:

> The teacher **made** Pierre finish the exercise before he went
> home.
>
> My parents always **made** me eat spinach when I was a child.

If used passively to convey the idea of being compelled or
forced, *make* is followed by the infinitive + *to*:

> Most of us were **made to** go to bed early when we were
> children.
>
> The prisoners were **made to** walk miles without food or
> drink.

Now look at the contrast with **let**, which in this context
conveys the feeling of not being compelled:

> The teacher **let** Pierre go home before he had finished the
> exercise.
>
> My parents **let** me stay out late when I was a teenager if I
> was with friends.
>
> (*let* + object + infinitive without *to*)

However, *let* cannot be used in the passive; **allow to** must
be used instead:

> I was **allowed to** stay out late when I was a teenager if I was
> with friends.

Appendix 1

Irregular verbs

Verb base	Past simple	Past participle	Verb base	Past simple	Past participle
be	was/were	been	lose	lost	lost
bear	bore	borne	make	made	made
beat	beat	beat	mean	meant	meant
become	became	become	meet	met	met
begin	began	begun	pay	paid	paid
bend	bent	bent	put	put	put
bet	bet	bet	read	read	read
bind	bound	bound	ride	rode	ridden
bite	bit	bitten	ring	rang	rung
bleed	bled	bled	rise	rose	risen
blow	blew	blown	run	ran	run
break	broke	broken	saw	sawed	sawn
bring	brought	brought	say	said	said
build	built	built	see	saw	seen
burn	burnt/burned	burnt/burned	sell	sold	sold
burst	burst	burst	send	sent	sent
buy	bought	bought	set	set	set
catch	caught	caught	sew	sewed	sewn
choose	chose	chosen	shake	shook	shaken
come	came	come	shine	shone	shone
cost	cost	cost	shoot	shot	shot
creep	crept	crept	show	showed	shown/showed
cut	cut	cut	shrink	shrank	shrunk
deal	dealt	dealt	shut	shut	shut
dig	dug	dug	sing	sang	sung
do	did	done	sink	sank	sunk
draw	drew	drawn	sit	sat	sat
dream	dreamt/dreamed	dreamt/dreamed	sleep	slept	slept
drink	drank	drunk	slide	slid	slid
drive	drove	driven	smell	smelt/smelled	smelt/smelled
eat	ate	eaten	sow	sowed	sown
fall	fell	fallen	speak	spoke	spoken
feed	fed	fed	spell	spelt/spelled	spelt/spelled
feel	felt	felt	spend	spent	spent
fight	fought	fought	spill	spilt/spilled	spilt/spilled
find	found	found	spin	spun	spun
fly	flew	flown	spoil	spoilt/spoiled	spoilt/spoiled
forbid	forbade	forbidden	spread	spread	spread
forget	forgot	forgotten	spring	sprang	sprung
forgive	forgave	forgiven	stand	stood	stood
freeze	froze	frozen	steal	stole	stolen
get	got	got	stick	stuck	stuck
give	gave	given	sting	stung	stung
go	went	gone	strike	struck	struck
grind	ground	ground	sweep	swept	swept
grow	grew	grown	swell	swelled	swollen
hang	hung, (hanged)	hung, (hanged)*	swear	swore	sworn
have	had	had	swim	swam	swum
hear	heard	heard	swing	swung	swung
hide	hid	hidden	take	took	taken
hit	hit	hit	teach	taught	taught
hold	held	held	tear	tore	torn
hurt	hurt	hurt	tell	told	told
keep	kept	kept	think	thought	thought
know	knew	known	throw	threw	thrown
lay	laid	laid	understand	understood	understood
lead	led	led	wake	woke	woken
lean	leant/leaned	leant/leaned	wear	wore	worn
learn	learnt/learned	learnt/learned	weep	wept	wept
leave	left	left	win	won	won
lend	lent	lent	wind	wound	wound
let	let	let	write	wrote	written
lie	lay	lain			
light	lit	lit			

* They hung the picture on the wall.
The prisoner was hanged at dawn.

Appendix 2

Phrasal verbs and phrasal nouns

In addition to the phrasal verbs and nouns already covered, the following list further contextualises the most frequently occurring phrasal verbs and phrasal nouns at First Certificate level.

break

Too much stress at work can lead to a nervous **breakdown**.

A cure for the common cold would be a scientific **breakthrough**.

After the **break-up** of her marriage, Rosemary decided to move to another town.

She **broke down** in tears when she heard the news of the murder.

The car kept **breaking down** so the journey took hours.

Thieves **broke into** the bank and stole thousands of pounds.

He **broke off** in the middle of a sentence as the doorbell rang.

As the fire spread, some prisoners managed to **break out** of the building and escape.

Some of the statues in the park have been **broken up** by vandals and completely destroyed.

bring

That music **brings back** memories of my youth.

The government will be **bringing in** a new law on guns next year.

It took doctors more than an hour to **bring** the woman **round** after she lost consciousness.

I was **brought up** in a small village in Hungary.

burst

The door flew open and a masked man **burst into** the room.

She **burst out** laughing so loudly that people near her were quite startled.

call

The manager was **called away** during the meeting by an urgent message.

I'll **call for** you around 6 o'clock but I might be a little late.

The football match was **called off** owing to the bad weather.

care

I **don't care** for this new coffee; do you like it?

carry

Don't stop what you're doing – **carry on** with your painting and I'll watch you!

catch

Do you think this craze for wearing black lipstick will **catch on**? I've seen quite a few girls with black lips recently.

After being away ill, Jeff had quite a lot of work to **catch up on** before he could look at what was in his in-tray.

check

If you intend **checking in** after 18.00 hours, please inform hotel reception in advance.

Check-in times at the airport vary depending on the length of your flight.

clear

'You kids **clear off** or I'll call the police,' the caretaker yelled.

Make sure you **clear out** all your drawers before I sell that old furniture.

I'm having a big **clear-out** before I buy any new furniture.

If the weather **clears up** later, shall we go for a walk?

come

I **came across** this old picture when I was clearing out the cellar.

House prices have **come down** in recent months owing to the recession.

He **came round** from the operation within an hour and was soon up and about.

He's **come up against** a number of difficulties in the past but he's never allowed them to upset his plans.

count

If you're organising a skiing trip, **count** me **in** – I love skiing.

You can always **count on** Viktor to help you if you've got a problem.

cross

When she saw the cost of the skiing trip, she **crossed** her name **out** as she couldn't afford to go.

cut

The recent **cutbacks** in staffing levels have meant that some people have been made redundant.

Now that we have less income we'll have to **cut back** our expenses and try to save money.

Cutting down on food is not a very sensible way of saving money.

I'm on a diet which means I have to **cut out** all fatty foods.

do

The government is planning on **doing away with** rural post offices which run at a loss.

During the drought people had to **do without** watering their gardens or washing their cars.

draw

How much money shall I **draw out of** the bank account for our holiday?

drop

If you're going past the college, could you **drop** me **off**, please?

The lecture was so boring that she **dropped off** and didn't wake up until everyone was leaving.

Young people who feel that society has nothing to offer them may end up as **dropouts** with no fixed address and no means of supporting themselves.

fall

Since being away Freya has **fallen behind** with her work and is finding it difficult to catch up with the rest of the class.

We had hoped for a quiet weekend, but with the arrival of unexpected friends our plans **fell through**.

get

I can see what you're **getting at**, but I don't agree with your ideas.

The lorry was parked in such a way that no other traffic could **get by**.

The long, cold, dark evenings are really **getting** me **down** – I wish spring would come.

How are you **getting on with** your new job – do you like it?

Whenever there's washing-up to do, my brother always manages to **get out of** doing it.

I always meant to learn a foreign language but somehow I never **got round to** it.

give

His red face and nervous manner when he was questioned about the theft were a complete **giveaway**.

The spy stayed hidden for months, but a light at his window one night eventually **gave** him **away** and he was caught.

She refused to **give in** to the pain and continued working despite being very ill.

I've **given up** eating chocolate because it's so bad for my teeth.

go

A number of students have **gone down with** food poisoning.

What does your allowance **go on**? I spend most of mine on food and travel.

Once the tide has **gone out**, we'll be able to walk along the beach.

The detective **went over** the suspect's statement and checked every detail.

Do you think this red shirt **goes with** these trousers, or do the colours clash?

hang

What are you doing **hanging about** here so late? Shouldn't you be at home?

He **hung up** in the middle of what I was saying.

hold

The supplies of fresh water **held out** for a few days but then dried up completely.

I missed my flight owing to a **hold-up** on the motorway.

keep

I think you ought to tell the police everything that happened and not **keep** anything **back**.

The management sacked some of the workforce but **kept on** the younger people.

You will have to work very hard if you want to **keep up with** the others who have been learning Russian for two years already.

knock

The team was **knocked out** in the first round of the competition and went home feeling very disappointed.

The blow from the cricket ball **knocked** him **out** and he had to be carried off the pitch.

leave

Don't **leave out** any questions when you sit an examination.

let

The holiday was an awful **let-down** after the description in the brochure, so we have written and complained to the tour company.

Although Katya admitted breaking the window, she was **let off** as the accident could have happened to anyone.

live

My university course was excellent and certainly **lived up to** my expectations.

look

The authorities are **looking into** the possibility of a bypass round the town in order to reduce traffic pollution.

She is a very efficient director and **looked up to** by everyone who works with her.

make

If you're looking for Sam, I've just seen him **making for** the sports stadium.

I think there's a ship on the horizon but I can't quite **make** it **out**.

You shouldn't use so much **make-up** – it's bad for your skin.

Ron says he's taking part in the next Olympics but I don't believe him; I think he's **making** it **up**.

He **made up for** forgetting his girlfriend's birthday by taking her out to dinner.

pass

The king **passed away** peacefully during the night after a short illness.

Some of the soldiers who had been standing in the heat for hours **passed out**.

pay

That's the girl who hit my little brother, and one day I'll **pay** her **back** because she hurt him quite badly.

The bank is not willing to lend you any more money until you have **paid off** your debts.

pick

Things have **picked up** for the family since they won the lottery.

pull

That house which was badly damaged in the fire will have to be **pulled down** as it's unsafe.

The driver **pulled away** without looking and hit a pedestrian who had just stepped off the pavement.

The bus **pulled up** outside the school to let the children get off.

put

I can **put off** my meeting until tomorrow if you would like me to stay at home with you today.

The entrance examination is so difficult that a lot of people are **put off** applying to the college.

If the hotel is full, do you think your parents would **put** me **up** for the night?

His behaviour was so intolerable that his wife, who was not prepared to **put up with** it, left home to live by herself.

rub

Try not to make any mistakes as you won't be able to **rub** them **out**.

run

Guess who I **ran into** when I was shopping – an old school friend whom I hadn't seen for ages!

During the heatwave many shops **ran out of** bottled water.

He accidentally **ran over** a fox while driving along a dark country lane.

see

We'll come to the airport to **see** you **off** when you leave on Sunday.

Will you **see to** sending this video tape to the TV company? I promised we'd put it in today's post.

set

Losing the contract was a **setback** to the firm's business plans.

Her spell in hospital **set** her **back** a little but she is making a quick recovery.

The warm weather has **set in** for the season.

The earthquake **set off** a series of tremors which lasted for three days.

There are at least six nurses sharing that two-room apartment; it's rather a strange **set-up**, but I think they work shifts so they're not ever there together.

show

He's a marvellous actor but a terrible **show-off**, and people find his constant need for attention very irritating.

Sally's very late but I'm sure she'll **show up** eventually.

stand

Despite the financial scandal his family **stood by** him throughout his difficulties.

What does the badge you're wearing **stand for**?

If I were you, I wouldn't **stand for** Jim's rudeness.

Who's **standing in for** Mr Jones while he's away?

If you wear that bright orange dress, you'll certainly **stand out** in the crowd.

She always **stood up for** him when he was criticised by other people.

The president **stood up to** the tour schedule very well considering her age.

stick

Although he found the factory job very tedious, he **stuck** it **out** until he had earned enough to buy a car.

stop

It's a long drive from Caen to Geneva, so I think I'll **stop off** in Dijon for a few hours.

The two-day journey from Ostend to Prague has a **stop-over** in Munich.

take

I **take after** my father both physically and temperamentally.

The tour of the sights **took in** both the old and the new city centres.

I was completely **taken in** by his hard-luck story and didn't discover the truth until days later.

Don't **take on** more work than you can manage.

Many small companies accept being **taken over** by larger ones in order to survive.

I **took to** him as soon as we met and we've remained friends ever since.

tie

She's a busy person; if you want to meet her, it's difficult to **tie** her **down** as she has so many commitments.

try

She borrowed the new car **to** try it **out** before deciding whether or not to buy one.

turn

His application for a work permit was **turned down** because his visa had expired.

What looked as if it would be a dull play **turned out** to be a really lively evening.

She **turned up** without warning but we were all pleased to see her.

wear

The gold has **worn off** this ring and it looks as if it's silver underneath.

Ella loved looking after her young grandchildren, but at the end of the day she felt **worn out** by their high spirits.

wipe

The fall in share prices **wiped out** any profits people had been hoping to make.

work

Lucien's a brilliant mathematician and **works out** these maths problems in no time at all.

Eddie goes to the gym early each morning for a **work-out**.

write

I take notes during the lectures and **write** them **up** afterwards.

CAMBRIDGE
EXAMINATIONS, CERTIFICATES AND DIPLOMAS
ENGLISH AS A FOREIGN LANGUAGE

University of Cambridge
Local Examinations Syndicate
International Examinations

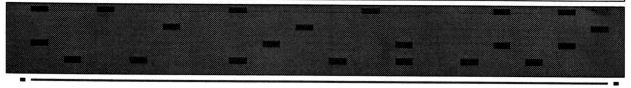

For Supervisor's use only

Shade here if the candidate is
ABSENT or has WITHDRAWN

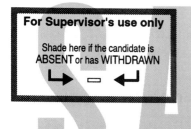

X

Examination Details	9999/01	99/D99
Examination Title	First Certificate in English	
Centre/Candidate No.	AA999/9999	
Candidate Name	A.N. EXAMPLE	

• Sign here if the details above are correct

• Tell the Supervisor now if the details above
  are not correct

Candidate Answer Sheet: FCE Paper 1 Reading

Use a pencil

Mark ONE letter for each
question.

For example, if you think **B** is
the right answer to the
question, mark your answer
sheet like this:

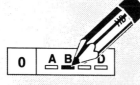

0   A B C D

Change your answer like
this:

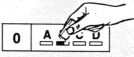

0   A C D

1	A B C D E F G H I
2	A B C D E F G H I
3	A B C D E F G H I
4	A B C D E F G H I
5	A B C D E F G H I

6	A B C D E F G H I
7	A B C D E F G H I
8	A B C D E F G H I
9	A B C D E F G H I
10	A B C D E F G H I
11	A B C D E F G H I
12	A B C D E F G H I
13	A B C D E F G H I
14	A B C D E F G H I
15	A B C D E F G H I
16	A B C D E F G H I
17	A B C D E F G H I
18	A B C D E F G H I
19	A B C D E F G H I
20	A B C D E F G H I

21	A B C D E F G H I
22	A B C D E F G H I
23	A B C D E F G H I
24	A B C D E F G H I
25	A B C D E F G H I
26	A B C D E F G H I
27	A B C D E F G H I
28	A B C D E F G H I
29	A B C D E F G H I
30	A B C D E F G H I
31	A B C D E F G H I
32	A B C D E F G H I
33	A B C D E F G H I
34	A B C D E F G H I
35	A B C D E F G H I

© UCLES/K&J

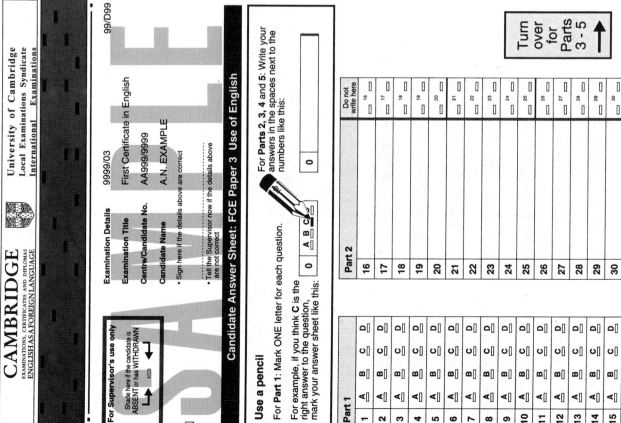

Part 3

	Do not write here
31	☐0 ☐1 ☐2
32	☐0 ☐1 ☐2
33	☐0 ☐1 ☐2
34	☐0 ☐1 ☐2
35	☐0 ☐1 ☐2
36	☐0 ☐1 ☐2
37	☐0 ☐1 ☐2
38	☐0 ☐1 ☐2
39	☐0 ☐1 ☐2
40	☐0 ☐1 ☐2

Part 4

	Do not write here
41	☐ 41
42	☐ 42
43	☐ 43
44	☐ 44
45	☐ 45
46	☐ 46
47	☐ 47
48	☐ 48
49	☐ 49
50	☐ 50
51	☐ 51
52	☐ 52
53	☐ 53
54	☐ 54
55	☐ 55

Part 5

	Do not write here
56	☐ 56
57	☐ 57
58	☐ 58
59	☐ 59
60	☐ 60
61	☐ 61
62	☐ 62
63	☐ 63
64	☐ 64
65	☐ 65

SAMPLE

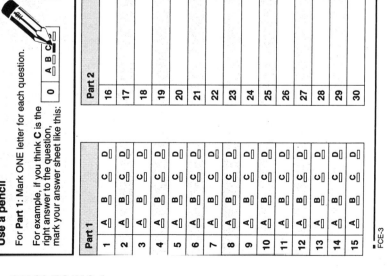

CAMBRIDGE
EXAMINATIONS, CERTIFICATES AND DIPLOMAS
ENGLISH AS A FOREIGN LANGUAGE

University of Cambridge
Local Examinations Syndicate
International Examinations

99/D99

For Supervisor's use only
Shade here if the candidate is
ABSENT or has WITHDRAWN →

Examination Details	
Examination Details	9999/03
Examination Title	First Certificate in English
Centre/Candidate No.	AA999/9999
Candidate Name	A.N. EXAMPLE

• Sign here if the details above are correct

• Tell the Supervisor now if the details above are not correct

☒

Candidate Answer Sheet: FCE Paper 3 Use of English

Use a pencil

For **Part 1**: Mark ONE letter for each question.

For example, if you think **C** is the right answer to the question, mark your answer sheet like this:

0 A☐ B☐ C■ D☐

For **Parts 2, 3, 4 and 5**: Write your answers in the spaces next to the numbers like this:

0 | 0

Part 1

	A	B	C	D
1	☐	☐	☐	☐
2	☐	☐	☐	☐
3	☐	☐	☐	☐
4	☐	☐	☐	☐
5	☐	☐	☐	☐
6	☐	☐	☐	☐
7	☐	☐	☐	☐
8	☐	☐	☐	☐
9	☐	☐	☐	☐
10	☐	☐	☐	☐
11	☐	☐	☐	☐
12	☐	☐	☐	☐
13	☐	☐	☐	☐
14	☐	☐	☐	☐
15	☐	☐	☐	☐

FCE-3

Part 2

	Do not write here
16	☐ 16
17	☐ 17
18	☐ 18
19	☐ 19
20	☐ 20
21	☐ 21
22	☐ 22
23	☐ 23
24	☐ 24
25	☐ 25
26	☐ 26
27	☐ 27
28	☐ 28
29	☐ 29
30	☐ 30

Turn over for Parts 3 - 5 ↑

DP152/99

© UCLES/K&J

CAMBRIDGE
EXAMINATIONS, CERTIFICATES AND DIPLOMAS
ENGLISH AS A FOREIGN LANGUAGE

University of Cambridge
Local Examinations Syndicate
International Examinations

For Supervisor's use only

Shade here if the candidate is
ABSENT or has WITHDRAWN

↳ ▭ ↵

X

Examination Details	9999/04	99/D99
Examination Title	First Certificate in English	
Centre/Candidate No.	AA999/9999	
Candidate Name	A.N. EXAMPLE	

• Sign here if the details above are correct

- -

• Tell the Supervisor now if the details above
  are not correct

Candidate Answer Sheet: FCE Paper 4 Listening

| Mark test version below |
| A | B | C | D | E |
| ▭ | ▭ | ▭ | ▭ | ▭ |

Use a pencil

For **Parts 1** and **3**:
Mark ONE letter for
each question.

For example, if you
think **B** is the right
answer to the
question, mark your
answer sheet like this:

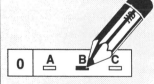

| 0 | A ▭ | B ▬ | C ▭ |

For **Parts 2** and **4**:
Write your answers in
the spaces next to the
numbers like this:

| 0 | |

Part 1

1	A ▭	B ▭	C ▭
2	A ▭	B ▭	C ▭
3	A ▭	B ▭	C ▭
4	A ▭	B ▭	C ▭
5	A ▭	B ▭	C ▭
6	A ▭	B ▭	C ▭
7	A ▭	B ▭	C ▭
8	A ▭	B ▭	C ▭

Part 2

		Do not write here
9		▭ 9 ▭
10		▭ 10 ▭
11		▭ 11 ▭
12		▭ 12 ▭
13		▭ 13 ▭
14		▭ 14 ▭
15		▭ 15 ▭
16		▭ 16 ▭
17		▭ 17 ▭
18		▭ 18 ▭

Part 3

19	A ▭	B ▭	C ▭	D ▭	E ▭	F ▭
20	A ▭	B ▭	C ▭	D ▭	E ▭	F ▭
21	A ▭	B ▭	C ▭	D ▭	E ▭	F ▭
22	A ▭	B ▭	C ▭	D ▭	E ▭	F ▭
23	A ▭	B ▭	C ▭	D ▭	E ▭	F ▭

Part 4

		Do not write here
24		▭ 24 ▭
25		▭ 25 ▭
26		▭ 26 ▭
27		▭ 27 ▭
28		▭ 28 ▭
29		▭ 29 ▭
30		▭ 30 ▭

© UCLES/K&J

RICHMOND PUBLISHING
19 Berghem Mews
Blythe Road
London W14 0HN
UK

©Diana L. Fried-Booth, 1997
Published by Richmond Publishing®
First published 1997

*All rights reserved. No part of this book may be reproduced, stored in a retrieval
system or transmitted in any form, electronic, mechanical or otherwise, without the
prior permission in writing from the publishers.*

ISBN: 84-294-4604-4
Depósito legal: M. 6013-1997
Printed by Mateu Cromo, S.A.

The author and publishers would like to thank all those teachers and
students who commented on the manuscript, and the teachers and students
who tried out the materials in their classes, in particular: **Argentina** Lilly
Alpert. **Australia** Holroyd High School, Sydney; Nicholas and Sue for
researching the Bunyip. **Greece** Asimenia Featham; Lyn Hughes. **Portugal**
Andy Martins Anceriz; Paul B. Carney. **Mexico** Rosalinda Reyna, Maddox
Academy; Carlos Tenorio and Ian Gardner, Tenorio Gardner Consultores
Lingüisticos, S.C. **Spain** Tony Hare, CESA, Alicante; all the teachers and
students at the EOI, Alicante; Juan Garcia Iborra, EOI, Murcia; Duncan
McBain, APPLE, Murcia; Charles Stedman, Speaker's Corner, Castellón;
Vicente Marco, English Centre, Almassora; Carmen Moreno and colleagues,
EOI, Valencia; David Spencer, International House, Madrid; Hilary Plass and
Alex Carter, Thamesis School, Madrid; Cathy Westmacott, Windsor Academy,
Madrid; Seamus McGeary, Casal School of English, Barcelona. **UK** Phil Jakes
for his helpful and perceptive comments, especially on the Grammar
Reference; Lyn Hudson and colleagues, King's School of English, Beckenham,
Kent; Annette Korthaus, Isabel C. Oestreich, Konrad Sippel, Tseng Shu-Wei
and all the overseas students at Wells Cathedral School, Somerset.

AUTHOR'S ACKNOWLEDGEMENTS
I am grateful to the many teachers and students whose advice,
encouragement and co-operation have been invaluable in developing this
book. I am also indebted to Sarah Thorpe and the entire team at Richmond
Publishing, most especially Frances Hayward. I particularly want to thank
Tony Garside, my editor, for his unfailing patience, guidance and good
humour throughout the entire project. And finally, I wish to thank Dominic
and Xanthé who have always been prepared to look critically and helpfully
at the material from their own generation's point of view, and Howard for
his support in countless ways.

RECORDINGS
Recordings were produced by Martin Williamson (Prolingua) and recorded
by Leon Chambers at Studio AVP with Gareth Armstrong, Carol Boyd, Lynne
Brackley, Tyler Butterworth, Elly Fairman, James Goode, John Graham, Nigel
Greaves, Ruth Jones, Alex Langdon, Nicolette McKenzie, Richard Pearce, Jill
Shilling, Nicola Vickery and Jo Wyatt.

PUBLISHER'S ACKNOWLEDGEMENTS
Thanks to the following for permission to reproduce material in this
publication:

AA Magazine for the adapted texts, page 126; A. P. Watt Ltd acting on behalf
of the estate of A. Blackwood for the adapted story 'Disappearance', page
170; Channel 4 Television for the adapted texts from 'Baka – People of the
Rain Forest', pages 88–89; The European for the articles 'Colloquial
Interpretations', page 11, 'At the heart of things', page 12, 'The girl can't
help it – nor can the boy', The European Magazine, page 20, 'Be aware of
Greeks bearing menus', The European Magazine, page 22, 'Where the stories
have all been told', Élan, page 44, 'Notice board', The European Magazine,
page 58, 'Glamorous new face in the boardroom', page 61, 'Inter-Rail
competition', The European Magazine, page 80, 'Learning about life in the
army', The European Magazine, page 179, '50 years of living with Pippi', The
European Magazine, page 198, 'Donna Karan crosses the Atlantic', Élan, page
204; Lennart Frick of Kerstin Kvint Literary and Co-production Agency for
the foreign language Pippi Longstocking book titles, page 197; Ewan
MacNaughton Associates for the article from The Daily Telegraph 'No room
in the fast lane for snail mail!' by Lesley Garner, page 122 and recorded
material; Fiona Hook for the article 'Can't work, don't make me', Ritz
Newspaper, page 193; Friends of the Earth for the advertisement, page 82;
Greenpeace for use of the logos, page 83; The Guardian for the article 'Time
for a feast', Guardian Education, page 21, 'Work till you drop', page 96, 'Trees
of the World' (illustration), Guardian Weekend, page 84, 'Height of

Madness', Guardian Review, page 155; Helmsley Speer Inc. for use of the line
drawing of the Empire State Building, page 161; HMSO for the extracts from
the Highway Code, reproduced by permission of the Controller of Her
Majesty's Stationery Office, page 128, © Crown Copyright; Ladybird
Children's Classics for the adapted text taken from 'Swiss Family Robinson',
page 81; Nineteen Magazine for the quiz 'Best Friend', page 26; The Observer
for the Language Collage, Observer Schools Report: Language Special, page 9,
'The global kitchen; South America', page 69; Solo Syndications for the
article from The Evening Standard 'Reading your stars', page 56; The Times
Newspaper Group, ©Times Newspapers Limited, for the articles 'Relative
Values', page 29, 'Whigfield', Sunday Times Style section, page 45, 'A day in
the life of', Sunday Times, page 50, 'My hols', Sunday Times Travel section,
page 78, 'Tomorrow's World of Shopping' and illustration, Sunday Times
Style section, pages 73–74, 'Game, set, and British matched', The Times Car
95, page 129 and recorded material, 'Hamsters reveal clue to man's violence',
Sunday Times, page 175, 'The good life goes on, underground', Sunday
Times, page 190, 'Hello house', The Times, page 212, 'Step into my parlour',
Sunday Times Style section, page 202; Youth Hostel Association for their logo
and the extract from their information leaflet, page 136; University of
Cambridge Local Examinations Syndicate for permission to reproduce the
sample OMR sheets, pages 237, 238, 239.

DESIGN/LAYOUT Jonathan Barnard
COVER DESIGN Geoff Sida, Ship
LAYOUT Gregor Arthur
PICTURE RESEARCH AND DIRECTION Simon James Collier for the Okai Collier
Company Ltd
STUDIO PHOTOGRAPHY Gareth Boden

ILLUSTRATIONS
Gregor Arthur page 9; **Jonathan Barnard** page 155; **Kathy Baxendale** pages
14 (*handwriting*), 15, 46, 53, 83, 88, 101, 107, 127, 128 (*handwriting*), 143,
144, 165; **Graham Berry** (The London Art Collection) pages 63, 194, 195;
Paul Davis (Garden Studio) pages 100 (*right*), 102; **Bob Dewar** (Cartoon
City) pages 17, 33, 49, 124, 128, 164, 166; **Richard Draper** page 93;
Hardlines pages 64, 73, 162, 178; **Chris Harner** pages 71, 135, 161;
Celia Hart page 201; **Paul Hess** (Garden Studio) pages 25, 200; **Steve Noon**
(Garden Studio) page 70; **Sharon Smith** page 100 (*left*); **Kath Walker** pages
30, 31, 75, 103, 105, 140, 145, 197; **Darrell Warner** (Blue Chip Illustration)
pages 14, 65, 139, 159, 180, 181, 186; **Mark Watkinson** (Garden Studio)
pages 86, 87, 131, 150, 167.

PHOTOGRAPHS
Thanks to the following for permission to reproduce material in this
publication: Diana L. Fried-Booth for the photographs on pages 13, 16,
34(*top*), 174; Howard Fried-Booth for the photographs on pages 34(*bottom*),
48, 53, 70, 174, 182, 203; Allsport pages 24 (*Damon Hill both*), 160 (*rock
climbing*), 201; Anthony Blake Photo Library page 69; Ardea Photo Library
page 175; Barnaby's Photo Library page 149; BFI page 44; J. Allan Cash pages
54 (*top left, middle highway background*), 63, 91 (*top*), 158 (*top*), 160 (*campsite*);
Colorific! page 179 (*left*); Electric Pictures/BFI page 138; European Newspaper
page 11; Friends of the Earth page 82; Ronald Grant Archive page 146 (*top
right, top left, bottom left*); Robert Harding Photo Library pages 54 (*middle
right*), 63, 85, 162 (*sand dunes*); Andre Heller/Partridge Consultancy page 144;
Hulton Getty Photos page 142 (*middle*); Gamma page 197; Greenhill Photos
page 176; Hutchinson Library pages 64, 106 (*top*); Kobal Collection page 138;
Katz Pictures page 202; Mary Evans Photos page 142 (*far right*); Network
Photographers pages 11 (*top*), 145, 183; NHPA pages 84, 162 (*forest*); Pearson
Television page 143; Popperfoto pages 24 (*Queen Sofia young*), 142 (*left*); Rex
Features pages 24 (*Tom Hanks both, Antonio Banderas both, Queen Sofia older,
Emma Thompson both*), 42 (*top left, middle bottom, bottom right, top right,
middle top*), 45, 50, 51, 54 (*tiger*), 91 (*top left*), 118, 146 (*bottom right*); Pictor
pages 54 (*bottom middle*), 67, 91, (*bottom right*), 104, 156 (*London*), 157, 158
(*bottom*), 162 (*glacier*), 204 (*all*), 205 (*all*); Still Pictures pages 89, 90, 178;
Telegraph Colour Library page 49; The Times Newspaper page 125 (*top*), 130;
The Sunday Times Newspaper/Martin Bell page 29; Tony Stone Images pages
10 (*bottom left*), 54 (*top right*), 64, 67, 68, 91 (*bottom left*), 106 (*left*), 110, 156
(*LA, Buenos Aires, Paris, Athens, Tokyo*), 160 (*beach, Hong Kong, canoe*), 162
(*ploughed field*); VSO Photos page 179 (*right*); Zefa page 12.

Every effort has been made to trace the owners of copyright, but if any
omissions can be rectified, the publishers will be pleased to make the
necessary arrangements.